Typological Studies on Languages in Thailand and Japan

Hituzi Linguistics in English

No.1	Lexical Borrowing and its Impact on English Makimi Kimura-Kano
No.2	From a Subordinate Clause to an Independent Clause Yuko Higashiizumi
No.3	ModalP and Subjunctive Present Tadao Nomura
No.4	A Historical Study of Referent Honorifics in Japanese Takashi Nagata
No.5	Communicating Skills of Intention Tsutomu Sakamoto
No.6	A Pragmatic Approach to the Generation and Gender Gap in Japanese Politeness Strategies Toshihiko Suzuki
No.7	Japanese Women's Listening Behavior in Face-to-face Conversation Sachie Miyazaki
No.8	An Enterprise in the Cognitive Science of Language Tetsuya Sano et al.
No.9	Syntactic Structure and Silence Hisao Tokisaki
No.10	The Development of the Nominal Plural Forms in Early Middle English Ryuichi Hotta
No.11	Chunking and Instruction Takayuki Nakamori
No.12	Detecting and Sharing Perspectives Using Causals in Japanese Ryoko Uno
No.13	Discourse Representation of Temporal Relations in the So-Called Head-Internal Relatives Kuniyoshi Ishikawa
No.14	Features and Roles of Filled Pauses in Speech Communication Michiko Watanabe
No.15	Japanese Loanword Phonology Masahiko Mutsukawa
No.16	Derivational Linearization at the Syntax-Prosody Interface Kayono Shiobara
No.19	Typological Studies on Languages in Thailand and Japan Tadao Miyamoto et al.

Hituzi Linguistics in English No. 19

Typological Studies on Languages in Thailand and Japan

Edited by:
Tadao Miyamoto, Naoyuki Ono,
Kingkarn Thepkanjana, Satoshi Uehara

Hituzi Syobo Publishing

Copyright © Tadao Miyamoto, Naoyuki Ono, Kingkarn Thepkanjana, Satoshi Uehara 2012
First published 2012

Editors: Tadao Miyamoto, Naoyuki Ono, Kingkarn Thepkanjana, Satoshi Uehara

All rights reserved. Except for the quotation of short passages for the purposes of criticism and review, no part of this publication may be reproduced, stored in a retrieval system, or transmitted in any form or by any means, electronic, mechanical, photocopying, recording or otherwise, without the written prior permission of the publisher.
In case of photocopying and electronic copying and retrieval from network personally, permission will be given on receipts of payment and making inquiries. For details please contact us through e-mail. Our e-mail address is given below.

Hituzi Syobo Publishing
Yamato bldg. 2F, 2-1-2 Sengoku Bunkyo-ku Tokyo, Japan
112-0011

phone +81-3-5319-4916 fax +81-3-5319-4917
e-mail: toiawase@hituzi.co.jp
http://www.hituzi.co.jp/
postal transfer 00120-8-142852

ISBN978-4-89476-607-5
Printed in Japan

Contents

Contents — v
About the Contributors — ix
Preface — xiii

Chapter Introductions — 1

Chapter 1 Syntactically naughty? : Prosody of final particles in Thai — 13
Pittayawat Pittayaporn and Pirachula Chulanon

Chapter 2 Etymological inquiry in a quest for the universality of human cognition: Focusing on word formation by sound symbolism — 29
Hiroyuki Eto

Chapter 3 Polyfunctionality in Pwo Karen: The case of ʔàʔ- (<T-B pronominal prefix *ʔa-) — 41
François Langella

Chapter 4 Global distribution of nominal plural reduplication — 57
Vipas Pothipath

Chapter 5	On the distinction between transitive and intransitive verbs in Thai	77
	Kingkarn Thepkanjana	

Chapter 6	Parallels between motion and resultative constructions	103
	Naoyuki Ono	

Chapter 7	The cognitive theory of subjectivity in a cross-linguistic perspective: Zero 1st person pronouns in English, Thai and Japanese	119
	Satoshi Uehara	

Chapter 8	A contrastive case study of pronominal forms in English, Japanese and Thai: A parallel corpus approach	137
	Theeraporn Ratitamkul and Satoshi Uehara	

Chapter 9	Directives in Japanese and Thai group discussions: Communal versus individual	159
	Ataya Aoki	

Chapter 10	The use of unconventional means of communication in Japanese and American blog comments	173
	Barry Kavanagh	

Chapter 11	"Green stink" and "fragrant taste": Synaesthetic expressions in Thai	195
	Naruadol Chancharu	

Chapter 12 A neuro-typological approach to writing systems 211
Tadao Miyamoto

Index 235

About the Contributors

ATAYA AOKI is a lecturer at the Department of Eastern Languages at Chulalongkorn University, Thailand. She received her PhD in Linguistic Communication at Tohoku University in 2010. From 2000 to 2010, she taught Thai at Miyagi Gakuin Women's University in Sendai, Japan, while also working as an International Tourism Specialist at the Sendai City Economic Affairs Bureau. Her research interests include cross-cultural communication, social interaction and comparative linguistics. <awesome.sendai@gmail.com>

NARUADOL CHANCHARU is currently a PhD candidate in Linguistics at the University of Cambridge, where he also obtained his MPhil in Linguistics in 2011. Before his receiving the Ananda Mahidol Foundation scholarship (King of Thailand's scholarship) to pursue his studies in the UK, he obtained his BA (first-class honours) in English in 2004, MA in English in 2007, and MA in Linguistics in 2010 from Chulalongkorn University. His research interests include issues in cognitive semantics (e.g. polysemy networks, conceptual metaphor and metonymy), grammaticalisation theory (e.g. grammaticalisation of modal markers, contact-induced grammaticalisation) and linguistic typology (e.g. typological studies of negative and prohibitive constructions). <naruadol@hotmail.com>

PIRACHULA CHULANON is a philosophy major at the Faculty of Arts, Chulalongkorn University, and is currently in the honors program in Linguistics. His interest in the philosophy of language has brought him to the field of linguistics, in which he studies theoretical topics, including the architecture of Grammar and the relationship between language and other cognitive systems. <sp472105@hotmail.com>

HIROYUKI ETO is an associate professor of English and linguistics at the Graduate School of International Cultural Studies of Tohoku University. He received his PhD in Germanic philology from Georgetown University in 2000 and his LittD in English philology from Sophia University (Japan) in 2002. His principal research interests lie in the areas of the intellectual history of linguistics, philosophy of language, and English-language teaching on the basis of historical English studies and liberal arts education. His recent publications include *Philologie vs. Sprachwissenschaft* (2003), "JAPAN: History of Linguistics" in *The encyclopedia of languages and linguistics* (2006), *Multiple perspectives on English philology and history of linguistics* (2010) and the Japanese translation of *Publication Manual of the American Psychological Association* (2011). <etoh@intcul.tohoku.ac.jp>

BARRY KAVANAGH is a lecturer teaching English, Intercultural communication and Media literacy courses at Aomori University of Health and Welfare in Aomori, Japan. He is also a PhD candidate at the Graduate School of International Cultural Studies of Tohoku University. His research interests include sociolinguistics, discourse analysis and pragmatics. <baz_kavanagh@yahoo.co.jp>

FRANÇOIS LANGELLA is currently taking his MA in linguistics at Chulalongkorn University. His research interests primarily focus on the minority languages of Mainland Southeast Asia. His thesis is a description of noun phrases in Southern Zhuang, a Central Tai language spoken in Southern China. <flangella@gmail.com>

TADAO MIYAMOTO is a professor of psycholinguistics, teaching at the Graduate School of International Cultural Studies of Tohoku University. He is also director of the Research Center for Language, Brain and Cognition affiliated with the Graduate School. He obtained his second BA, MA and PhD in linguistics from the Department of Linguistics of the University of Victoria, Canada, where he currently holds an adjunct professor position. He is the author of *Light verb construction in Japanese: The role of verbal nouns* (1999), and also the co-author (with Joseph F. Kess) of *Japanese psycholinguistics: Classified and annotated bibliography* (1994) and *Japanese mental lexicon: Psycholinguistic studies of kana and kanji processing* (1999). These books were all published by John Benjamins. His research interests include the evolution of language, writing system and neuro-imaging studies of language. <professortadaomiyamoto@yahoo.co.jp>

NAOYUKI ONO is a professor of the Department of Linguistic Communication in the Graduate School of International Cultural Studies at Tohoku University. His research interest encompasses theoretical and empirical issues in Lexical Semantics and Linguistic Typology. He is the author of a book on lexical-semantic analysis of Japanese and English based on the Generative Lexicon framework (2005) and the editor of two volumes on resultative constructions in various languages across the world (2007, 2009). <nono@intcul.tohoku.ac.jp>

PITTAYAWAT PITTAYAPORN is currently a faculty member at the Department of Linguistics, Faculty of Arts, at Chulalongkorn University. His research interests cover two distinct but interrelated domains. In the domain of synchronic phonology, he investigates tones, metrical structure as well as prosody. In historical linguistics, his research includes tonal changes, language contact, and linguistic prehistory. He also has a strong areal focus on the languages of Mainland Southeast Asia, especially Tai-Kadai and Mon-Khmer languages. <Pittayawat.P@chula.ac.th>

VIPAS POTHIPATH is a lecturer in the Department of Thai, Faculty of Arts, at Chulalongkorn University, where he obtained his BA in Thai (1995) and MA in linguistics (1999). He worked extensively on typology and the evolution of cardinal numeral-noun constructions, which was the subject of his 2008 PhD thesis at the University of Edinburgh. His research interests center on typology, historical linguistics and cognitive linguistics. <vipas_pothipath@live.com>

THEERAPORN RATITAMKUL is a lecturer at the Department of Linguistics, Faculty of Arts at Chulalongkorn University. She received her PhD in linguistics at the University of Illinois at Urbana-Champaign in 2007. Her research interests include argument realization in East Asian and Southeast Asian languages, psycholinguistic perspectives on argument realization, and argument realization in child language. <theeraporn@gmail.com>

KINGKARN THEPKANJANA is an associate professor of linguistics at the Department of Linguistics, Faculty of Arts, at Chulalongkorn University. She received her PhD in linguistics at the University of Michigan, Ann Arbor, in 1986 and was a visiting scholar at the Harvard-Yenching Institute at Harvard

University from 2001 to 2002. Her research interests include serial verb constructions, grammaticalization, polysemy and transitivity alternations. <Kingkarn.T@chula.ac.th>

SATOSHI UEHARA is a professor of Japanese language and linguistics of the Center for the Advancement of Higher Education and the Graduate School of International Cultural Studies at Tohoku University. He received his PhD in linguistics at the University of Michigan in 1995, and was a visiting scholar at Harvard University in 2002-3. His research interests include cognitive linguistics, linguistic typology and pragmatics, and his research focuses on Japanese and other East and Southeast Asian languages. He is the author of *Syntactic categories in Japanese: A cognitive and typological introduction* (Kurosio Publishers, 1998) and a number of international journal and edited volume papers. <uehara@intcul.tohoku.ac.jp>

Preface

This book is a collection of papers, most of which were presented at the Chulalongkorn-Tohoku Cognitive and Typological Linguistics Symposium held in August 27–28, 2010 in Bangkok, Thailand. This symposium was jointly hosted by the Department of Linguistics at the Faculty of Arts of Chulalongkorn University and the Research Center for Language, Brain and Cognition (LBC) affiliated with the Graduate School of International Cultural Studies of Tohoku University. The LBC is an intra-university institute, aiming at understanding the biological nature of human language.

Funding-wise, it was supported by Chulalongkorn University's Center of Excellence Program for Language, Linguistics and Literature (2008–2012) headed by Prof. Kingkarn Thepkanjana, who was also the main organizer of the symposium. However, originally, this symposium was planned both by her and Prof. Satoshi Uehara of Tohoku University, who visited the Center on a regular basis. Their objective was to bring together a group of researchers specialized in cognitive linguistics and linguistic typology at the Faculty of Arts of Chulalongkorn University and also a group of researchers affiliated with the LBC of Tohoku University for exchanging their research findings.

As a reciprocal endeavor, the LBC has promised the Center of Excellence Program that it would assume the responsibility of publishing the collection of papers presented at this symposium into a book. To do so, it established an editing committee of four: Professors N. Ono, K. Thepkanjana, S. Uehara and T. Miyamoto. The primary concern of the editors was to assess the quality of the papers to be included in the book. Hence, all the submitted papers were sent to reviewers, and individual contributors reworked their reviewed papers. During this process, we unfortunately had to eliminate two papers which did not meet the academic standard we had established.

Meanwhile, we contacted Hitsuji Shobo, one of the most prominent publishers in Japan in Linguistics and Language Sciences, asking if the publisher was interested in publishing our collection of papers as a book. Once the papers had been approved for quality, we were able to bring about this volume of work in this book, entitled *Typological Studies on Languages in Thailand and Japan*. I hope that this body of research will attract the interest of not only those specialized in cognitive and typological linguistics but also those interested in the Thai and Japanese languages, or in linguistics in general.

Tadao Miyamoto
Editor-in-Chief
Director of the Research Center for Language, Brain and Cognition
The Graduate School of International Cultural Studies, Tohoku University

Chapter Introductions

Chapter 1   On Thai final particles and their prosodic characteristics

Final particles have always been an intriguing topic in Thai linguistics. They are grammatical morphemes that occur at the end of phrases and convey a range of grammatical, discourse or sociolinguistic information. From a syntactic perspective, final particles display behaviors that could be considered 'naughty' in the sense that they can occur after a variety of structures: a complete sentence, a word, or even by themselves. However, in their paper entitled *Syntactically naughty? Prosody of final particles in Thai*, PITTAYAWAT PITTAYAPORN and PIRACHULA CHULANON claim that from a prosodic perspective, the distribution of final particles is best characterized as intonational clitics that occur on the right edge of intonational phrases. Moreover, they have also shown that stress plays a major role in determining the shape of the final particles. That is, in marked circumstances, final particles function as prosodic words upon receiving stress. By default, when they are not stressed, they are then merely attached to the preceding intonational phrase. In sum, final particles, from a syntactic glance, appear to be a highly problematic class of words, but from a prosodic point of view they are quite regular. Their seemingly 'naughty' pattern in the distribution is in fact rigorously constrained by prosodic structure rather than by syntactic structure. This study shows that Thai final particles resemble function words found in other languages in respect to their prosodic behaviors.

Chapter 2   On word formation by sound symbolism

The fundamental lexical issue of whether the link between referents and symbols representing these referents is arbitrary or non-arbitrary has been debated since the dawn of the Greek philosophy era. As it is well known, Aristotle in *On Interpretation* [*PeriHermeneias*, Περὶ Ἑρμηνείας] regards the arbitrariness of signs as one of the fundamental principles of linguistic science. In modern days, the same idea was advocated by Saussure in *Cours de linguistique générale*. HIROYUKI ETO's paper, which is entitled *Etymological inquiry in a quest for the universality of human cognition: Focusing on word formation by sound symbolism*, is basically antithesis to this Arbitrary Hypothesis, supporting the idea that, as Plato in *Cratylus* [Κρατύλος] suggests, sound symbolism plays an important role in word formation. In opting for the Non-arbitrary Hypothesis, this study cites two sets of data. One is the Japanese onomatopoetic word, *pika-don* and its related words; and the other is the Indo-European stem, *bl-* , and its cognate words.

First, the Japanese word *pika-don*, referring to atomic bombs, which was described as a combination of flashing light, *pika*, and the sound of a thunderous blast, *don*, is associated with a rather 'primitive' way of creating a new word from the sound imitation, since other than using this primitive way, there was no way of describing the nature of the unprecedented bomb blasts. The author applies this non-arbitrary nature of word formation to his etymological inquiry. Many English words beginning with *bl-* evoke the image of 'expansion' because of the sound sequence of /b/ and /l/. This sound symbolism is not specific in modern English. OE (Old English) words beginning with *bl-* and the IE (Indo-European) root **bhel-* share the same symbolic value based on the identical sound sequence. Relying on an extensive set of words, which cognate with these roots, this paper demonstrates the author's point that sound symbolism is one of the principle ways of creating new words. An implication of his demonstration is that sound symbolism would be able to broaden the possibility of etymological inquiry in a quest for the universality of human cognition.

Chapter 3　On the proto-Tibeto-Burman prefix *ʔa-

Karenic languages belong to the Tibeto-Burman language family, one of the five language families spoken in Southeast Asia, along with Tai-Kadai, to which Thai belongs. Karen speakers live in an area straddling the Thai-Burmese border. The dialect studied in the paper, which is entitled *Polyfunctionality in Pwo Karen: The case of ʔaʔ--* (<*T-B pronominal prefix *ʔa-),* is a dialect of Pwo Karen, a member of the Southern Branch of Karenic languages, and spoken in Dong Dam, a village of about 400 inhabitants located in Lamphun province, Northern Thailand. It shares with a vast number of Tibeto-Burman languages a reflex of the Proto-Tibeto-Burman prefix **ʔa-*, which has gathered considerable attention in the field of Tibeto-Burman linguistics, due to its large functional range. Supported by the Karen Linguistics Project directed by Prof. Theraphan Luangthongkum of Chulalongkorn University, FRANÇOIS LANGELLA conducted fieldwork in Dong Dam village in order to investigate which of the six semantic functions of the Proto-Tibeto-Burman prefix *ʔa- identified by Matisoff (2003) are available to Dong Dam Pwo Karen. It was found that only three semantic functions are attested in Dong Dam Pwo Karen: The 3rd person possessive, verb nominalizers and phonological bulk providers. The three other functions that are missing in Dong Dam Pwo Karen are its vocative and referential uses with kinship terms, subject agreement markers and aspectual markers. Further to this, the paper discusses whether it makes sense in the case of Dong Dam Pwo Karen to distinguish between a pronominal prefix and a non-pronominal prefix, as argued by Solnit in the case of another Karenic language, Eastern Kayah Li (Solnit 1997). It is argued that in absence of morphosyntactic evidence, it is more adequate to recognize only one prefix ʔàʔ- in Dong Dam Pwo Karen, and to account for its multiple functions by means of a semantic map.

Chapter 4   On cross-linguistic survey of nominal plural reduplication

Reduplication is a morphological process by which the entire root or stem or its part is repeated for semantic or grammatical purposes. As imagined, the repetition of form can easily suggest a greater number of referents (e.g. Indonesian *kota-kota* [town-town] 'various cities and towns'). Such correspondence of linguistic form and its meaning is known as *linguistic iconicity*. Accordingly, it is reasonable to assume that NPR (nominal plural reduplication), which is iconic in nature, is likely to be a commonly attested linguistic feature, and is widely distributed throughout most parts of the world. This is an assumption made based on Rubino's (2005) research on areal distribution of reduplication, which claims that the phenomenon is cross-linguistically wide and regular. In fact, however, it has not been attested how extensively the world's languages use reduplication as a means of forming plurals.

In his paper entitled *Global distribution of nominal plural reduplication*, VIPAS POTHIPATH explores the geographical distribution of NPR in a synchronic sample of 190 languages across the globe by constructing a large-scale language database depending mainly on their *reference grammars*. The main finding of his endeavor is that although NPR is an instance of iconic reduplication and languages with reduplication are very common, the overall number of languages with NPR appears to be somewhat smaller than expected. Only one third of the language he surveyed were found to utilize NPR as a means of expressing plurality. Even though it is being extensively utilized in the two regions, i.e. Australia and New Guinea as well as Southeast Asia and Oceania, this strategy is not found among the languages in Western Europe. An implication of this study is that further expansion of this line of inquiry will enhance our understanding not only of NPR but also the universality associated with reduplication itself, which is one of the essential features of human language.

Chapter 5   On classifying Thai verbs

Although classifying verbs into transitive or intransitive is a fundamental issue in any grammar, this could be an especially tricky matter in such languages as Thai, where (i) the semantic criteria of (in)transitivity is vague, and (ii) omitting linguistic elements in discourse is prevalent. However, based on Dowty's (1991) prototype approach, in the paper entitled *On the distinction between transitive and intransitive verbs in Thai*, KINGKARN THEPKANJANA substantiates Thai native speakers' intuition behind the verb categorization. In doing so, she has, as criteria, spelled out the parameters associated with the Proto-Agent and Proto-Patient as semantic features, such as [+/-actional], [+/-telic], [+/-volitional] and [+/-punctual]. Based on this semantic feature approach, she classifies verbs not only into three major classes, namely, transitive, intransitive and ambivalent verbs, but further into their sub-classes.

First, the transitive verbs are defined as being high in transitivity, which in turn is defined by such semantic features as [+actional], [+telic] and [+volitional]. Transitive verbs are further subcategorized into three classes based predominantly on the semantic roles associated with two features: [D(irect) O(bject) highly affected] and [DO highly individuated]. Second, intransitive verbs are defined as those which are irrelevant to [DO highly affected] and [DO highly individuated]. These verbs are further classified into three subclasses based on the following five semantic features: [actional], [telic], [volitional], [punctual] and [Agent high in potency]. Third, there is a group of ambivalent verbs, which appear both with and without DOs. These verbs are sub-classified into two types based on whether they take direct objects or not. However, these potential objects could not denote created entities or targets of actions. In short, these are basically regarded as either transitive verbs or intransitive verbs depending on to what extent the *absence* of their potential objects is obligatory or non-obligatory.

Based on the above analysis, the author has concluded that there is no clear-cut distinction between transitive and intransitive verbs in Thai; and the classification of Thai verbs can be accounted for in terms of a transitivity continuum, which is gradient in nature.

Chapter 6 On resultative construction and event-framing typology

In cognitive typology, one of the most well investigated topics is Talmy's idea that languages fall into two categories, verb-framed and satellite-framed languages, depending on how they encode primary semantic components of motion events in verbs and satellite phrases (Talmy 2000). However, the validity of this typology in the domains of event types other than that of motion event has not been substantially evaluated.

NAOYUKI ONO's paper entitled *Parallels between motion and resultative constructions* first examines the validity of Talmy's idea from a typological perspective of English and Japanese resultative constructions. It then demonstrates the clear parallelism between motion and resultative constructions based on various factors including the observation as that verb-framed languages show the systematic lack of the satellite-framed pattern for both motion and resultative consturctions. In so doing, he provides robust evidence to the validity of Talmy's typology.

Second, this paper makes a rather unique claim: verb-framing and satellite-framing are two strategies for encoding event frames, which may be used in a single language as competing options for describing the same event. In other words, the event typology arises not from distinct language types, but from the inventory of lexical resources for encoding different framing options. In this so-called 'lexical resource view' of the event-framing typology, the question then arises as to what lexical resources comprise different encoding strategies. The answer would be that at least English and Japanese would be able to make use of lexical resources, which are, in essence, the semantic properties of the particular ad-positions involved (e.g. Eng: *to* or *into*; Jap: *ni* (dative)). Employing such evidence as semantic alteration in reading among *goal*, *bound path* and *change-of-state* associated with ad-positional phrases, the author illustrates that the above answer is in fact correct. In sum, this study treats the verb-framed and satellite-framed patterns introduced by Talmy (2000) not as language types but rather as descriptions of alternative encoding strategies.

Chapter 7   On subjectivity in Thai and Japanese

Typologically Thai and Japanese are classified into the same "zero pronominal" language type, where pronominal reference can freely take the form of zero whenever it is contextually recoverable. In this paper, which is entitled *The cognitive theory of subjectivity in a cross-linguistic perspective: Zero 1st person pronouns in English, Thai and Japanese*, SATOSHI UEHARA opts for the cognitive theory of subjectivity to identify a subtype of zero pronouns called "deictic zero". His argument is that these two languages differ drastically from each other in their use of deictic zero, and, accordingly, in their default degree of subjectivity in the linguistic expressions of events involving the speaker.

Focusing on the so-called ISPs (internal state predicates), predicates of mental states, such as emotions and desires, he examines whether zero 1st person pronouns of the experiencer subject in these two languages behave differently or not. His findings indicate differences. For instance, ISPs in Japanese can take only the first person pronoun for their subjects; and to be used with third person subjects, they have to co-occur with some evidential markers such as *garu* 'show the signs of being'. In contrast, ISPs in Thai totally lack such person restriction (like those in English) and need to be accompanied, or replaced, by some marker of exclamation to indicate any perception or sensation specific to the speaker. In other words, the difference in this respect between the two zero pronominal languages emerges most notably in their lexicalization patterns of expressions of sentient beings' internal states; and in Japanese, ISPs are lexicalized into "deictic predicates", while in Thai they are not. In sum, typologically speaking, Thai and Japanese may look the same in the behavior of "zero pronominal", but a careful examination reveals that these two languages are characteristically different from each other.

Chapter 8   On pronominal use in Thai and Japanese texts

It is widely acknowledged that the languages of East and Southeast Asia differ from Western languages like English in terms of referential expressions. Referents in East and Southeast Asian languages, such as Japanese and Thai, can be left unexpressed, hence assuming not only the lexical and pronominal forms but also the null form. Thus, there arise interesting questions as to how these forms get chosen in discourse. The questions put forward by THEERAPORN

RATITAMKUL and SATOSHI UEHARA are (i) to what extent do pronominal forms vary in English, Japanese and Thai? and (ii) what are the factors that influence referential choices in Thai? In an examination of these questions, an English short story, *The Last Leaf*, and its Thai and Japanese translations were analyzed for their pronominal use. In their work entitled *A contrastive case study of pronominal forms in English, Japanese and Thai: A parallel corpus approach*, particular attention was paid to English subject pronouns and their counterparts in Thai and Japanese.

Their data reveal that English pronouns are not always translated into pronouns in Thai and Japanese. It is observed that the Thai translations contain a largest proportion of overt pronouns, followed by nouns, and that the occurrence of zero pronouns is the fewest. The Japanese text, on the other hand, exhibits a different pattern. More than half of the forms used in the Japanese translation are ellipses, the remaining two-thirds are pronominal forms and the rest are nouns. In essence, Thai is distinct from Japanese in the use of overt forms: (i) lexical terms are used for self-reference; (ii) kin terms are used to convey intimacy; and (iii) pronominal forms are used to indicate the speaker's attitude to and social relationship with the addressee and the referent mentioned in discourse. The authors conclude that recoverability from context and socio-pragmatic meanings of overt referential expressions are the two important factors that influence referential choices in Thai.

Chapter 9   On rapport management between Thais and Japanese

Group communication is a natural activity in any society, and participation in discussions is regarded as a standard form of decision-making and equitable involvement in organizations. In particular, communication in small groups can symbolize how group members define and enact their sense of self and their group (Lesch 1994); and its communication patterns can also be regarded as a reflection of the larger society. ATAYA AOKI's paper, which is entitled *Directives in Japanese and Thai group discussions: Communal versus individual*, investigates how native groups of Japanese and Thai proceeded toward a set goal, and how their speech behavior revealed aspects of social relations in their respective groups. Her focus is on the directive speech acts, which can be classified as asking for opinion or suggesting ways to work out the problem. She assembled six experimental discussion groups in order to attain comparable sets of data:

three groups of Japanese speakers, and another three groups of Thai speakers. The topic of discussion was a problem-solving situation that required the group to reach a consensus. The scenario was an accident scene in which the participants could only rescue seven people out of ten survivors. Her analysis of the direction of directive speech acts and conversational sequences presents two findings. First, the Japanese tended to deliver directives towards the group rather than towards specific individuals whereas the Thais preferred the opposite. Second, the Japanese interacted in a predictable and reciprocal pattern while the Thais showed no established pattern and participated in the conversation independently. These differences suggest that in a group situation, Japanese speakers' cognition is oriented toward the communal body and relationships are managed at a collective level, whereas Thai speakers' cognition is oriented toward individuals and relationships are managed in an independent level.

Chapter 10   On Japanese and American blog comments

This paper attempts to examine the applicability of Hall's (1976) theoretical framework within the computer mediated communicative environment. High context cultures, such as Japan, are described as having an ambiguous and vague approach to communication, which tends to be implicit and non-verbal. In contrast, low context cultures, such as America, are described as using more direct, verbal and explicit forms of communication.

In the paper entitled *The use of unconventional means of communication in Japanese and American blog comments*, through an examination of Japanese and American personal diary weblog comments, BARRY KAVANAGH illustrates that unconventional means of communication (UMC), such as emoticons and unconventional phonetic spelling, is used in higher frequency within the Japanese blog comments than within the American blogs. In total 47% of Japanese comment sentences had a UMC attached to them compared to 17% of English sentences. These UMC's on a faceless communication medium act as a means to bridge the gap amongst their users, to explicitly construct emotion and to promote harmony. The fact that the use of these UMC's allows Japanese comment writers to express their emotion explicitly can be regarded to constitute a piece of counter-evidence to Hall's cultural framework stating that high context cultural communication is vague, implicit and ambiguous. By the same token, the infrequent use of the UMC's by the American blog writers constitutes a piece of counter-evidence to Hall's framework since the writers from this low context culture are not making use of the UMC' in an explicit manner. Hall's framework can therefore be challenged in terms of its applicability to online communication and the use of UMC's.

Chapter 11 On cross-sense modality transfer in Thai

In his paper entitled *"Green stink" and "fragrant taste": Synaesthetic expressions in Thai*, NARUADOL CHANCHARU investigates synesthetic expressions, i.e. linguistic expressions that encode cross-sense modality transfer, with a special emphasis on Thai data. The term 'synesthesia' is used to refer to a condition in which the stimulation of one sensory modality is accompanied by one of the other modalities. Synesthesia is also used in language studies, referring to a linguistic phenomenon in which a linguistic expression encodes the perception of one sense modality through another: e.g. *Mary has a sweet voice*. One of the controversial issues is its directionality of 'transfer'. Synesthetic transfers are claimed to be hierarchically distributed, going from the lower to the higher sensory modes: TOUCH > TASTE > SMELL > SOUND > SIGHT. It is also claimed that the predominant source and target of synesthetic transfer are TOUCH and SOUND, hence suggesting the presence of some cognitive constraints.

This study attempts to identify the overall distributional hierarchy of transfer in Thai, and also to determine the predominant source and target domains of synesthesia. To fulfill the objectives, two groups of five native-speaking Thai university students participated in one half-hour brainstorming session. They were given information on the definition and examples of synesthetic expressions, and were in turn asked to provide more examples of synesthetic expressions. The data collected from these two sessions was tested against the 13-million-word Thai National Corpus and the web-based search engine Google for actual occurrences and contextual use. The main finding is that there are 10 pathways of synesthetic transfer. These pathways all have TOUCH as the predominant source and SOUND as the predominant target except for only two cases of downward transfer: COLOR → SMELL and SMELL → TOUCH. While claiming that in terms of distribution, one potentially universal feature is TOUCH as the predominant source of transfer, the author also speculates that the predominant destination of transfer can be culturally variable: SIGHT for some cultures and SOUND for others.

Chapter 12   On neuro-typology of writing systems

In the field of linguistics, writing systems have not been well investigated under the assumption that while language is innate, writing systems are mere cultural artifacts, lacking the intrinsic nature associated with human language, which uniquely separates us from other species of animals. In spite of his false assumption of alphabeto-centrism, it is Gelb (1963) who first demonstrated that the study of writing systems could be a meaningful sub-discipline for understanding the nature of language.

In the paper entitled *A neuro-typological approach to writing systems*, TADAO MIYAMOTO illustrates that even though writing systems are divided into various types based generally on script types, they could also be classified based on the notion of orthographic depth, which in turn is uniquely manifested in terms of brain activation. In other words, it might be possible to classify writing systems based on the difference in brain activation. To examine this possibility, he examined previous neuro-imaging studies on single word reading. Based on neuro-imaging studies on the Italian and English alphabet, Japanese Kana, Korean Hangul, Chinese Hanzi and Japanese Kanji, he was able to demonstrate the clear correlation between orthographic depth associated with these writing systems and the activation patterns, which are defined in terms of a dual-cortical system and the presence/absence of an anterio-posterior network.

An implication of his study is then that (i) neuro-imaging could be employed for the classification of writing systems; and (ii) it could be possible to establish a new linguistic sub-field, which could be termed 'neuro-typology', where neuroimaging techniques are utilized for linguistic-typological studies.

References

Gil, David & Bernard Comrie. 2005. (eds), *The world atlas of language structures*, 114–117. Oxford: Oxford University Press.
Dowty, David. 1991. Thematic proto-roles and argument selection. *Language* 67(3). 547–619.
Gelb, I. J. 1963. *A study of writing*. 2nd edition. Chicago: University of Chicago Press.
Hall, E. 1976. *Beyond culture*. New York: Doubleday.
Lesch, Christee L. 1994. Observing theory in practice: Sustaining consciousness in a coven. In Lawrence R. Frey (ed.), *Group communication in context: Studies of natural groups*, 57–82. Hillsdale, NJ: Lawrence Erlbaum Associates.

Matisoff, James. 2003. *Handbook of Proto-Tibeto-Burman: System and philosophy of Sino-Tibetan reconstruction*. (UC Publications in Linguistics 135). Berkeley & Los Angeles: University of California Press.

Rubino, Carl. 2005. Reduplication. In Martin Haspelmath, Matthew S. Dryer, David Gil & Bernard Comrie (eds), *The world atlas of language structures*, 114–117. Oxford: Oxford University Press.

Solnit, David. 1997. *Eastern Kayah Li: Grammar, texts, glossary*. Honolulu: University of Hawai'i Press.

Talmy, Leonard. 2000. *Toward a cognitive semantics*. Massachusetts: MIT Press.

Tsui, Amy B. M. 1994. *English conversation*. Oxford: Oxford University Press.

Zimmerman, Don H. & Candace West. 1975. Sex roles, interruptions and silences in conversation. In B. Thorne & N. Henley (eds), *Language and sex*, 105–129. Rowley, MA: Newbury House.

Chapter 1

Syntactically naughty? : Prosody of final particles in Thai

Pittayawat Pittayaporn and Pirachula Chulanon

1. Introduction

Final particles have always been a fascinating yet puzzling topic in Thai linguistics. Semanticists and pragmatists are challenged by the range of meaning conveyed by these grammatical morphemes (Bhamoraput 1972; Cooke 1989; Prasithrathsin 2001). Sociolinguists are amazed by their being elaborately interwoven with complex social organization (Iwasaki & Inkapirom 2005; Peyasantiwong 1981). Syntacticians and phonologists are similarly at a loss when confronting these function words, whose syntactic and phonological behaviors are quite different from other morphemes in Thai.

While final particles have been variously defined by different researchers (for example Bhamoraput 1972; Cooke 1989; Peyasantiwong 1981), they can be roughly characterized as grammatical morphemes that occur at the end of phrases and may convey a range of grammatical, discourse, or sociolinguistic information. These morphemes can be classified into three types according to their functions: (a) interrogative particles, marking yes/no questions, (b) modality particles, denoting the speaker's modal or epistemic knowledge, and (c) status particles, indexing gender, social status, and the relationship between participants of the discourse. The three classes of particles are exemplified in (1).

(1) a. Interrogative Particles
nɔ́ːj   nɔ̌ːn   nāːn   máj
Noi   sleep long-time INT

"Did Noi sleep for a long time?"

b. Modality Particles
nɔ́ːj nɔ̄ːn nāːn   na-H%¹
Noi   sleep long-time FP
"Listen, Noi sleeps for a long time."

c. Status Particles
nɔ́ːj nɔ̄ːn nāːn   kʰráp
Noi   sleep long-time FP
"Noi sleeps for a long time." (formal, male speaking)

In (1a), the interrogative particle /máj/ turns the sentence to which it attaches into an interrogative sentence. In contrast, the particles in (1b) and (1c) do not change the structural type of the sentence but add discourse and social information to it. In (1b), the modality particles /na/ "COMMON GROUND' signals that the speaker expects some response from the addressee. In (1c) the status particle /kʰráp/ 'MALE, FORMAL' signals that the speaker is male and that the relationship between the addressee and the speaker himself requires a moderate to high degree of politeness (Cooke 1989; Prasithrathsin 2001).

From a syntactic point of view, final particles display behaviors that could be considered "naughty". Although these particles typically occur at the end of various types of syntactic units, the range of structures after which they are located seems to indicate that syntax alone does not adequately specify their locations within the utterance. They can occur after a variety of structures, from complete sentence as in (2a), to a word as in (2b), or even alone as in (2c).

(2) a. [nɔ́ːj nɔ̄ːn nāːn]   kʰráp
     Noi   sleep long-time FP
     "Noi sleeps for a long time." (formal, male speaking)

b. [mêː]   kʰráp
   mother   FP
   "Mom" (formal, male speaking)

c. kʰráp

FP

"Yes" (formal, male speaking)

From a phonological point of view, final particles show a great variability in form, especially given the fact that morphophonemic alternation is virtually absent in Thai. As illustrated in (3) below, a number of final particles in Thai may take different shapes in different contexts.

(3) a. nɔ́ːj   kāmlāŋ   ˈnɔ̄ːn   kʰa-L%
Noi   PROG   sleep   FP
"Noi is sleeping." (formal, female speaking)

b. nɔ́ːj   nɔ̄ːn   nāːn   ˈkʰaʔ-L%
Noi   sleep   long-time   FP
"Noi sleeps for a long time." (formal with a sarcastic tone, female speaking)

c. mêː   ˈkʰaː-H%
mother   FP
"Mom!" (formal with mild impatience, female speaking)

Adopting the framework of Prosodic Phonology (Nespor & Vogel 1986), we account for these two aspects of the prosody of final particles in Thai, namely, their distribution and phonological characteristics. We argue that final particles are best characterized as intonational clitics (Zec & Inkelas 1992; Zec 2005), whose possible locations are not directly conditioned by syntactic structures but rather by prosodic structure. More specifically, they only occur on the right edge of intonational phrases.

Their unusual phonological behaviors are also shown to result from the facts that they are prosodically deficient and have to undergo phonological modification in response to general prosodic requirements imposed by the language. More specifically, the particles show the observed phonological variability because they, unlike lexical words, do not form prosodic words, and thus remain unstressed in unmarked cases. When they are forced to become stressed, however, they must undergo augmentation processes to satisfy the constraints on the shape of Thai prosodic words, resulting in a systematic alternation of certain particles.

2. Final particles and the intonational phrase

One of the biggest challenges for linguists posed by final particles in Thai is their apparent syntactically "naughty" behaviors. In other words, the distribution of these function words is extremely hard to generalize in terms of syntax. Any attempt to specify their locations in terms of syntax would end up with a non-unified list of structures that can be followed by a final particle (e.g. Prasithrathsint 2001). However, if we look at these structures from the viewpoint of Prosodic Phonology, all of them can be identified with a single type of prosodic constituent—the intonational phrase.

In the view of the theory of Prosodic Phonology (Nespor & Vogel 1986; Selkirk 1981), a string of phonological segments is organized into a hierarchical structure, grouping sequences of sound into layers of prosodic constituents, parallel to syntactic constituents. Segments are grouped into syllables, syllables into feet, and feets into phonological words, which are also known as prosodic words. The constituents above phonological words are phonological phrases, intonational phrases and utterances. This hierarchy is schematized in (4).

(4)   (   ) Utterance (U)
      (   )(   ) Intonational Phrase (ι)
      (   )(   )(   )   ) Phonological Phrase (φ)
      ( )( )( )( )( )   ) Phonological Word (ω)

The constituents in the prosodic hierarchy are motivated in the first place by the need to provide proper domains for the application of phonological rules which cannot be accounted for by syntax. Syntactic constituent structure and prosodic constituent structure are systematically related by virtue of mapping rules or constraints from the former to the latter (Selkirk 1981; Truckenbrodt 1999). However, a prosodic constituent is not necessarily isomorphic with some syntactic constituents. A classic example of such non-isomorphism is shown in (5). None of the phonological phrases in the second line (except the last one) corresponds to any definable syntactic constituent, as shown in the first line.

(5)   [This [is [the cat [that caught [the rat [that stole [the cheese]]]]]]]

(This is the cat)(that caught the rat)(that stole the cheese)

Although prosodic constituents are claimed to be derivable, in part at least, from syntactic constituents, it is only the prosodic structure that is referred to by the phonological component. This explains the frequent failure of syntactic domains to accommodate phonological processes. In accordance with this hypothesis, Truckenbrodt (1999) suggests that the phonological rules that have been thought to refer to syntax must be recast in terms of prosodic constituents. This is consistent with our claim here that for the distribution of final particles in Thai, while prosodically governed, the syntactic constituent structure is not directly relevant.

The type of prosodic constituent we are focusing on here is the intonational phrase, which is the prosodic constituent that serves as the domain for the characteristic intonational contours of a language (Selkirk 1984: 197). A sentence may be divided into one or more intonational phrases and one sentence may have more than one possible intonational phrasing. In Thai, the intonational phrase is realized phonetically with one pitch contour, delimited by a final stressed syllable (Luksaneeyanawin 1983). To illustrate, the sentence in (6) consists of two phonological phrases, each ending with a stressed syllable and forming one pitch contour.

(6) (nɔ́ːj làp saˈnìt)ι (lɛ́w tʰɯ̌ŋ lāmɤ̄ː ʔɔ̀ːk māː)ι
     Noi asleep tight then conn sleep-talk out come
     "Noi was fast sleep before she started to talk in her sleep."

Final particles in Thai can occur after a diverse set of syntactic units. They can occur after sentences, topic phrases, syntactic phrases and words that occur in isolation, as well as clauses that do not fit at all with any syntactic constituents. Although syntactically diverse, these units that host final particles all constitute intonational phrases. Consider the examples that follow.

(7) a. (nɔ́ːj nɔ̄ːnˈ nāːn)ι na-L%
       Noi sleep long-time FP
       "It's just that Noi sleeps for a long time."

b. (ˈnɔ́j)ι là
   Noi   sleep
   "And Noi?"

c. (nɔ́ːj)ι na-L%   (nɔ̄ːn saˈbāːj)ι
   Noi   FP   sleep   comfortable
   "Noi, she sleeps comfortably."

d. (nɔ́ːj làp   saˈnìt)ι ja-L% (lɛ́w tʰŭŋ   lāmɣ̄ː   ʔɔ̀ːk ˈmāː)ι
   Noi   asleep tight   FP   then   conn   sleep-talk out   come
   "Noi was fast asleep before she started to talk in her sleep."
   (non-restraint, female speaking)

e. (nɔ́ːj ˈlâw)ι na-H%   (wâː   mêː   líəŋ   ˈmáː)ι
   Noi   relate   FP   comp   mother raise   horse
   "Noi told us that her mother raised horses, if I remember correctly."

In (7a), the final particle /na/ 'COMMON GROUND' follows a sentence consisting of one single intonational phrase. In (7b), the particle /là/ 'TOPIC SWITCH' occurs after a proper name, which functions as subject of an omitted predicate and by itself forms an intonational phrase. In (7c), the final particle /na/ 'COMMON GROUND' occurs after a topic phrase, which constitutes a separate intonational phrase. In (7d), where the sentence is composed of more than one coordinate clause, the final particle /ja/ 'FEMALE, NON-RESTRAINT' occurs finally to one of the clauses, which also forms an intonational phrase. The fact that an optional pause is possible after the final particle /ja/ is a good diagnostic that the sentence is divided into two separate intonational phrases. Most crucially, in (7a) the particle /na/ occurs after the matrix clause of a subordinate sentence, which does not form a syntactic constituent but form an intonational phrase. These examples show clearly that the final particles are not hosted by syntactic units but by the intonational phrase.

In sum, the fact that the different types of syntactic units that precede the final particles in Thai all form intonational phrases leads to the conclusion that the final occurs to the right of intonational phrases. This generalization means that syntax is not directly relevant in determining potential sites for final particles. Rather, it is prosody that governs their distribution.

3. Final particles as clitics

In understanding the behaviors of final particles, another crucial question that needs to be answered is what kind of elements they are. The generalization that final particles select for the right edge of the intonational phrase discussed above suggests that it is prosody that underlies the peculiar behaviors of these function words. In this section, we will show that they are best characterized as a sub-class of function words, namely, clitics with the intonational phrase as their host.

Cross-linguistically, in contrast to lexical words, function words often do not have prosodic word status and, therefore, are exempted from certain metrical and prosodic constraints of the language. For example, lexical words in English must have one primary stress, e.g. *Tímothy*. However, function words like *for* are not stressed and must be prosodically dependent on the following noun, for example, *for Tímothy* (Selkirk 1995). This is also the case for Thai, in which function words normally lack word-level stress. Consistent with their status as function words, Thai final particles also show the same prosodic deficiency with respect to prominence. They do not carry word stress, which suggests that they do not have prosodic word status, as illustrated by the data in (8).

(8) a. ˈnɔ́ːj   ˈnɔ̄ːn   saˈbāːj
     Noi   sleep   comfortable
     "Noi sleeps comfortably."

  b. ˈnɔ́ːj   ˈnɔ̄ːn   saˈbāːj   máj
      Noi   sleep   comfortable   INT
      "Does Noi sleep comfortably?"

  c. ˈnɔ́ːj   ˈnɔ̄ːn   saˈbāːj   kʰráp
      Noi   sleep   comfortable   FP
      "Noi sleeps comfortably." (formal, male speaking)

In the three examples in (8), none of the final particles carries word stress. In (8a) the whole sentence is composed of only lexical words, all of which receive word stress. In (8b) the final particle /máj/ 'INTERROGATIVE' is the only element that does not have word stress. This is also the case with other final particles, such as with the final particle /kʰráp/ in (8c). The failure of final particles to receive word stress in these cases suggests that final particles do not form prosodic words by themselves.

The prosodic deficiency characteristic of Thai final particles together with their dependency on a prosodic host implies that they belong to the sub-class of function words known as clitics. According to Zec (2005), two classes of function words display differences in prosodic behaviors and in distribution: i.e. free function words and clitics. Free function words readily receive prosodic word status, given that they satisfy all the word-shape requirements of the language. For example, free function words in Standard Serbian receive prosodic word status if they are minimally disyllabic. In contrast, clitics are excluded from having an independent prosodic status and must depend on some prosodic host with their possible locations being constrained by that host, accordingly. For example, Serbo-Croatian clitics must be hosted by an independent prosodic word. They occur either before or after the host prosodic words, depending on their lexically-specified position in reference to their hosts.

In short, the primary difference between the two classes of function words lies in their readiness to assume prosodic word status. While free function words form prosodic words, clitics are excluded from having prosodic word status. In this classification of function words, Thai final particles must be characterized as clitics. Taking into account the fact that they always occur to the right of intonational phrases, they are thus best viewed as intonational clitics, a class of function words well-attested in languages like Tzotzil, Kinande and Gokana (Zec & Inkelas 1992). The clitics identified in these languages occur in positions that can be generalized with respect to an edge of the intonational phrase and not in any other terms, similar to final particles in Thai.

Assuming that clitics together with their host create a recursive structure (Zec & Inkelas 1992; Zec 2005), the prosodic structure of final particles in Thai can be represented as in (9).

(9) a. ((   )ι FP)ι

    b. ((nɔ́ːj nɔ̄ːn saˈbāːj)ι kʰráp)ι
       Noi   sleep   comfortable   FP
       "Noi sleeps comfortably." (formal, male speaking)

As a clitic, the final particle does not receive prosodic word status, and remains without word stress. Consequently, the particle must be attached to the preceding prosodic constituent. The intonational phrase thus serves as the prosodic host for the particle. The particle is attached to the right of the smaller intonational phrase, and at the same time, occupies the right edge of the larger one.

In sum, final particles in Thai are best characterized as intonational clitics that select for the right edge of the intonational phrase. It is this prosodic deficiency that explains the peculiar prosodic behaviors of the particles. In the following section, we will show that their phonological variability is attributable to their status as clitics.

4. Phonological variability of final particles

Another conspicuous characteristic of final particles in Thai is their variability with respect to their phonological shape. Although Thai generally lacks morphophonemic alternation all together, some final particles may take different surface forms as exemplified in (3). The key to understanding this phonological peculiarity is the prosodic deficiency of the final particles. More specifically, we argue that certain final particles show such variability because they are function words that may receive stress in marked circumstances. By default, they are unstressed because they, like other types of function words, are excluded from receiving prosodic word status. However, they are forced to undergo phonological modifications in specific marked contexts to satisfy weight requirements of the language on stressed syllables.

4.1 Phonological variability of final particles as stress-governed alternation

To understand the phonological variability of final particles, one important fact needs to be highlighted. Only a relatively small subset of Thai final particles actually shows such variability. Crucially, these particles are unified in their phonological character. In unmarked contexts, they typically appear as an open syllable with a short vowel. In other words, they surface as single light syllables by default. In marked structural contexts, they are stressed and become heavy by way of either glottal stop epenthesis or vowel lengthening.[2] The data in (10) shows the normal and stressed forms of particles showing phonological variability in contrast with those that do not.

(10) a. Normal   Stressed
        [kʰa]   [ˈkʰaʔ], [ˈkʰaː]   'FEMALE, FORMAL'
        [si]   [ˈsiʔ], [ˈsiː]   'EXPECTABLE'
        [na]   [ˈnaʔ], [ˈnaː]   'COMMON GROUND'
        [ca]   [ˈcaʔ], [ˈcaː]   'INTIMATE'

    b. [kʰráp]   [ˈkʰráp]   'MALE, FORMAL'
        [jāŋ]   [ˈjāŋ]   'PERFECT INTERROGATIVE'
        [rɔk]   [ˈrɔk]   'CORRECTION OF UNDERSTANDING'

In (10a), the female formal particle is realized either as unstressed and light [kʰa] in general contexts or stressed and heavy [kʰaʔ] or [kʰaː] under marked circumstances (see §4.3). The other particles in this group follow the same pattern. In contrast, the male formal particle in (10b) is a closed syllable by default and, therefore, realized as heavy [kʰráp] regardless of whether they receive word stress or not. Other particles in this group also show no variability, as expected for Thai words. The difference between the particles in (10a) and (10b) thus lies in the phonological shape of their unstressed forms. While the former are by default realized as light monosyllables, the latter are realized as heavy. This stress-governed alternation is crucial to understanding the phonological variability of the alternating clitics.

4.2 Weight requirements on Thai prosodic words

In Thai, within a prosodic word with more than one syllable, the final syllable is normally the one that receives word stress (Bennett 1994; Bennett 1995). This generalization is illustrated in (11), which shows that lexical words in Thai must be headed by a stressed syllable but function words are systematically exempted from this requirement.

(11) a. (ˈcʰáːŋ)_ω   'elephant'
        (wí.tʰīː)_ω   'method'
        (ˌrát.tʰa.ˈbāːn)_ω   'government'
        (ˌpʰāː.ˌsăː.ˈsàːt)_ω   'linguistics'

    b. [kɔ]   'LINKER'
        [ca]   'IMMINENT'

[lɛ] 'and'

The lexical words in (11a) all have one primary stress. When they consist of more than one syllable, like in [wí.tʰīː] 'method', or [ˌrát.tʰa.ˈbāːn] 'government', their head is the rightmost syllable within the word. In contrast, the function words in (11b) by default occur as [kɔ] 'LINKER' [ca] 'IMMINENT' [lɛ] 'and' without word stress. This prosodic exception is exactly one of the characteristics of final particles.

Another requirement governing the shape of the prosodic word in Thai is the one that requires each stressed syllable to be heavy. In Thai, a stressed syllable can be either closed (CVC, CVVC), or open with a long vowel (CVV), but, importantly, not open with a short vowel (CV). In other words, a prosodic word that consists of one single light syllable is disallowed (Bennett 1994; Bennett 1995). The examples in (12) illustrate this fact.

(12) a. (ˈmáː)_ω   'horse'   *(ˈmá)_ω
     b. (ˈtāj)_ω   'kidney'   *(ˈtā)_ω
     c. (sa.ˈbāːj)_ω 'comfortable, fine' *(sa.ˈbā)_ω
     d. (ka.ˈtʰíʔ)_ω 'coconut milk'   *(ka.ˈtʰí)_ω

The lexical words in (12) all have one primary stress on the rightmost syllable. These head syllables are all heavy. Crucially, these well-formed prosodic words contrast sharply with the forms on their right. These hypothetical forms are unacceptable because their head syllables are stressed but light. Recall that final particles in Thai that show phonological variability all have unstressed and light variants. Given the weight requirement of stressed syllables, the acceptability of the light forms of these function words is expected from the fact that they are not prosodic words.

4.3 Weight requirement and phonological variability

Taking into account the two requirements on the prosodic word in Thai just discussed, the variability of light final particles can be understood as an effect of general prosodic constraints of the language on the prosodic word status of the particles. In other words, the contexts in which the stressed forms are found force the final particles to assume prosodic word status (Bennett 1994; Bennett 1995). There are two special contexts in which they are forced to surface in their stressed forms.

The first context is when they are the only word in the utterance, while the second context is when they are under focus. The examples in (13) illustrate that stand-alone particles invariably appear in their stressed forms.

(13) a. ˈkʰráp
 FP
 "Yes." (formal, male speaking)

 b. ˈkʰaʔ-L%
 FP
 "Yes." (formal, female speaking)

 c. ˈkʰaː-L%
 FP
 "Yes." (formal with a mild degree of annoyance, female speaking)

The examples in (13) show final particles that occur alone in the intonational phrase. The form [ˈkʰráp] of the male formal status particle in (13a) is stressed but does not show any segmental phonological effect. When the female formal particle occurs alone, it appears with either a final glottal stop, like [ˈkʰaʔ] in (13b), or a lengthened vowel, like [ˈkʰaː] in (13c). Therefore, the epenthesis and vowel lengthening of final particles in this context can be straightforwardly explained as repair strategies to satisfy the weight requirement of stressed syllables. More specifically, the augmentation is triggered because the sole syllable of the particles must serve as the bearer of the sentential stress, which is obligatorily heavy.

Another context where light final particles appear in their stressed forms is when they are under focus, as illustrated in (14).

(14) a. nɔ́ːj   nɔ̄ːn   ˈnāːn   kʰa $_F$ -L%
     Noi   sleep long-time   FP
     "Noi sleeps for a long time." (formal female speaking)

 b. nɔ́ːj   nɔ̄ːn   nāːn   ˈkʰaʔ $_F$ -L%
     Noi   sleep long-time   FP

"Noi sleeps for a long time."
(formal with a sarcastic tone, female speaking)

c. nɔ́ːj   nɔ̄ːn   nāːn   ˈkʰaːᵢ_F   -L%
    Noi   sleep long-time FP
"Noi sleeps for a long time."
(formal with a mild slight annoyance, female speaking, female speaking)

As shown in (14) above, these final particles appear in their stressed forms when they are under focus (cf. Truckenbrodt 1995; Zec 2005). The particle in (14a) is not focused and not stressed. In contrast, the female formal particles in (14b) and (14c) are focused and appear stressed. They differ from their default unstressed form with respect to syllable structure. It is realized with a final glottal stop, and with a lengthened vowel, respectively. Although the two forms differ, they are both metrically heavy.

The data in (14) thus illustrates the effect of focus on the syllable structure of the particles. More concretely, the occurrence of the stressed forms means that final particles are forced to be stressed when they are under focus. Similar to the case of stand-alone particles, the epenthesis and vowel lengthening final particles in this context can be straightforwardly explained as repair strategies to satisfy the requirement that stressed syllables are obligatorily heavy.

In sum, the phonological variability of final particles in Thai is viewed as an effect of an interaction between general prosodic constraints of the language and the prosodic contexts that the final particles find themselves in. As lexical words must obligatorily correspond to prosodic words, they can never be prosodically deficient. They must always occur with one stressed and heavy syllable. In contrast, as function words, final particles may or may not receive stress depending on the context. By default, they occur unstressed because they are clitics, which are excluded from having prosodic word status. This lack of obligatory stress allows certain particles to appear as light. On the other hand, when final particles occur alone or under focus, they are forced to become stressed, which causes the particles to become heavy. In this sense, the peculiar phonological variability of Thai final particles is in fact not surprising given that they, unlike lexical words, can occur with or without stress.

5. Conclusion

Final particles in Thai may at first glance appear to be a highly problematic class of words, but from a prosodic point of view they are quite regular. Their seemingly "naughty" pattern in the distribution is in fact rigorously constrained, but by prosodic structure rather than by syntactic structure. Each of the syntactic entities after which final particles may occur corresponds to a single prosodic category–the intonational phrase. That is, the possible location of final particles is the right edge of intonational phrases. Their dependency on other prosodic constituents of a particular type suggests that they should be characterized as clitics, to be specific, intonational clitics.

Moreover, final particles may also seem, at first glance, exceptional because they show variability in their surface forms despite the general absence of morphophonemic alternation in the language. From a phonological point of view, this seemingly peculiar phonological behavior can be explained in terms of the general prosodic constraints of the language. The alternation is found only in final particles whose unmarked forms are metrically light and unstressed. When these particles are stressed in specific marked contexts, they become heavy in order to satisfy the general requirement that stressed syllables be heavy. In conclusion, final particles, though generally perceived to be syntactically naughty, prove to be prosodically well-behaved.

Acknowledgements

The authors are grateful to Abigail Cohn, John Whitman, Draga Zec, Nikola Predolac and Hye-Sook Lee for their feedback at various stages of this paper. We also thank the audience at the 80th Annual Meeting of the Linguistics Society of America, the International Workshop on "Intonation Phonology: Understudied or Fieldwork Languages", and the Chulalongkorn-Tohoku Cognitive & Typological Linguistics Symposium. All shortcomings this paper may have are, of course, ours. This work was supported by the Higher Education Research Promotion and National Research University Project of Thailand, Office of the Higher Education Commission (HS1231A).

Notes

1 We assume that some final particles are lexically toneless. The pitch that appears on each of them is a realization of boundary tones, symbolized by H% or L%.
2 Many particles also show apparent tonal variability in addition to the variability in the syllable structure. Pittayaporn and Tansiri (to appear) argue that these particles lack lexical tone and that the observed pitch patterns are in fact an intonational phenomenon.

References

Bennett, J. Fraser. 1994. Iambicity in Thai. *Studies in the linguistic sciences* 24. 39–57.
Bennett, J. Fraser. 1995. *Metrical foot structure in Thai and Kayah Li: Optimality-Theoretic studies in the prosody of two Southeast Asian languages*. Urbana-Champaign, IL: University of Illinois at Urbana-Champaign dissertation.
Bhamoraput, Amara. 1972. *Final particles in Thai*. Providence, RI: Brown University MA Thesis.
Cooke, Joseph R. 1989. Thai sentence particles: Forms, meaning and formal-semantic variations. In Joseph R. Cooke (ed.), *Thai sentence particles and other topics*, 1–90. Canberra: Department of Linguistics, Research School of Pacific Studies, the Australian National University.
Hall, T. Allan. 1999. The phonological word: A review. In T. Alan Hall & Ursula Kleinhenz (eds), *Studies on the phonological word*, 1–22. Amsterdam: John Benjamins.
Inkelas, Sharon. 1989. *Prosodic constituency in the lexicon*. Palo Alto, CA: Stanford University dissertation.
Inkelas, Sharon. 1999. Exceptional stress-attracting suffixes in Turkish: Representations versus the grammar. In René Kager, Harry van der Hulst & Wim Zonneveld (eds), *The prosody-morphology interface*, 134–187. Cambridge: Cambridge University Press.
Inkelas, Sharon, C. Orhan Orgun & Cheryl Zoll. 1997. The implications of lexical exceptions for the nature of grammar. In Iggy Roca (ed.), *Derivations and constraints in phonology*, 393–418. Oxford: Clarendon.
Iwasaki, Shoichi & Preeya Inkaphirom. 2005. *A reference grammar of Thai*. Cambridge, UK: Cambridge University Press.
Luksaneeyanawin, Sudaporn. 1983. *Intonation in Thai*. Edinburgh: University of Edinburgh dissertation.
Nespor, Marina & Irene Vogel. 1986. *Prosodic Phonology*. Dordrecht, Holland: Riverton, USA: Foris Publications.
Peyasantiwong, Patcharin. 1981. *A study of final particles in conversational Thai*. Ann Arbor, MI: University of Michigan dissertation.
Prasithrathsint, Amara. 2001. Syntactic distribution and communicative function of the /kh/ polite particles in Thai. *Journal of Language and Linguistics* 20. 11–23.
Selkirk, Elizabeth. 1978. On prosodic structure and its relation to syntactic structure. In Thorstein Fretheim (ed.), *Nordic Prosody II*, 111–140. Trondheim: TAPIR.
Selkirk, Elizabeth. 1981. On the nature of phonological representation. In Terry Myers, John Laver & John M. Anderson (eds), *The cognitive representation of speech*, 379–388. Amsterdam: North Holland
Selkirk, Elizabeth. 1984. *Phonology and syntax: The relation between sound and structure*.

Cambridge, MA: MIT Press.

Selkirk, Elizabeth. 1995. The prosodic structure of function words. In Jill Beckman, Laura Walsh Dickey & Suzanne Urbanczyk (eds), *Papers in Optimality Theory*, 439–470. Amherst, MA: GLSA

Truckenbrodt, Hubert. 1995. *Phonological phrases: Their relation to syntax, focus, and prominence*. Cambridge, MA: MIT dissertation.

Truckenbrodt, Hubert. 1999. On the relation between syntactic phrases and phonological phrases. *Linguistic Inquiry* 30. 219–255.

Zec, Draga. 2005. Prosodic differences among function words. *Phonology* 22. 77–112.

Zec, Draga & Sharon Inkelas. 1992. The place of clitics in the prosodic hierarchy. In D. Bates (ed.), *The proceedings of the Tenth West Coast Conference on Formal Linguistics*, 509–519. Stanford: CSLI.

Chapter 2

Etymological inquiry in a quest for the universality of human cognition: Focusing on word formation by sound symbolism

Hiroyuki Eto

1. Word formation by means of sound symbolism

1.1 "Pika-don"

Sixty-six years ago, in August 1945, just before Japan surrendered to the allied forces, America dropped two atomic bombs on Hiroshima and Nagasaki. Very few people around the world of that time, whether military or civilian, had any advance information about this new-type of bomb, because this highly-classified weapon of mass destruction had been planned and developed in complete secrecy.

Not surprisingly, therefore, the victims of the atomic bombs in Hiroshima and Nagasaki, as well as virtually all the Japanese people during the war time, had no concept of this new weapon. But they realized from its devastating power not previously experienced that it was totally different from what they knew from daily air raids. So they coined a new word *pika-don* for these new bombs in order to distinguish them from existing, conventional ones. This word is neither obsolete nor slang today, but is contained as an entry in most standard Japanese dictionaries and Japanese-English dictionaries.

The process of creating this new word is very simple. It is a perceptual representation of the victims' vivid experience of the great suffering that immediately followed. Soon after the bomb was released, it is said that they first caught a strong blinding flash of light and then heard the sound of a huge explosion. Thus the atomic bomb was described as a combination of flashing light, *pika*, and the sound of a thunderous blast, *don*. In short, the atomic bomb was so named in Japanese because it gave off a blinding flash, *pika*, followed by a huge explosive sound, *don*, with the unbelievably strong atomic blast.

1.2 Symbolic and suggestive value of "pika" and "don"

This Japanese word *pika-don* is a very good example of explaining word formation by means of sound symbolism. As explained above, *pika-don* can be divided into two elements: *pika* and *don*. The first element *pika* is now used in everyday conversation in the following way:

> *pikarito, pikatto*: with a flash
> *pikarito hikaru, pikatto hikaru*: give out a flash
> *pika-pika suru*: glitter, sparkle, flash, shine, twinkle
> *pika-pika no*: glittering, sparkling, flashing, shining, brand-new
> *pika-pika ni suru*: polish, shine, brush

Thus the word *pika*, describing the manner of flashing light, has an indispensable semantic relationship with the image of "light".

The Japanese word for "light, shine" (noun) is *hikari*, and that for "shine, gleam, twinkle" (verb) is *hikaru*. There are several theories regarding the etymology of *hikari* and *hikaru*. Some of them hypothesize that these words derived in the following manner from *pika* that represents the image of flash light: *pika* → *pikari* → *hikari, hikaru* (cf. Watanabe 1989: 233). I support this hypothesis from a viewpoint of sound symbolism.

In linguistics dictionaries, sound symbolism is usually defined as "a (fancied) representative relationship between the sounds making up a word and its meaning" (Chalker & Weiner 1994: 367). To put it another way, sound symbolism has a kind of suggestive value (Jespersen 1922: 408; Firth 1964: 184) to depict various perceptual phenomena with human articulate sounds, that is, linguistic representation or iconic description of natural phenomena in which no sounds occur. So the word *pika* is sound-symbolic, or synesthetic, in nature. When we perceive flashing light, we do not usually hear any sound. But we express the perception of light with the sound-like word *pika* as if it were heard.

On the other hand, *don*, the second element of *pika-don*, is a perfect example of the direct imitation of the sound (Jespersen 1922: 398). To be accurate, it is an onomatopoeia formed in imitation of the sound of a huge explosion of the atomic bomb. When a bomb explodes, such a great roar as *bang* or *dong* strikes our ear suddenly. Clearly the Japanese word *don* originates in the sound *dong*, the sound of a thunderous blast.

This onomatopoetic element *don* is also used in our everyday speech today as an independent word in the following manner:

don to naru: go bang
don toiu bakuhatuon: a loud bang
don to tataku: beat drums loudly; knock at the door loudly

In another context, *don-don* is used to describe rapidity, vigorousness, readiness, etc., which symbolizes the rapid and vigorous sound itself.

Onomatopoeia, combination of two Greek words *onoma* (name) and *poios* (making, creating), originally means "creating a name". It is defined as "the formation of a word with sounds imitative of the thing which they refer to; the use of such a word" (Chalker & Weiner 1994: 237). Accordingly, onomatopoeia is created by imitating a natural sound associated with what is named.

The etymological analysis of the word *pika-don* shows a rather "primitive" way to create a new word from the sound imitation. This is a good example to claim that a certain sound carries particular meaning in and of itself. It is well known that Aristotle in *On Interpretation* and Saussure in *Cours de linguistique générale* regard the arbitrariness of signs as one of the fundamental principles of linguistic science. But I support the idea that, as Plato in *Cratylus* suggests, sound symbolism — sound imitation and iconization of sound — played an important role in word creation, particularly in the primitive stage. One important question arises here: Is this connection of a particular sound with a particular image a language specific or universal in nature?

2. Sound symbolism of the English initial *bl-*

2.1 Etymology of "black"

In present-day English *black* and *white* are regarded as antonyms, words totally opposite in meaning to one another. As the OED says, *black* is "the proper word for a certain quality practically classed among colours, but consisting optically in the total absence of colour, due to the absence or total absorption of light, as its opposite *white* arises from the reflection of all the rays of light" (Simpson & Weiner 1989: vol.2, 238).

This is true not only of expression of color, but also of figurative and metaphorical use of *black* and *white*. The idiom "in black and white", for example, means "absolutely right or wrong, good or bad, with no grades between them". *White* means figuratively "morally or spiritually pure, innocent and untainted", whereas *black* "full of gloom, very depressed, tragic, etc." Synchronically the meaning range of *white* is opposed to something characterized as *black*.

The interesting — in a sense, strange — fact is that the word *black* is cognate with such words as French *blanc*, Spanish *blanco*, Italian *bianco*, all of which mean "white, shining white". In addition, the modern English word *blank* meaning "an empty space" or "a space left to be filled in a document" derives from the same origin with *black*. We may mostly associate "shining" and "an empty space" with *white*, not with *black*. Etymologically speaking, however, *black* was associated with the meaning of "shining" and "an empty space". Diachronically *black* covered a part of semantic range of *white*.

An etymological survey of *black* clarifies this interesting semantic phenomenon (cf. Buck 1949; Hoad 1986; Klein 1971; Onions 1966; Skeat 1879–1882). In Old English (OE) there existed two forms for *black*: blæc and blac. The former means "black, dark" as used in present-day English, but the latter "bright, shining, glittering, flashing". In the OE period, the notions of *black* (blæc) and *white* (blac) were distinguished by the slight differentiation of vowels.

Still in the Middle English (ME) period those two words were difficult to distinguish in meaning. Regarding the etymology of *black*, the OED explains as follows:

> OE. *blæc, blac* (def. *blace*) = OHG. *blah-, blach-* (in comb.); a word of difficult history. In OE., found also (as the metres show) with long vowel *blāce, blācan*, and thus confused with *blác* shining, white:– OTeut. *blaiko- (see BLAKE), as is shown by the fact that the latter also occurs with short vowel, *blăc, blăcum*; in ME. the two words are often distinguishable only by the context, and sometimes not by that... In Eng. *black* has quite displaced the original colour-word SWART, which remains in the other Teutonic languages. (Simpson & Weiner 1989: vol.2, 238)

As stated in this quotation, in the OE period *blæc* (black) was confused with *blac* (white), and still in the ME period both words could only be distinguished by the context. In other words, it was difficult to tell *blæc* (black) from *blac* (white) morphologically because both words are quite alike with only one subtle difference in the length of the vowel. They can be regarded as one and the same word. Why, then, is it possible for one word to carry two such totally opposite meanings?

The etymological meaning of *black* is "shining, light". This means at the same time "the total absence of color". This sense of "total absence of color", or *blankness*, may also have represented "black, dark" due to "the absence or total absorption of light" (Simpson & Weiner 1989: vol.2, 238). Until the word *white* appeared in the English language in the late 10th or early 11th century, *black* had signified both "dark (black)" and "shining (white)".

2.2 Symbolic character of *bl-*

After examining the etymology of *black*, we have to tackle a further question: Why did OE *blac* have the meaning of "shining, bright, white, pale"? The clue to the solution seems to lie in the symbolic character of the initial *bl-*.

The following list shows OE words beginning with *bl-* (cf. Bosworth-Toller 1898; Clark Hall 1960; Sweet 1896):

blāc: bright, shining, flashing, pale
blācian: to turn pale
blācung: turning pale, pallor
bladesian: to flame, blaze, be hot
bladesnung: odor
bladesung: shining, lightening
blæc: dark
blæcan: to bleach, whiten
blæcce: black matter
blæce: irritation of the skin, leprosy
blæcern: lamp, candle, light
blæco: pallor
blæcða: leprosy
blæd: blade
blæd: blowing, blast, breath, spirit
blædan: to puff up, inflate
blædnes: blossom, fruit
blædre: blister, pimple

blǣge: gudgeon, bleak
blǣgettan: to cry
blǣhǣwen: light blue
blǣse: firebrand, torch, lamp
blǣsere: incendiary
blǣst: blowing, breeze, flame
blǣstan: to blow, belch forth
blǣstm: flame, blaze
blandan: to blend, mix, trouble, disturb
blāt: livid, pale, wan
blātian: to be livid, pale
blāwan: to blow, breathe, inflame
blāwend : inspirer
blāwende: blowing hard
blāwere: blower
blāwung: blowing, blast, inflammation
blēd: shoot, branch, flower, blossom, leaf, foliage, fruit
blēdan: to bleed
blegen: blain
blendan: to blind, deprive of sight
blendnes: blindness
bleo: color
blētsian: to consecrate, ordain
blētsung: consecration
blican: to glitter, shine, gleam, sparkle, dazzle
bliccettan: to glitter
blice: exposure
blīcian: to shine
blind: dark, obscure, opaque
blindnes: blindness
bliss: bliss, merriment, happiness
blissian: to be glad, rejoice, exult
blīðe: blithe, joyous, cheerful, pleasant
blōd: blood
blōstm: blossom
blōwan: to blow

blysian: to burn, blaze

These OE words beginning with *bl-* can be roughly categorized into three semantic groups:

- Visual image: shining, bright, flashing; pale, bleach, whiten; dark
- Other sensory image: blow, blast, inflate; breathe, bleed; odor
- Figurative use in connection with expansion: blade, blossom, fruit; inflammation, flame, fire; cry; pimple, leprosy; success, glory, consecration (<shining)

To summarize these three categories, the initial *bl-* in OE words represents "physical — particularly spatial — expansion, extension, effusion, swelling". This may originate in the combination of the phonemes /b/ ([voiced bilabial] plosive) and /l/ (liquid). The combination of plosive and liquid sounds (bursting and flowing) may have symbolic value of expanding, shining, blowing, swelling, etc., and be used figuratively in connection with expansion. OE *blac* is thus a sound-symbolic word that evokes the image of "shining, bright, white, pale".

In present-day English, words beginning with *bl-* have a variety of meanings: *black, bladder, blade, blame, bland, blank, blanket, blast, blaze, bleach, bleak, bleed, blend, bless, blind, blink, blister, block, blond, blood, bloom, blossom, blot, blow, blown, blue, bluff, blunder, blunt, blur, blush*, etc. So various that it is not easy to categorize these words into a few semantic groups. In its long history English vocabulary mingles Anglo-Saxon, Norman French, Greek and Latin, and so on. Being such a hybrid language, present-day English contains words beginning with *bl-* that have various origins with different meanings from different sources.

Compared with present-day English, OE words with the initial *bl-* are more sound-symbolic, and it is easier to interpret the symbolic nature of their sound. In general, when we exemplify sound-symbolic words, we should go back as further as possible to words of an older, "more primitive", stage before the influx of foreign elements.

3. Sound symbolism of the IE root *bhel- and beyond

3.1 Symbolic character of the IE root *bhel-

We may go back much further to a far more primitive stage, examining the reconstructed Indo-European (IE) root *bhel-, from which the OE words with the initial bl- is supposed to have derived. This IE root is semantically divided into the following four groups (cf. Watkins 2000: 9–10; Pokorny 1989: 118–124):

*bhel-[1]: To shine, flash, burn; shining white and various bright colors.
*bhel-[2]: To blow, swell; with derivatives referring to various round objects and to the notion of tumescent masculinity
*bhel-[3]: To thrive, bloom. Possibly from bhel-[2]
*bhel-[4]: To cry out, yell.

These four meaning groups of *bhel- can be rearranged into the following three semantic categories:

- Physical (particularly spatial, visual, acoustic) expansion, extension, effusion, swelling: *bhel-[1], *bhel-[2]
- Figurative use in connection with physical expansion: *bhel-[3]
- Acoustic expansion: *bhel-[4]

We understand that the common image of these three categories is "expansion". This perceptional image can be regarded as the sound-symbolic character of the IE root *bhel-. As with the case of bl-, *bhel- also consists of a plosive sound bhe and a liquid sound l. Both bl- and *bhel- can be analyzed as follows:

bl-: /b/ (plosive) + /l/ (liquid) → expansion
*bhel-: bhe (plosive) + l (liquid) → expansion

3.2 Universality of human cognition of sound-symbolic values

As we have seen in the example of the OE words beginning with bl- and the IE root *bhel-, both create the image of "expansion, extension, spread". This is attributed to the symbolic character of the combination of plosive and liquid sounds.

Not only bl-, but other combinations of plosive/fricative and liquid (e.g., *fl-, pl-*) are also of the same sound-symbolic value. They have the image of expansion, extension, spread: *flag, flap, flat, flaw, flee, flight, fling, flip, flit, float, flop, flow, fluent, fluid, flush, flux, fly; place, placate, placid, plane, plant, plate*, etc. Such sound sequences that we can associate with particular meanings are "phonesthemes" (Firth 1964). In addition to *bl-, fl-, pl-*, English has a lot of phonesthemes such as *cl-, gl-, dr-, kn-, sk-, sl-, sm-, sn-, sq-, st-, sw-, tw-* (cf. e.g. Käsemann 1992; Burridge 2002; Karasawa 2003; Oda 2010). Is this phenomenon that certain sound sequences evoke particular images unique to English or observable in other languages?

The same "expansion" image created by /b/ can also be observed in the Chinese language. Most characters pronounced as *ha, ba, pa* have meaning of "expansion, extension, spread", because, I assume, the initial plosive/fricative sounds represent an "explosive" image:

巴: lie on the stomach, flatten
把: spread the palm of one's hand
波: rippling wave
爬: move on the stomach
芭: flower blooming flatly
派: separating and spreading
破: bursting, explosion
耙: till/flatten the soil
播: scatter
馬: horse, smash one's way
麻: plant growing straight

In Japanese, too, words pronounced as *ha (fa), ba, pa* used in various semantic settings have the "spreading" image in common:

ha, ba [刃]: blade
ha, ba, pa [羽]: blade, wing
ha, ba [歯]: tooth
ha, ba [葉]: leaf

In addition, the combination of "h" (fricative) and "r" (liquid) in Japanese also has the symbolic value of expansion, extension, spread:

hara　[原]: field, place
hara　[腹]: belly
hari　[針]: needle, sting
hari　[梁]: beam
haru　[張る]: stretch, spread
haru　[貼る]: paste
haru　[春]: spring (i.e., "swelling of buds")
hare　[晴]: clear up (i.e., "spreading blue sky")
hare　[腫れ]: swelling, tumor

Similar processes of the word/root-creation through sound symbolism are observed here in languages having no known linguistic relationship or historical contact. The phenomenon observed in the OE initial *bl-*, the IE root **bhel-*, and the above-described Chinese and Japanese words may, however, be no coincidence, for it can perhaps be attributed to the universality of the human brain and sense organs. As long as the human sense organs are of a universal structure, the activity of linguistic representation through human perception may result in similarities. This interpretation will make it possible to hypothesize the universality of human cognition.

4. Concluding remarks

One of the chief concerns of historical linguistics is to reconstruct the physically unreachable cultures with the help of words, which play the most important role in this endeavor as symbolic representations of a bygone reality. As each word has its own story, or history, we can retrace the process from word to thought to idea to a particular world view through the historical survey of the meaning of words, that is, etymological inquiry. This may enable us to reclaim what was once the intellectual property of ancient people and to understand their real and concrete ideas.

As long as written evidence is available, we can depend on what is remaining in a written form for etymological research. Without it, it is theoretically possible to reconstruct the form of missing words and the root of a word by an analogical approach to the systematic sound change. Even if we have reconstructed the IE root **bhel-* and assumed what it signified, it is still difficult to explain why this root had the symbolic image of "swelling, exploding". The sound-symbolic interpretation of particular words or word elements provides an insightful explanation for this.

Though Jespersen comments that "no language utilizes sound symbolism to its full extent" (1922: 406), sound symbolism provides insight into etymological inquiry. In addition, by collaboration with other disciplines, particularly with cognitive sciences and neuro-sciences that examine human cognition scientifically, sound symbolism — not as a result of mere speculation, but with scientific, cognitive, evidence — may be able to broaden the possibility of etymological inquiry in a quest for the universality of human cognition of particular sound-symbolic values.

References

Bosworth, Joseph & T. Northcote Toller. 1898. *An Anglo-Saxon dictionary: Based on the manuscript collections of the late Joseph Bosworth*; edited and enlarged by T. Northcote Toller. Oxford: Oxford University Press.

Buck, Darling Carl. 1949. *A dictionary of selected synonyms in the principal Indo-European languages*. Chicago: The University of Chicago Press.

Burridge, Kate. 2002. *Blooming English. Observations on the roots, cultivation and hybrids of the English language*. Cambridge, UK: Cambridge University Press.

Chalker, Sylvia & Edmund Weiner. 1994. *The Oxford dictionary of English grammar*. Oxford: Clarendon Press.

Clark Hall, J. R. 1960. *A concise Anglo-Saxon dictionary*. 4th ed. Toronto: University of Toronto Press.

Firth, J. R. 1964. *The tongues of men and speech*. R. Mackin & P. D. Strevens (eds), London: Oxford University Press. [Rpt. ed. of *Speech* (1930)]

Hoad, T. F. (ed.). 1986. *The concise Oxford dictionary of English etymology*. Oxford: At the Clarendon Press.

Jespersen, Otto. 1922. *Language. Its nature, development and origin*. London: George Allen & Unwin.

Karasawa, Kazutomo. 2003. Problems with the etymology of OE *dream*. *Asterisk, A Quarterly Journal of Historical English Studies* 12(2). 129–136.

Käsemann, Hans. 1992. Das englische phonästhem *sl-*. *Anglia* 110. 307–346.

Klein, Ernest. 1971. *A comprehensive etymological dictionary of the English language*. Amsterdam: Elsevier.

Oda, Tetsuji. 2010. The sound symbolism of *sc-* in Old English heroic poetry. In T. Oda & H. Eto (eds), *Multiple perspectives on English philology and history of linguistics*, 56–90. Bern: Peter lang.

Onions, C. T. (ed.). 1966. *Oxford dictionary of English etymology*. Oxford: At the Clarendon Press.

Pokorny, Julius. 1989. *Indogermanisches etymologisches Wörterbuch*. 2. Aufl. Bern: Francke.
Simpson, J. A. & E. S. C. Weiner (eds), 1989. *The Oxford English dictionary*. 2nd ed. Oxford: Clarendon Press.
Skeat, Walter W. 1879–1882. *An etymological dictionary of the English language*. Oxford: At the Clarendon Press.
Sweet, Henry. 1896. *The student's dictionary of Anglo-Saxon*. Oxford: At the Clarendon Press.
Watanabe, Shoichi. 1989. *Eigo gogen no sobyo* (*Outline of English etymology*). Tokyo: Taishukan.
Watkins, Calvert. 2000. *The American heritage dictionary of Indo-European roots*. 2nd ed. Boston: Houghton Mifflin Company.

Chapter 3

Polyfunctionality in Pwo Karen: The case of ʔàʔ- (<T-B pronominal prefix *ʔa-)

François Langella

1. Introduction

Karenic languages are spoken in an area straddling the Thai-Burmese border. Following Thurgood's classification (2003), Pwo Karen belongs to the Southern group of the Karenic family. The dialect studied in this paper is that spoken in Dong Dam village, a village of about 400 inhabitants located in Lamphun province, Northern Thailand. I shall refer to this dialect as Dong Dam Pwo Karen.

The morpheme that is the topic of this paper has been a subject of continual interest in the field of Sino-Tibetan linguistics. The main reason for this is probably that reflexes of Proto-Tibeto-Burman *ʔa- are found in a wide array of Tibeto-Burman languages, and that they occur in various environments in these languages. This ubiquity and versatility have initially led Wolfenden (1929) to reconstruct two distinct proto-elements to account for this phenomenon. Such analysis has fallen out of favor, and empirical research based on a larger sample of languages has recognized that the various semantic functions of *ʔa- are all "outgrowths of one and the same proto-element" (Matisoff 2003: 104, whose reconstruction I follow. See also Benedict 1972, as well as Lehman 1975 who reaches similar conclusions).

In his Handbook of Proto-Tibeto-Burman (2003), Matisoff spells out six semantic functions attested across the Tibeto-Burman family, which I have used as a point of departure to investigate the range of functions covered by Dong Dam Pwo Karen ʔàʔ-. Of these six functions, three are not found in Dong Dam

Pwo Karen, of which two will be dealt with in Section 2. Drawing on Solnit's analysis of Eastern Kayah Li (1997), I have divided the remaining four functions into two groups: pronominal functions (Section 3) and non-pronominal functions (Section 4). Finally, in Section 5, I discuss whether this division makes sense in the case of Dong Dam Pwo Karen. Section 6 summarizes the findings presented in the paper.

Before starting this survey of the functions of Dong Dam Pwo Karen ʔàʔ-, some remarks on selected aspects of the language's morphosyntax are in order. Dong Dam Pwo Karen exhibits morphosyntactic features that are quite typical of Mainland Southeast Asian languages (Enfield 2005): it is largely isolating and analytic, has lexical tones and a numeral classifier system and makes extensive use of verb serialization.[1] More directly relevant to this study, all noun modifiers follow the head noun, except for possessive modifiers, which occur in phrase-initial position. Furthermore, nouns can be divided into free and bound nouns. A free noun can stand alone, meaning that it can head a noun phrase and fill an argument slot in a clause, as opposed to bound nouns, which need some kind of morphological prop to behave as free nouns. I have used a numeral classifier construction in order to distinguish between the two types of nouns. A free noun must be able to fill the empty slot in the following frame: _____ + Numeral + Classifier. For example, dāuʔ 'house' is a free noun since it can directly enter in construction with khéi phlau [two CLF], as in dāuʔ khéi phlau 'two houses'. On the other hand, -kjùʔ 'sheath' is a bound noun, since *kjùʔ khéi bei (intended meaning: 'two sheaths') is syntactically ill-formed.

2. Functions not attested in Dong Dam Pwo Karen

2.1 With kinship terms

Matisoff (2003) reports that *ʔa- is often found prefixed to kinship terms, both in their vocative (1) and referential (2) uses.

(1) a-pa 'Father!' (Lahu)

(2) wa or əwa 'father' (Kachin) (Benedict 1972: 121)

Dong Dam Pwo Karen ʔàʔ- does not occur with kinship terms in their vocative use. A child from Dong Dam village simply uses the prefix-less form phá 'Father!' to call his father. ʔàʔ- does occur with kinship terms in their referential uses but always anaphorically refers to a third person possessor: ʔàʔ-phá thus means 'his/her/their father', not 'father'. Note that in Kachin, ə- alone does not carry this possessive meaning, and a distinct morpheme, kə-, is used if such a meaning is intended: kəwa 'his father' (Benedict 1972: 121).

2.2 "Aspectual" verbal prefix

In the "aspectual verbal prefix" function, *ʔa- is prefixed to a verbal root and involves valency-changing operations such as transitivizing/intransitivizing or causativizing/decausativizing processes (Matisoff 2003: 122). For example, the Jingpho verb rái 'to be' becomes ʔərái 'to arrange, to prepare', literally 'to make (something) come into being'. This function goes unreported for all the Karenic languages formerly described (Benjakul 1997; Jones 1961; Kaewsilpa 1982; Kato 2003; Solnit 1997), and Dong Dam Pwo Karen is no exception.

3. Pronominal functions

This section deals with two separate functions in Matisoff's classification. In both these functions, *ʔa- anaphorically refers to a third person entity, attached to a noun in one and to a verb in the other. Matisoff (2003: 121) calls these two functions "third person possessive" and "verbal prefix showing agreement to a third person subject", respectively. The third person possessive function is further divided into two subfunctions. In (3a), Lai Chin ʔa- is prefixed to the noun referring to the possessed entity, rool 'food', standing in for an already established possessor.[2] In (3b), Lahu ɔ̀- is prefixed to the possessed entity and preceded by the lexical possessor vàʔ 'pig'.

(3) Third person possessive (examples from Matisoff 2003: 121)
    a. "Pronominal possessor": ʔa-rool 'his/her food' (Lai Chin)
    b. "Prefixed to the thing possessed": vàʔ ɔ̀-šā 'the flesh/meat of a pig' (Lahu)

In (4), the Lai Chin prefix ʔa- occurs prefixed to a verb, anaphorically referring to a third person subject.

(4) ʔa-kal 'he/she goes' (Lai Chin, Matisoff 2003: 121)

3.1 Dong Dam Pwo Karen pronominal system

We now turn to Dong Dam Pwo Karen. The pronominal system of Dong Dam Pwo Karen is summarized in Table 1.

Table 1. Dong Dam Pwo Karen Pronominal System

Person	Possessor-N	Subject-V	V Object
1SG	(jā) càʔ-N	(jā) càʔ-V	V jā
1PL	(xɯ) ʔàʔ-N	(xɯ) ø-V	V xɯ
2	(nē) nàʔ-N	(nē) nàʔ-V	V nē
3	ʔàʔ-N	ø-V	

A noticeable feature of the Dong Dam Pwo Karen pronominal system is the presence of two sets of pronouns, free pronouns jā/xɯ/nē and bound pronouns càʔ-/naʔ-/ʔàʔ-. The frame test introduced in Section 1 equally applies to these pronouns. In the possessive constructions in (5), the second person free pronoun nē may be directly quantified by khéi ɣá (5a), while this cannot be so for the second person bound pronoun nàʔ- in (5b), which, indeed, forms an inseparable whole with the head noun dāuʔ 'house'.

(5) a. nē   khéi   ɣā   nàʔ-dāuʔ
     2   two   CLF   2-house
     'the house of you two'

    b. *nàʔ-khéi   ɣā   dāuʔ
      2-two   CLF   house
      (Intended: 'the house of you two')

Bound and free pronouns thus contrast in their distribution: only free pronouns may occur as object arguments, while they are optional, and indeed often absent, when referring to the subject or possessor entity. Bound pronouns, in contrast, do not occur in object function, while they are obligatory in subject function and in possessive constructions, as shown in (6).

(6) a. (jā)   càʔ-eŋ   phàʔla   ʔa
     1SG   1SG-eat   betel   a.lot
     "I eat a lot of betel."

b. *jā   eŋ   phàʔla   ʔa
   1SG   eat   betel   a.lot
   (Intended: "I eat a lot of betel.")

c. (jā)   càʔ-dāuʔ
   1SG   1sg-house
   'my house'

d. *jā   dāuʔ
   1SG   house
   (Intended: 'my house')

These distributional facts suggest that bound pronouns form a person-marking paradigm, close to what Bresnan and Mchombo (1987) call a system of "anaphoric agreement", as opposed to a "grammatical agreement" system. In grammatical agreement, found for example in French, a noun phrase bears the argument relation with the verb and an inflectional suffix marks agreement with this noun phrase on the verb root, in a somehow redundant manner. In anaphoric agreement, the noun phrase that may at first sight appears to function as the clausal subject "has only a non-argument function — either as an adjunct or as a topic or focus of the clause or discourse structure", while "the verbal affix functions as an incorporated pronominal argument of the verb" (Bresnan & Mchombo 1987, cited in Bhat 2004: 17). In a similar fashion, the bound pronoun in possessive constructions can be regarded as an "incorporated" possessor modifying the head noun, which can be optionally preceded by a noun or free pronoun specifying the identity of the possessor, presumably for pragmatic effects. A possessive construction can thus be described as the following schema (R) Pro-D, in which R stands for the possessor and D for possessed entity.

Another remarkable particularity of Dong Dam Pwo Karen is that it is asymmetrical in two respects. Firstly, free pronouns are asymmetrically distributed across the three persons. Free pronouns are only found to express the first and second persons: Dong Dam Pwo Karen does not have a third person free pronoun. Such a gap is not unusual in typological terms (Bhat 2004; Dixon 2010). Secondly, the third person bound pronoun ʔàʔ- is not used as an "incorporated pronominal argument to the verb" (7a), but only to signal a third person possessor (7b).

(7) a. (phɔ́i)   ø-ʔeŋ phàʔla   ʔa
       grandma   3-eat betel   a.lot
       "Grandma eats a lot of betel."

   b. phlāu   làʔ-ɣā   no   ʔàʔ-dāuʔ
      person   one-CLF   that   3-house
      'that person's house'

Finally, a few words on number marking. In accordance with Corbett's Animacy Hierarchy (Corbett 2000, cited in Bhat 2004), number marking in Dong Dam Pwo Karen is restricted to the existence of two first person pronouns, marked for number, singular jā and plural xɯ. Although the first person singular has a dedicated bound pronoun, càʔ-, there is no dedicated first person plural bound pronoun. Rather, it seems that the first person plural xɯ is treated as a third person pronoun, since it pairs up with the third person ʔàʔ- in possessive constructions, and the first person plural is zero-marked on the verb. Alternatively, one could argue that third person marking has been extended to the marking of the first person plural. It remains unclear at this stage which analysis should be preferred over the other.

3.2 Pronominal ʔàʔ- in Dong Dam Pwo Karen and other Karenic languages

The examination of the pronominal system reveals that only the third person possessive function is available to Dong Dam Pwo Karen ʔàʔ-. In this function ʔàʔ- is a member of the pronominal paradigm {càʔ-, nàʔ-, ʔàʔ-} marking reference to a third person possessor, which can optionally be specified before the prefixed head noun.

Table 2 recapitulates the facts presented in the previous sub-section and contrasts them with two other Karenic languages: Hpa-An Pwo Karen (Kato 2003) and Eastern Kayah Li (Solnit 1997).

Table 2. Comparison of Reflexes of TB *ʔa- in Three Karenic Languages

	Dong Dam PK ʔàʔ-	Hpa-An PK ʔə-	Eastern Kayah Li ʔa
Morphological status	bound form	bound form	free form
3rd p. subject	no	in sub. clauses only	yes
In possessive constructions	R ʔàʔ-D	R (ʔə-)D	Rʔa D

Table 2 shows that the reflexes of Proto Tibeto-Burman *ʔa- in the two Pwo Karen dialects and Eastern Kayah Li contrast with each other in terms of their morphological status. Interestingly, this seems to correlate with their functional range, since only in Eastern Kayah Li, which only have free pronouns, is ʔa found to function in subject position without restrictions. Furthermore, Hpa-An Pwo Karen sits halfway between Dong Dam Pwo Karen and Eastern Kayah Li, since, on the one hand, ʔə- is found prefixed to the thing possessed (like Dong Dam Pwo Karen), but not compulsorily (unlike Dong Dam Pwo Karen), and, on the other hand, it may function as a subject (like Eastern Kayah Li), although only in subordinate clauses (unlike Eastern Kayah Li).

4. Non-pronominal functions

4.1 Verb nominalizer

In Tibeto-Burman languages, reflexes of *ʔa are frequently used to derive nouns from verbs, such as in Jingpho wák 'to notch' → ʔəwák 'a notch'. In Dong Dam Pwo Karen, ʔàʔ- is hardly ever found in this use. The sole example I could find that resembles the Jingpho example is sa 'to bear fruits' → ʔàʔ-sa 'the fruits (of a tree)', illustrated in (8).

(8) a. khu.sa làʔ-thaɯ jō   sa   jāuʔ
       mango one-CLF this bear.fruit already
       "This mango tree is already giving fruits."

    b. khu.sa làʔ-thaɯ jō   ʔàʔ-sa ʔo   jāuʔ
       mango one-CLF this   -fruit exist already
       "This mango tree, it already has fruits."
       (Literally: "This mango tree, its fruits already are/exist.")

However, (8) remains an isolated example in my data, which casts doubt on the nominalizing function of ʔàʔ- in this example. A safer option at this stage would be to consider that the morpheme *sa* can function both as a verb and as a noun. Consequently, I would rather treat ʔàʔ- in (8a) as a third person possessive pronoun prefixed to the head noun *sa* 'fruits', as the literal translation between parentheses suggests.

Much more widespread is the use of ʔàʔ- to derive free nouns from adjectival roots, with the meaning 'the adjV one', for example *du* 'big' → ʔàʔ-du 'the big one'.³ Evidence that the derived forms are nouns can be found in their ability to be quantified (9a), and indeed to take noun modifiers (9b) or function as core arguments (9c).

(9) a. ʔàʔ-du   khéi   phlau
        -big   two   CLF
        'the two big ones (i.e. fish baskets)'

    b. ʔàʔ-pi   jō
        -small   this
        'this small one (i.e. fish basket)'

    c. càʔ-thái   ʔàʔ-séŋ   jāuʔ
        1SG-weave   -new   already
        "I've already woven a new one (i.e. lid of a fish basket)."

An important property of the derived nominals in (9) is that all refers to entities that the speaker assumes to be identifiable by the addressee, as a result of being possibly pointed at at the time of the utterance, such as in (9a) and (9b), or of having been previously mentioned, such as (9c), that answers the addressee's initial enquiry about the missing lid of a fish basket. This equally applies whether ʔàʔ- attaches to an adjectival root or to a bound noun (see Section 4.2).

4.2 Phonological "bulk-provider"

Before getting into the details of this function, let me first go back to Matisoff's (2003: 117) definition of phonological "bulk-provider", for the sake of clarity. Very frequently this prefix is added to roots that are already nouns, merely to give them a bit more of phonological bulk, providing them with the salience to serve as constituents in larger constructions.

According to Matisoff, this use is attested both with nouns that are already free nouns and with bound nouns. Furthermore, it may or may not involve "semantic specialization", meaning that it may or may not involve some sort of meaning increment to the noun it is attached to.⁴ When no semantic specialization is involved, the main function of *ʔa- may be to preserve the integrity of the rythmic pattern of the utterance. An example provided by Matisoff is the Lahu pair bo ~ ɔ̂-bo, which both mean 'favor, grace, advantage'. In contrast, semantic specialization is at work in Burmese ʔəmyak 'knot in timber', derived from the noun myak 'eye'.

My data does not show any cases not involving semantic specialization, and all instances of ʔàʔ- do bring some kind of meaning increment to the affixed noun. However, this may merely reflect the fact that my data comes, for the most part, from elicitation sessions, which carries the risk that informants will focus on giving to each word its own semantic contribution to the sentence, thus downplaying the role of prosody.

Keeping this caveat in mind, uses of ʔàʔ- with both free and bound nouns always involve in my data a relational interpretation, meaning that the addressee is invited to construe the referent of the affixed noun in relation to some other entity. This typically involves a possessive relationship. To further the discussion, it is worth noting that the morphological status of a noun (free vs. bound) is not without consequences on the type of possessive relationship that it can enter into with a modifier noun. This is illustrated in example (10).

(10) a.   pàʔnè   ʔàʔ-rōŋ
          buffalo   -pen
          'the buffalo's pen'

     b.   ʔ sāuʔ ʔàʔ   -rōŋ
          Sau   -pen
          (Intended meaning: 'Sau›s pen', i.e. the pen that belongs to Sau.)
          (Actual meaning: 'Sau›s pen', i.e. ʔ the pen to keep Sau in.)

(10a) and (10b) are two examples of possessive constructions following the schema [(possesso)R ʔàʔ-(possessee)D] presented in Section 3.1. The oddity of (10b) shows that when the D slot is filled by a bound noun such as -rōŋ 'pen', the range of semantic relationships holding between the possessor and the possessed entity is restricted. In other words, only a noun specifying the kind of possessed entity being talked about can fit the R slot. Therefore, when ʔàʔ- occurs prefixed to a bound noun it can only refer to a specifying noun other than a third person owner. Accordingly, càʔ-rōŋ [1SG-pen] and nàʔ-rōŋ [2-pen] are at best very odd, since they respectively mean that the speaker and the addressee are the tenants of the pen.

To summarize, when ʔàʔ- is prefixed to a free noun, it can straightforwardly be interpreted as a third-person possessive pronoun, and a member of the three-member paradigm {cà-, nà-, ʔàʔ-}. Cases when it is affixed to a bound noun are more complex insofar as it is not anymore aligned with the first and second personal pronouns cà- and nà-. If ever a phonological "bulk-provider" function has to be distinguished, it is possibly in this use with bound nouns, which, as seen above, need some kind of prop, or "phonological bulk" to occur as autonomous constituents. A related question is whether ʔàʔ- remains pronominal in this function. This forms the topic of the next section.

5. Discussion: Pronominal versus non-pronominal ʔàʔ-

5.1 Eastern Kayah Li: pronominal ʔa and formative prefix ʔa-

In both Benedict's Sino-Tibetan Conspectus (1972) and Matisoff's Handbook of Proto-Tibeto-Burman (2003), ʔàʔ- and its cognate forms in other Tibeto-Burman languages are taken to be modern reflexes of a sole Tibeto-Burman pronominal element: *ʔa-. Lehman (1975) follows this view, but leaves open the possibility that two prefixes may be distinguished in modern Tibeto-Burman languages, on the basis of the functions they fulfill in these languages. Solnit's analysis of Eastern Kayah Li (1997: 41–46) precisely echoes Lehman's point of view, insofar as he distinguishes the "unmarked third person pronoun" ʔa from the formative prefix ʔa-, "which allows the [bound] Noun to occur as a free Form without adding any other semantic coloration". Solnit (1997: 43) adduces the following example as evidence for the non-pronominal nature of ʔa- in Eastern Kayah Li.

(11) vē   sínɛ   ʔo,   mané   ʔaplɔ   ʔo   to
     1s   gun   exist   but   exist NEG
     "I have a gun, but no bullets."

In (11), Solnit argues, "it would be inaccurate to analyze ʔaplɔ [...] as a possessive construction 'its small-round-thing'". Since -plɔ 'small round thing' is a bound noun and cannot function as a main constituent on its own, and since ʔaplɔ does not refer to the bullets of a particular gun such as the one referred to in the first clause but "simply names the general category 'bullet'", it follows that ʔa- is no more than a "colorless" morphological device used to derive a free noun from a bound noun. The resulting form is thus best analyzed as "a sort of abbreviation of the compound noun sínɛ plɔ 'bullet'".

Although the uses of reflexes of *ʔa- in Eastern Kayah Li and in Dong Dam Pwo Karen show similarities, the genetic relation between the two languages is of course no sufficient reason to replicate Solnit's analysis with the Dong Dam Pwo Karen data. Whereas Solnit is able to differentiate two morphemes on the basis of their morphological status, free pronoun ʔa and prefix ʔa-, there is only one bound form ʔàʔ- in Dong Dam Pwo Karen.[5] Beyond morphology, the pragmatic properties of free nouns derived from bound nominal roots provide evidence against distinguishing between a pronominal and a non-pronominal ʔàʔ-.

5.2   Pragmatic properties of constructions involving the prefix ʔàʔ-

The use of derived nouns involving the prefix ʔàʔ- is subject to a major discourse-level restriction, namely that the speaker assumes that his interlocutor will be able to identify which kind of entity he is referring to. I will refer to this constraint as the identifiability constraint.[6] The following exchange, from which (9c) was extracted, took place between a basket weaver and a villager inquiring about the missing lid of a fish basket. The use of both ʔàʔ-phlī and ʔàʔ-séŋ is licensed by the shared knowledge of what kind of lid and which new thing, respectively, are being talked about.

(12) A: ʔàʔ-phlī   ʔo   phàʔlē
         -lid   be.at   where
     B: ɣéɣōŋ,   càʔ-thái   ʔàʔ-séŋ   jāuʔ
         broken   1SG-weave   -new   already
     A: "Where is the/its lid?"
     B: "(It's) broken. I have already woven a new one."

Although I would cautiously reckon that more naturalistic data are needed to confirm my hypothesis, I am inclined to consider that, in utterances such as (12) ʔàʔ- retains its pronominal function, and that 'its lid' is the appropriate gloss for ʔàʔ-phlī.

Furthermore, it is not obvious that compounds of the form [free specifying noun-bound noun] can be analyzed as the full-fledged expressions of nouns sharing the structure [ʔàʔ-bound noun], as Solnit proposes for Eastern Kayah Li. As illustrated in (13), such compounds contrast with possessive constructions, usually, but not systematically, involving a lesser degree of specificity: (14a) does so, (13b) may do so, but (13c) does not.[7]

(13) a. chéŋ-ja 'chicken' vs. chéŋ ʔàʔ-ja 'the flesh, meat of a chicken'
 b. mi-kɔ̄ŋ ‹a rice kratip› vs. mi ʔàʔ-kɔ̄ŋ 'a rice kratip, a kratip of rice'
 c. dāuʔ-khlāuʔ or dāu ʔàʔ-klāuʔ 'behind the house, the back of the house'

Finally, some high-frequency bound nouns are found to occur with other prefixes, such as tàʔ- or thàʔ-:

(14) a. ʔàʔ-sa   làʔ   ʔo   dāiʔ   ba
     -fruits   NEG   exist   yet   NEG
 "It (i.e. the tree) is not giving fruits yet."
 (Literally: "Its fruits do not exist yet.")

 b. tàʔ-sa   làʔ   ʔo   ba
    fruits   NEG   exist   NEG
 "There are no fruits."
 (Literally: "Fruits do not exist.")

(15) a. ʔàʔ-ja 'its flesh, meat'   ʔàʔ-dəi 'its eggs'
 b. thàʔ-ja 'meat'   thàʔ-dəi 'eggs'

The contrast between the forms referenced under (a) and those referenced under (b) in (14) and (15) parallels that opposing the possessive constructions from the compounds in (13). For example, ʔàʔ-ja 'the meat, its meat' could refer to the meat or flesh of a particular animal, whereas thàʔ-ja 'meat' refers to meat in general.[8] The origins of the prefixes tàʔ- and thàʔ- remains unsure, although it can be hypothesized that the latter thàʔ- comes from the coalescence of the free noun thə̀ 'thing, stuff' and the pronominal prefix ʔàʔ-. Indeed, my informant once tried to make the meaning of thà-dəi 'eggs' more transparent to me by spelling it out as thə̀ ʔàʔ-dəi 'eggs of something'.

6. Closing remarks

To summarize, I wish to present the findings of this paper in the form of a semantic map, following Haspelmath's notational convention (Haspelmath 2003). The square area in Figure 1 delimits the functional range of Dong Dam Pwo Karen ʔàʔ-.

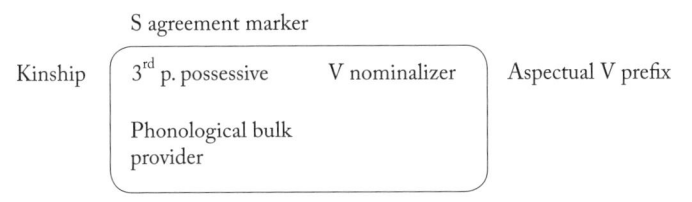

```
                    S agreement marker
                 ┌─────────────────────────────┐
   Kinship       │  3ʳᵈ p. possessive    V nominalizer  │    Aspectual V prefix
                 │                             │
                 │  Phonological bulk          │
                 │  provider                   │
                 └─────────────────────────────┘
```

Figure 1. Semantic map showing the functional range of Dong Dam Pwo Karen ʔàʔ-.

Of the six functions attributed to modern reflexes of *ʔa- across Tibeto-Burman languages, three go unattested in the case of Dong Dam Pwo Karen ʔàʔ-. These are represented outside of the square area: with kinship terms, as an aspectual verb prefix and as a verb prefix referring to a third person subject. As for the three remaining functions, ʔàʔ- appears primarily as a third person possessive pronoun, and I have attempted to show that it retains its possessive interpretation even with bound nouns, in constructions that resemble what Matisoff describe as involving the use of *ʔa- as a "phonological bulk provider". Finally, the function of verb nominalizer is represented within the functional range of ʔàʔ-, although a proviso is necessary: it was only found to occur with adjectival verbs, in a rather different configuration than in Matisoff's examples.

Acknowledgements

This research is part of the Karen Linguistics Project directed by Prof. Theraphan Luangthongkum. I am grateful to the Thailand Research Fund and to the Faculty of Arts, Chulalongkorn University, for providing financial support for my field trip in March 2010.

Notes

1. There are four lexical tones on non-checked syllables, while checked syllables (final glottal stop -ʔ) only take two tones, low and high. Transcription is as follows:
Mid tone	a (no diacritic)
Low tone	à
High tone	ā
High rising tone	á

2. Following Dixon's use (2010), the term "possession", as well as its derivatives "possessor" and "possessed entity", spans the range of semantic relationships cross-linguistically observed to be expressed through a single construction, such as kinship, whole-part relationships, hyponymy, etc.
3. Following Solnit (1997) on Eastern Kayah Li, I assume that words denoting properties, usually corresponding to the category "adjective" in English, form a subcategory of verbs in Dong Dam Pwo Karen, which I will refer to as "adjectival verbs", "adjV" in short.
4. I borrow the term "semantic specialization" from Matisoff (2003: 109), who doesn't use it in a technical sense. As suggested by an anonymous reviewer, the term "metaphorization" might be more adequate, i.e. a knot in timber is conceptualized as an eye.
5. However, Solnit (1997) notes that ʔa- is an unusual prefix, insofar as it is not unstressed, and does not undergo vowel harmony.
6. I voluntarily avoid the term "definiteness". I prefer the notion of "identifiability" which, following Lambrecht (1994), is assumed to be a universal cognitive category, which closely correlates to the language-specific syntactic category of "definitness", in languages that have it.
7. In a similar fashion, Matisoff observes that in Lahu "free-headed compounds" (what I call here possessive constructions) of the type vàʔ ɔ̀-šā [pig ɔ̀-flesh] 'the pig's flesh, the flesh of a pig' are "more specific and definite in meaning [...] while the bound headed ones are vaguer and more general", e.g. vàʔ-šā 'pork' (Matisoff 1973: 71).
8. Interestingly, the form thàʔ- is also found attached to verbs: ɣe 'spicy' gives thàʔ-ɣe 'chilli' and ʔeŋ 'eat' gives thàʔ-ʔeŋ 'food'. The former example would contrast with ʔàʔ-ɣe 'the spicy one'.

References

Benedict, Paul. 1972. *Sino-Tibetan: A conspectus*. Cambridge: Cambridge University Press.
Benjakul, Lalin. 1997. *A syntactical study of the Pwo Karen dialect in Huay-Hom-Nok village, Tambon Tha Mae Lob, Mae Tha district, Lamphun province*. Bangkok: Mahidol University MA Thesis.
Bhat, D. N. S. 2004. *Pronouns*. New York: Oxford University Press.
Bresnan, Joan & Sam Mchombo. 1987. Topic, pronoun and agreement in Chichewa. *Language* 63. 741–782.
Corbett, Greville. 2000. *Number*. Cambridge: Cambridge University Press.
Dixon, Robert M. W. 2010. *Basic linguistic theory*. Vol.1 & 2. Oxford: Oxford University Press.
Enfield, Nicholas J. 2005. Areal linguistics and mainland Southeast Asia. *Annual Review of Anthropology* 34. 181–206.

Jones, Robert B. 1961. *Karen linguistic studies: Description, comparison, and texts.* (UC Publication in Linguistics 25). Berkeley & Los Angeles: University of California Press.

Kaewsilpa, Chutima. 1982. *A description of Pho Karen: A Tibeto-Burman language in Thailand.* Bangkok: Mahidol University MA thesis.

Kato, Atsuhiko. 2003. Pwo Karen. In Graham Thurgood & Randy LaPolla (eds), *The Sino-Tibetan languages*, 632–648. London: Routledge.

Haspelmath, Martin. 2003. The geometry of grammatical meaning: Semantic maps and cross-linguistic comparison. In Michael Tomasello (ed.), *The new psychology of language*, vol. 2, 211–243. New-York: Erlbaum.

Lambrecht, Knud. 1994. *Information structure and sentence form: Topic, focus, and the mental representations of discourse referents.* Cambridge: Cambridge University Press.

Lehman, Frederic K. 1975. Wolfenden's non-pronominal a- prefix in Tibeto-Burman. *Linguistics of the Tibeto-Burman Area* 2(1). 19–44.

Matisoff, James. 1973. *The grammar of Lahu.* UC Publications in Linguistics 75. Berkeley & Los Angeles: University of California Press.

Matisoff, James. 2003. *Handbook of Proto-Tibeto-Burman: System and philosophy of Sino-Tibetan reconstruction.* UC Publications in Linguistics 135. Berkeley & Los Angeles: University of California Press.

Peansiri, Ekniyom. 1982. *A study of informational structuring in Thai sentences.* Honolulu: University of Hawai'i PhD dissertation.

Solnit, David. 1997. *Eastern Kayah Li: Grammar, texts, glossary.* Honolulu: University of Hawai'i Press.

Thurgood, Graham. 2003. A subgrouping of the Sino-Tibetan languages: The interaction between language contact, change and inheritance. In Graham Thurgood and Randy LaPolla (eds), *The Sino-Tibetan languages*, 632–648. London: Routledge.

Wolfenden, Stuart. 1929. *Outline of Tibeto-Burman linguistic morphology.* London: Royal Asiatic Society.

Chapter 4

Global distribution of nominal plural reduplication

Vipas Pothipath

1. Introduction

Reduplication is a morphological process widely distributed throughout most parts of the world. In this process, the entire root/stem or a part of it is repeated for semantic or grammatical purposes (Rubino 2005: 114), as in (1) and (2).

(1) Turkish (Altaic; Turkey; Kornfilt 1997: 433)
    sepet 'basket'   sepet-sepet 'baskets'

(2) Wambaya (West Barkly; Australia; Nordlinger 1998: 43)
    bungmaji 'old man'   bung-mungmaji 'old men'

Reduplication has been shown to exhibit a rich variety of meanings with various word classes. For instance, when applied to verbs, reduplication is employed as a grammatical device to express the continuation or repetition of an action. Such a language is Warekena (Arawakan; Brazil): e.g. *tsapia* 'jump' versus *tsapi-pia* 'jump many times' (Aikhenvald 1998: 348). With adjectives and adverbs, reduplication may serve to express intensity. A straightforward case is found in Hunzib (Nakh-Daghestanian; Russia), e.g. *bat'iyab* 'different' versus *bat'-bat'iyab* 'very different' (Berg 1995: 34). Nevertheless, the notable function of reduplication to be discussed in this paper involves indicating plurality with nouns, as already exemplified in (1) and (2). This type of reduplication is henceforth referred to as *nominal plural reduplication* (or NPR).

The function of reduplication as the morphological means of forming plurals clearly reflects an iconic similarity between the linguistic forms and their meaning in terms of quantity. The repetition of form suggests a greater number of referents. The correspondence of linguistic form and its meaning as such is known as *linguistic iconicity*. Nominal plural reduplication therefore instantiates the principle referred to in Haspelmath (2008: 1) as "the iconicity of quantity"—that is, "greater quantities in meaning are expressed by greater quantities of form". Several iconic linguistic phenomena are to some extent universal (i.e. found in a number of languages regardless of genetic or geographic relationships), such as onomatopoeic words. Accordingly, it is reasonable to assume that NPR, which is iconic in nature, is likely to be a commonly attested linguistic feature, at least among languages with reduplication.

Reduplication has been particularly well-studied; however, NPR represents a reduplicative construction that has so far attracted relatively little attention in typological linguistics literature. Therefore, this paper will explore the areal distribution of NPR in the world's languages, illustrated on typological maps. The next section provides an overview of a few previous typological studies in relation to the areal distribution of reduplicatives and NPR in particular. Then, section 3 explicates the definitional criteria and the typological sample used in this study. Section 4 describes the global distribution of NPR, accompanied by typological maps. Finally, section 5 summarizes the paper and adds a few concluding remarks.

2. Previous work

Reduplication has received considerable attention from linguists, perhaps from Moravcsik (1978) onwards, for the several past decades. The reader is referred to the online Graz database on reduplication for a list of more than 2,000 bibliographical references on reduplication (cf. Hurch 2005). This section, however, will focus only on a few recent typological studies on reduplication, especially those which are relevant to NPR.

According to Rubino's (2005: 114–117) research on areal distribution of reduplication, the phenomenon is cross-linguistically regular. Reduplicative constructions occur in 311 out of 367 languages in the sample or 85 per cent of the languages shown on Map 1. The only clear area where reduplication is absent is western Europe. Still, this work does not examine how many of the world's languages use reduplication as a means of forming plurals.

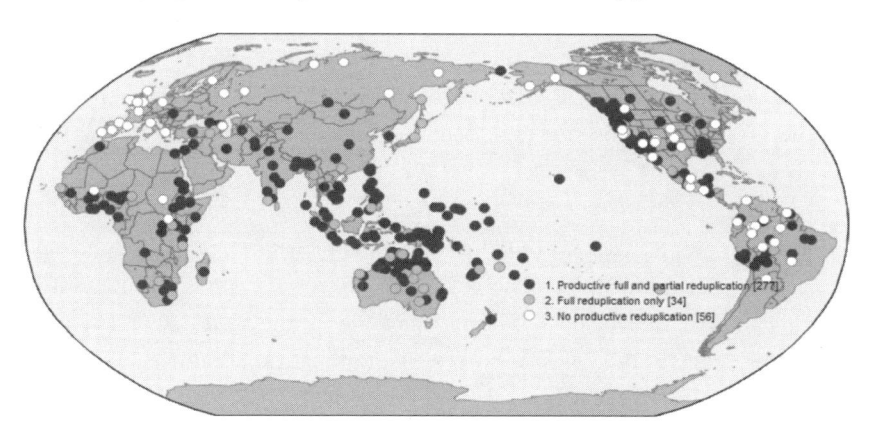

Map 1. Geographical distribution of reduplication
(Rubino 2005: 116–117, computer-generated).

Dryer (2005) investigates various grammatical devices which languages employ to indicate plurality on nouns. It is found that only 8 out of 957 languages in his sample use *complete reduplication* (i.e. the entire root is repeated, see example (1)) as a *primary* method for indicating plurality. The number of languages with this strategy is surprisingly small. This is because the languages indicating plurality by using *partial reduplication* (i.e. a part of the root is repeated, see example (2)) and the languages using reduplication as a *non-primary* method for expressing plurality are not counted in at all. Otherwise, the number of languages in which nouns form their plural by reduplication must be much higher than reported in Dryer's survey.

Kajitani (2005) explores 16 languages representing various genetic groups and geographical areas to test Uspensky's hypothesis (1972: 70 in Kajitani 2005: 93–94) about the preferential ranking of the four semantic properties of reduplication. These include *augmentation* (increase of quantity) of which NPR is an instance, *diminution* (decrease of quantity), *intensification* (increase of degree), and *attenuation* (decrease of degree). It was found that *augmentation* is universally preferred over the other three properties. The second preference is *intensification*, which is statistically preferred over *attenuation* and *diminution*. Considering the generalizations made by Kajitani along with the widespread occurrence of reduplication in the world's languages, it is reasonable to expect NPR to be fairly common. This is because *augmentation* is ranked first in the hierarchy. However, as mentioned in Kajitani (2005: 97), there are two types of *augmentation*: augmentation of *participants of an event* (comparable to NPR, see the subtypes of NPR in §3.1) and augmentation of *events* (e.g. repetition or continuation of an action). Therefore, when saying that *augmentation* is the most frequent type of reduplication, it does not necessarily mean that NPR must also be regularly found.

Hurch's (2005) *Graz Database on Reduplication* is a project that provides information on most aspects of reduplication, namely phonology, morphology, semantics, diachrony and productivity. The project also provides substantial examples taken from about 100 languages across the world. In relation to semantics, reduplication has a variety of grammatical meanings, including nominal pluralization which perhaps corresponds to NPR here. However, the project does not intend to do strict random sampling. It is stated clearly that some languages in the sample are taken into consideration because they contain interesting reduplication types or when the reference grammars provide satisfactory information on the reduplication system. Therefore, it is hard to know exactly how common NPR is.

3. Definitional criteria and language sample

3.1 Definitional criteria

Reduplication of nouns has been found to express various subtypes of nominal plurality (cf. Moravcsik 1978: 317–318). For the present study, languages surveyed are classified as having NPR when the reduplicative constructions express any kind of nominal plurality as below.

In many languages, reduplication plays an important role in plural formation with no special meanings. In such cases, the reduplicative constructions simply express '*more than one* individual', as illustrated in (3) – (5).

(3) Hausa (Afro-Asiatic; Nigeria; Jagger 2001: 65)
 àkàwu 'clerk' àkàwu - àkàwu 'clerks'

(4) Kilivila (Austronesian; Papua New Guinea; Senft 1996: 45)
 gwadi 'child' gugwadi 'children'

(5) Yaqui (Uto-Aztecan; Mexico; Dedrick & Casad 1999: 264)

káa 'house'   ka-káa 'houses'

Reduplication is also used to form plural nouns with the special plural meaning '*every* individual'. The examples in (6) – (8) illustrate this.

(6) Mandarin (Sino-Tibetan; China; Lin 2001: 69)
ren 'man'   ren-ren 'everybody'

(7) Maltese (Afro-Asiatic; Malta; Borg & Azzopardi-Alexander 1997: 272)
dar 'house'   dar-dar 'every house'

(8) Tamil (Dravidian; India; Annamalai & Steever 1998: 124–125)
vīti 'street'   vīti-vīti 'every street'

Certain languages employ reduplication to indicate plurality along with the meaning '*different kinds* of individuals'. The following examples are from Burmese, Semelai and Kambera.

(9) Burmese (Sino-Tibetan; Burma; Okell 1969: 46)
yawa 'village'   ăywaywa 'various villages'

(10) Semelai (Austro-Asiatic; Malaysia; Kruspe 2004: 220)
kraba 'official'   kraba-krabat 'various officials'

(11) Kambera (Austronesian; Indonesia; Klamer 1998: 41)
'ama bokul 'elder'   'ama-ama bokul 'various elders'

It is possible that in some languages, reduplication serves to convey the meaning '*each individual*'. Buru is an example of such a language.

(12) Buru (Austronesian; Indonesian; Grimes 1991: 75)
geba 'person'   geba-geba 'each person'

3.2 Language sample

The present study is based on a synchronic sample of 190 languages. The sample includes one representative language at least from most language families across the globe, plus a few representative languages from creoles and pidgins chosen from major geographical areas of the world. An attempt has been made to ensure that the sampling is as free as possible of genealogical and geographical biases. Nevertheless, the sample of 190 languages is somewhat biased towards a few large language families such as Indo-European, Austronesian and Australian languages, since these families contain many genera. It is assumed here that any living languages which are well-documented have an equal chance of representing the language groups. The sample includes both languages with NPR and those without. The selection of languages within the genera and/or the family is random. Regarding language classification, this study follows the classification presented in the *World Atlas of Language Structures* (Haspelmath, Dryer, Gil & Comrie 2005; henceforth *WALS*), one of the most up-to-date cross-linguistic databases for typological studies. The reader is referred to the appendix for a list of the sample languages, the examples of NPR and the references therein.[1]

The language data reported in the paper are mainly based on *reference grammars*. Since a large database is needed for the phenomenon in question, this methodology is thus more practical than eliciting information from native speakers through questionnaires or from texts. Also, reduplication is well-described in most reference grammars, so the data can be obtained directly from them. In addition, where necessary, the information was checked with language experts.

4. Geographical distribution

4.1 Overview

This section addresses the geographical distribution of NPR in the languages of the world. The text is accompanied by one single world map (Map 2) and 7 inset blown-up maps of certain zoomed areas (Maps 3–9). All maps were generated with the *Interactive Reference Tool of the World Atlas of Language Structures (WALS)*, developed by Hans-Jörg Bibiko (cf. Haspelmath et al. 2005) (used with permission). The single world map shows 190 languages, which are sorted into 2 categories: languages in which NPR is reported, marked as black, and those where NPR is not reported, marked as white. A couple of points need to be noted. That is to say, although the data were collected carefully and language experts have been consulted, it is hard to confirm the absence of NPR in some languages. The white dots representing 'NPR not reported' on the map do not necessarily mean that NPR is absent. In fact, the feature probably does exist but due to the fact that this grammatical feature is not productive, it has not attracted much attention from grammarians. It should be added that even though the languages are described as lacking NPR, they may indeed have other types of reduplication. Note also that a language is considered as having NPR here, no matter whether or not the NPR is productive in the language. The reader is referred to the appendix for a geographically and genealogically organized list of the sample languages as well as examples of NPR. Map 2 below shows the following areal-typological configurations with respect to NPR.

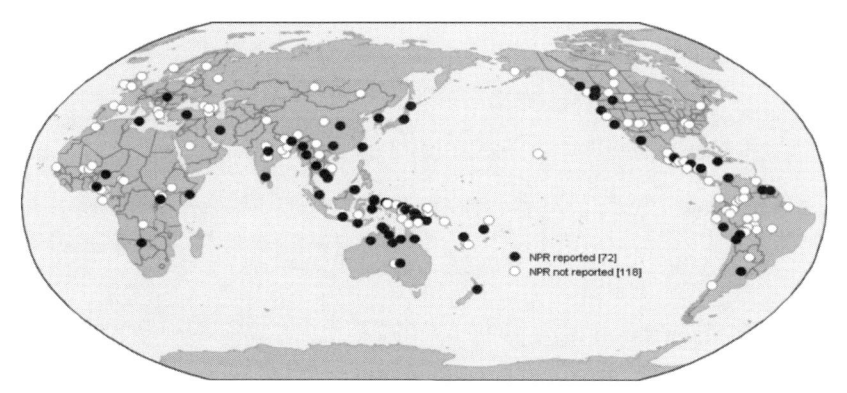

Map 2. Geographical distribution of NPR in the world's languages.

The first and most important finding is that although languages having reduplication are quite widely distributed throughout most parts of the world, as demonstrated on Map 1 (cf. Rubino 2005: 114–117), the overall number of languages in which nouns form their plurals by reduplication is a bit smaller than one might expect. Only 72 out of 190 languages in the current sample (i.e. about 38 per cent) are reported to have NPR. The finding suggests that although NPR occurs generally, it is not really a favoured grammatical device to form nominal plurals in the world's languages. As Map 2 shows, the particular concentrations of NPR are in only two macro-areas, namely Australia & New Guinea as well as Southeast Asia & Oceania.

4.2　Australia and New Guinea

Nominal plural reduplication is typical for Australia (Map 3). Almost all Australian languages in the sample (8 out of 10 languages) employ reduplication as a morphological device to express nominal plurality despite the fact that many of them have plural suffixes. It is not clear from the available sources, though, how NPR is functionally different from plural suffixes. However, according to the examples given in the appendix, the Australian languages seem to have NPR in human nouns.

In Australia, NPR occurs in different genera of Australian languages. The examples in (13) – (15) below illustrate this in Bunuba (Bunuban; Western Australia), Diyari (Pama-Nyungan; South Australia), and Wambaya (West Barkly; Northern Territory). In the survey, there are only 2 languages in which NPR is not reported, namely Gaagudju (Gaagudju; Northern Territory) and Arabana (Pama-Nyungan; South Australia).

(13)　Bunuba (Rumsey 2000: 69)
　　　ngarranayi 'mother'　　ngarrngarranyi 'mothers'

(14)　Diyari (Austin 1981: 105)
　　　kupa 'child'　　kupa-kupa 'children'

(15)　Wambaya (Nordlinger 1998: 43, 106)
　　　bungmaji 'old man'　　bungmungmaji 'old men'

Since almost all Australian languages examined have NPR, the existence of NPR in Australia is perhaps attributable to genetic inheritance rather than areal contact. Even though this speculation may seem possible, the genealogical affinity of the languages in the area is under discussion (cf. Dixon 2001: 64).

Another NPR hotbed can be found in the Pacific, including New Guinea. In the Pacific region, NPR is particularly well-attested in Papua New Guinea (Map 4), where a number of language groups are spoken. NPR in Papua New Guinea occurs in 7 out of 15 languages (or 5 out of 10 language families), i.e. about half of the languages explored in this area. These include Nagatman (Yale), Ambulas (Sepik), Kaki Ae (Eleman), Kilivila (Austronesian) and a few languages of the Trans-New Guinea family, namely Amele, Binandere and Nankina. Current distributions across different families in Papua New Guinea perhaps point to historical relationships in some way. The following examples are from Nagatman, Kaki Ae and Nankina.

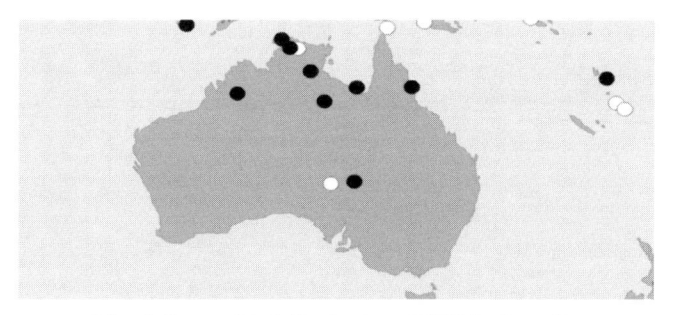

Map 3. Geographical distribution of NPR in Australia.

(16) Nagatman (Campbell & Campbell 1987: 36)
 iko 'boy'   ikoiko-wa 'only boys'

(17) Kaki Ae (Clifton 1997: 37)
 aua 'child'   aua'aua 'children'

(18) Nankina (Spaulding & Spaulding 1994: 112)
 mʌnji 'male.child'   mʌnji-mʌnji 'children'

Off Papua New Guinea, NPR remains widespread in the Pacific region, stretching from Taiwan in the north to New Zealand in the south. Languages having NPR in this area are mostly confined to the Austronesian family. The phenomenon is represented in many languages such as Atayal (Austronesian; Taiwan), Begak (Ida'an) (Austronesian; Malaysia), Kambera (Austronesian; Indonesia), Bislama (pidgins and creoles; Vanuatu), Rotuman (Austronesian; Fiji) and Maori (Austronesian; New Zealand), illustrated in (19) – (21).

(19) Atayal (Rau 1992: 116)
 btunux 'stone'   b-btunux 'stones'

(20) Begak (Ida'an) (Goudswaard 2005: 276)
 anak 'child'   anak-anak 'children'

(21) Rotuman (Vamarasi 2002: 27)
 oʔi 'parent'   oʔ- oʔi 'parents'

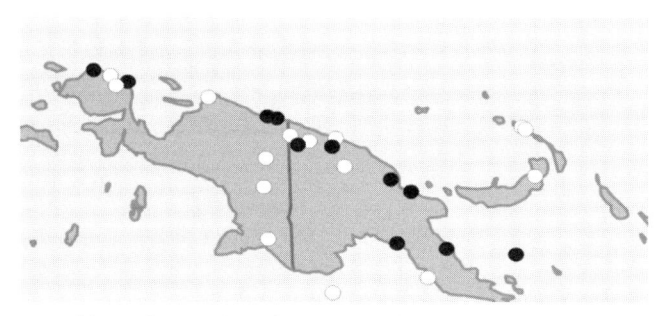

Map 4. Geographical distribution of NPR in New Guinea.

As the Austronesian family stretches from Taiwan to New Zealand, it is tempting to consider this as an Austronesian phenomenon. However, it seems likely that languages with NPR and languages without NPR can be found interspersed although such cases belong to the same genus. For example, Rotuman (Austronesian; Oceanic; Fiji) has NPR, whereas Erromangan (Austronesian; Oceanic; Vanuatu) does not. Then, one may wonder whether NPR is native to the Pacific languages. However, more data are required to answer this question and the issue goes beyond the scope of the current study.

4.3 Southeast Asia and Oceania

Another area that seems to be characterized by NPR is mainland Southeast Asia (Map 5). It is observed in 7 out of 10 languages in the region, representing 3 major language families in the region, namely Tai-Kadai, Sino-Tibetan, and Austro-Asiatic, as illustrated in (22) – (24). However, it does not occur in some of the Austro-Asiatic languages, namely Sapuan (Bahnaric; Laos), Khmu' (Palaung-Khmuic; Laos) and Sedang (Bahnaric; Vietnam). This may reflect that the areal pattern is stronger than the genetic bonds among the Southeast Asian languages, and also there appears to be areal influence in some way in the distribution of NPR in Southeast Asia and the Pacific region. An in-depth investigation of areal distribution and the productivity of NPR among Southeast Asian languages is required to test the hypothesis.

(22) Mulao (Jung & Zheng 1993: 34)
 kon^2 'table' kon^2-kon^2 'every table' (^{2} is the superscript tone marker)

(23) Burmese (Okell 1969: 46)

yawa 'village'   ăywaywa 'various villages'

(24) Semelai (Kruspe 2004: 220)
kraba 'official'   kraba-krabat 'various officials'

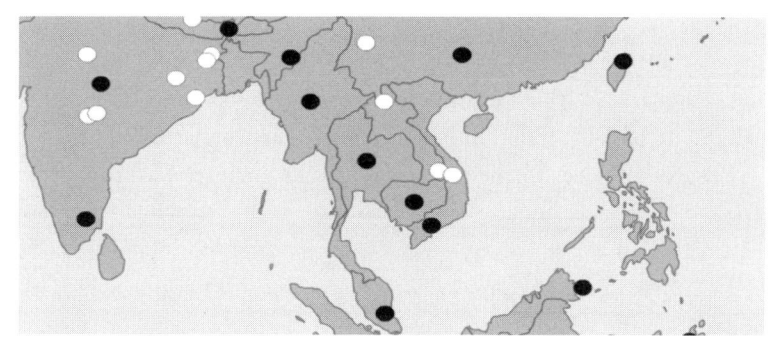

Map 5. Geographical distribution of NPR in Southeast Asia and adjacent areas.

4.4 North America

Outside of the main areas mentioned above, NPR can also be observed in some other regions although the situation does not seem to be particularly strong. The first to mention are the Americas. As Map 2 above demonstrates, the NPR area extends from the western coast of North America to the western coast of South America. Within the Americas, NPR is more common in North America than in South America.

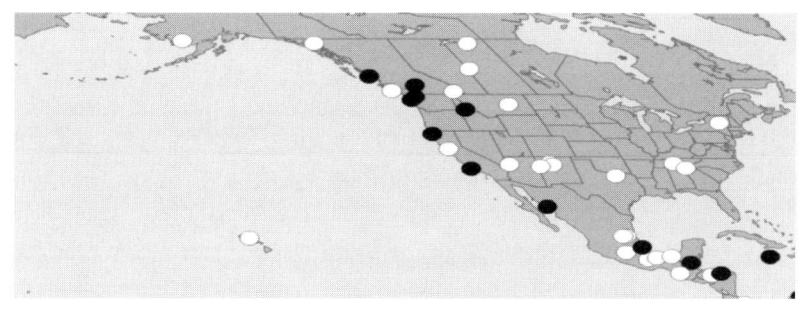

Map 6. Geographical distribution of NPR in North America.

In North America (Map 6), it appears that languages without NPR are in the majority. NPR is found in 11 out of 35 languages, representing 5 out of 25 language families. The phenomenon is geographically restricted, showing a regional concentration only on the western coast of the continent. One may see this area as extending from Canada in the north down to Mexico in the south. Examples are Tsimshian (Coast) (Penutian; Canada and US), Lillooet (Salishan; Canada), Yurok (Algic; California, US), Yaqui (Uto-Aztecan; Mexico) and Itzaj (Mayan; Mexico). One token (Jamaican Creole) comes from creoles, a group of languages in which reduplication seems to be common (Gooden 2007: 67). Examples of NPR found in North America are illustrated in (25) – (27). The NPR area stretches further southward to the north-eastern part of South America.

(25) Tsimshian (Coast) (Dunn 1979: 13)
 dasx 'squirrel' dikdasx 'squirrels'

(26) Lillooet (Eijk 1997: 56)
 s-ɣap 'tree' s-ɣap-ɣáp 'trees'

(27) Jamaican Creole (Kouwenberg et al. 2003: 107)
 buk 'book' buk-buk "many 'books'

4.5 South America

Within South America, NPR is relatively infrequent. However, two possible clusters of NPR are in the north-eastern part and the west-central part of the continent. There are only 7 out of 31 languages in which NPR is in evidence, representing 5 out of 24 language families plus 2 creoles. In north-eastern South America, this strategy occurs in Petch (Chibchan; Honduras) and Ika (Chibchan; Colombia) plus two creoles, namely Berbice Dutch Creole (creoles and pidgins; Guyana) and Ndyuka (creoles and pidgins; French Guiana and Suriname). Then it skips the central area to show up again in Quechua (Tarma) (Quechuan; Peru), Mosetenan (Mosetén; Bolivia), Aymara (Aymaran; Peru), Guaicuruan (Mocoví; Argentina) in the south-western part of the continent. The following examples show nominal plural reduplicative constructions in South America.

(28) Ika (Frank 1985/2003: 76)

ipa 'book'   ipapá 'a number of books'

(29) Mosetén (Sakel 2004: 58)
jedye' 'thing'   jedye'-jedye' 'things'

(30) Berbice Dutch Creole (Kouwenberg 2003: 258)
fɛnsrɛ 'window'   fɛnsrɛ- fɛnsrɛ 'a number of windows'

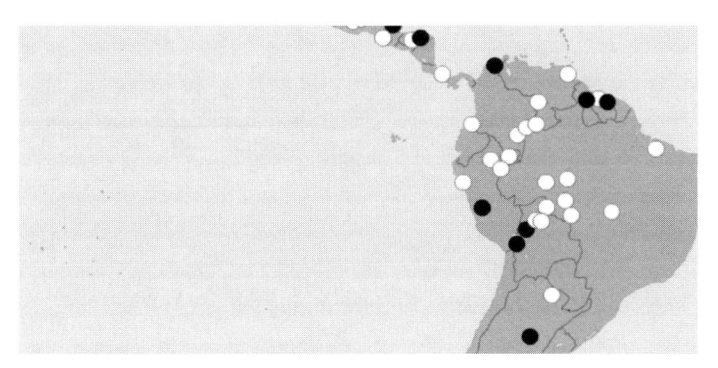

Map 7. Geographical distribution of NPR in South America.

4.6 Africa

Unlike the regions mentioned above, the phenomenon is relatively uncommon in Africa and Eurasia (a linguistic area containing the languages of Europe and most parts of Asia (cf. Dryer 1989)—only sporadic cases have been identified. In Africa, languages with NPR do not cluster in any particular area (Map 8). There are only 6 tokens observed in Africa, limited to representatives of Afro-Asiatic languages, namely Somali (Somalia), Hausa (Niger, Nigeria) and Maltese (Malta) and of Khoisan languages, namely ⊠Ani. In addition, two instances come from pidgins and creoles, namely Nigerian Pidgin (Nigeria) and Nubi (Uganda). The other African languages investigated are marked as white. Examples illustrating African nominal plural reduplicative constructions are (31) – (33) below.

(31) Maltese (Borg & Azzopardi-Alexander 1997: 272)
dar 'house'   dar dar 'every house'

(32) Nigerian Pidgin (Faraclas 1996: 243)
 mòto 'car'   mòto-mòto 'cars'

(33) ǁAni (Heine 1999: 57)
 aan 'child'   oan-oan 'boys'

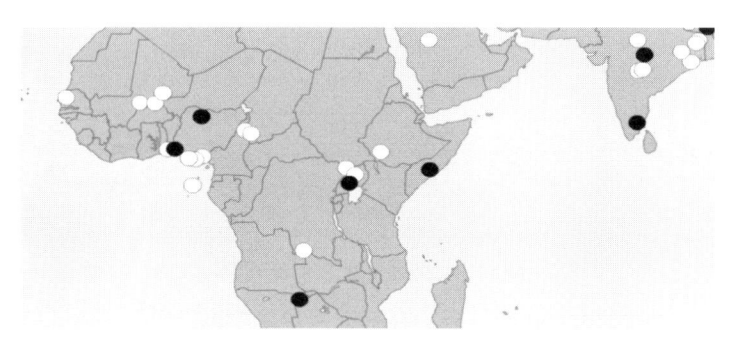

Map 8. Geographical distribution of NPR in Africa.

4.7 Eurasia

In Eurasia (see Map 2), NPR is quite infrequent in the western part of the region and exceptionally rare in Western Europe. Roughly speaking, most of the languages in this large area lack NPR. Exceptions to this areal tendency are found in the eastern part of Eurasia. There are only 9 instances of it among the 34 Eurasian languages in the sample. As illustrated in (34) – (36), NPR occurs in various language families, though. These include Japanese (isolate; Japan), Ainu (isolate; Japan), Korean (isolate; Korea), Persian (Indo-European; Iran), Hungarian (Uralic; Hungary), Turkish (Altaic; Turkey), Kolami (Dravidian; India), Tamil (Dravidian; Indian) and Korku (Austro-Asiatic; India). Interestingly, Persian is the only Indo-European language found to have NPR, probably due to the influence of neighbouring NPR languages.

(34) Persian (Iran; Mahootian & Gebhardt 1997: 340)
 bæcce 'child'   bæcce-mæce 'children'

(35) Turkish (Turkey; Kornfilt 1997: 433)
 sepet 'basket'   sepet-sepet 'baskets'

(36) Japanese (Japan; Iwasaki 2002: 78)
    yama 'mountain'   yama-yama 'mountains'

The area with virtually no NPR is the vast northerly Eurasian landmass including the Caucasian mountain zones, forming the largest homogenous *non*-NPR area. The area extends between Gaelic (Indo-European, Scotland) in the west and Mongol (Khamnigan) (Altaic, Mongolia) in the east. Almost all northern Eurasian languages display an absence of NPR with only few exceptions, such as Mandarin, Ainu and Korean.

As can be seen from Map 2, one clear area where NPR is completely absent is Western Europe. Given the fact that reduplication is atypical for Indo-European, it comes as no surprise that almost all European languages, except Hungarian, lack NPR.

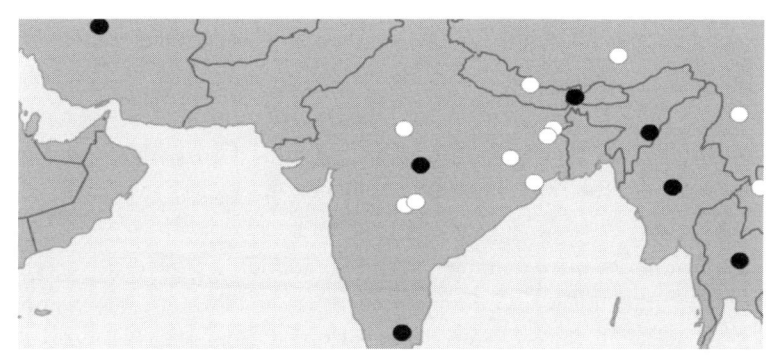

Map 9. Geographical distribution of NPR in South Asia and adjacent areas.

Languages with NPR occur only sporadically in South Asia, where there are four large language families, namely Indo-European, Dravidian, Austro-Asiatic and Sino-Tibetan. Interestingly, despite the fact that reduplication is very rich here (Rubino 2005), only 3 cases of NPR from different families are shown, namely Lepcha (Sino-Tibetan; Bhutan), Korku (Austro-Asiatic; India) and Tamil (Dravidian; India).

In summary, the following general tendencies can be observed. Although reduplication occurs all over the world, 38 per cent of the languages in the survey employ this strategy to form nominal plurals. There are two large areas in which NPR occurs with a remarkable density. One is Australia & New Guinea. The other is Southeast Asia & Oceania. Languages with NPR are moderately common in the Americas, overlapping appreciably with non-NPR languages. Instances of NPR are mostly found along the Pacific coast of the two continents. Apart from these areas, the distribution is fairly infrequent and geographically uneven. Unsurprisingly, this strategy is not reported for Western Europe where reduplication is extremely rare.

5. Concluding remarks

What the data from this paper make clear is that although NPR is iconic, this grammatical feature is not a universal characteristic of human languages as assumed. In addition, given the typology of NPR, the question may involve the search for typological correlation with other language types. At first glance, there appears to be a tendency for NPR to be particularly common in Southeast and East Asia and Australia, where optionality or absence of plural marking is found (cf. Haspelmath 2005). On the contrary, NPR is extremely rare in European languages in which plural marking systems are obligatory. To some extent, the presence of NPR may correlate with the language's general lack of morphological plurals, e.g. Mandarin (Sino-Tibetan), Thai (Tai-Kadai) and Khmer (Austro-Asiatic). This may hold as a tendency in creoles, the languages of Southeast and East Asia, and some Australian languages. However, as shown in the appendix, counter-examples to this correlation are generally observed, especially in other areas, for example, Lepcha (Sino-Tibetan; India; Southeast Asia & Oceania), Turkish (Altaic; Turkey; Eurasia) Somali (Afro-Asiatic; Somalia; Africa), Lillooet (Salishan; Canada; North America), and Aymara (Aymaran; Bolivia; South America). These languages appear to favor the obligatoriness of plural marking as well as nominal plural reduplication. The occurrence of NPR, therefore, does not seem to be related in any significant way to the presence of a plural marking system.

Finally, since there are languages with both NPR and regular plural forming strategies, it is reasonable to assume that NPR tends to express special plural meanings (cf. Moravcsik 1978: 317–318). This assumption is supported by Dryer's (2005) findings, that is to say, among the 957 languages in the sample, only 8 use *complete reduplication* as a *primary* method for forming nominal plurals. Therefore, NPR is perhaps a grammatical strategy employed to convey additional meanings other than plurality.

Acknowledgements

The research was supported by the Center of Excellence Program on Language, Linguistics and Literature (Chulalongkorn University Centenary Academic Development Project), Faculty of Arts, Chulalongkorn University, and the Higher Education Research Promotion and National Research University Project of Thailand (HS1231A), Office of the Higher Education Commission, Ministry of Education, Thailand. This is hereby gratefully acknowledged. The author would also like to thank the Department of Linguistics, the Max Planck Institute for Evolutionary Anthropology, Leipzig, Germany for permission to use the library facilities freely. Thanks are due to several people who kindly provided data for languages in the sample. Finally, the author is grateful beyond words to Associate Professor Dr. Kingkarn Thepkanjana for her tremendous and unwavering support.

Notes

The appendix to the paper can be found on the website of *The Center of Excellence for Language, Linguistics and Literature (CELLL):* http://ling.arts.chula.ac.th /CELLL/index.php.

References

Aikhenvald, Alexandra Y. 1998. Warekena. In Desmond C. Derbyshire & Geoffrey K. Pullum (eds), *Handbook of Amazonian languages*, vol. 3, 215–439. Berlin: Mouton de Gruyter.
Annamalai, Elayaperumal & Sandford B. Steever. 1998. Modern Tamil. In Sanford B. Steever (ed.), *The Dravidian languages*, 100–128. London: Routledge.
Austin, Peter. 1981. *A grammar of Diyari, South Australia*. Cambridge: Cambridge University Press.
Berg, Helma van den. 1995. *A grammar of Hunzib*. München: Lincom Europa.
Borg, Albert & Marie Azzopardi-Alexander. 1997. *Maltese*. London: Routledge.
Campbell, Carl & Jody Campbell. 1987. *Yade grammar essentials*. Ukarumpa: Summer Institute of Linguistics.
Clifton, John M. 1997. The Kaki Ae language. In Stefan A. Wurm (ed.), *Materials on languages in danger of disappearing in the Asia-Pacific region, vol.1: Some endangered languages of Papua New Guinea: Kaki Ae, Musom, and Aribwatsa*, 3–65. Canberra: Australian National University.
Dedrick, John M. & Eugene H. Casad. 1999. *Sonora Yaqui language structures*. Tucson: University of Arizona Press.

Dixon, Robert M. W. 2001/2006. The Australian linguistic area. In Alexandra Y. Aikhenvald & Robert M. W. Dixon (eds), *Areal diffusion and genetic inheritance: Problems in comparative linguistics*, 64–104. Oxford: Oxford University Press.

Dryer, Matthew S. 1989. Large linguistic areas and language sampling. *Studies in Language* 13. 257–292.

Dryer, Matthew S. 2005. Coding of nominal plurality. In Martin Haspelmath, Matthew S. Dryer, David Gil & Bernard Comrie (eds), *The world atlas of language structures*, 138–141. Oxford: Oxford University Press.

Dunn, John A. 1979. *A reference grammar for the Coast Tsimshian language*. Ottawa: National Museums of Canada.

Eijk, Jan van. 1997. *The Lillooet language: Phonology, morphology, syntax*. First Nations Language 1. Vancouver: University of British Columbia Press.

Faraclas, Nicholas G. 1996. *Nigerian pidgin*. London: Routledge.

Frank, Paul S. 1985/2003. *A grammar of Ika*. Philadelphia: University of Pennsylvania dissertation.

Gooden, Shelome. 2007. Morphological properties of pitch accents in Jamaican Creoles reduplication. In Magnus Huber & Viveka Velupillai (eds), *Synchronic and diachronic perspectives on contact languages*. Amsterdam & Philadelphia: John Benjamins.

Goudswaard, Nelleke E. 2005. *The Begak (Ida'an) language of Sabah*. Amsterdam: Vrije Universitet dissertation.

Grimes, Charles E. 1991. *The Buru language of Eastern Indonesia*. Canberra: Australian National University dissertation.

Haspelmath, Martin. 2005. Occurrence of nominal plurality. In Martin Haspelmath, Matthew S. Dryer, David Gil & Bernard Comrie (eds), *The world atlas of language structures*, 142–145. Oxford: Oxford University Press.

Haspelmath, Martin, Matthew S. Dryer, David Gil & Bernard Comrie (eds). 2005. *The world atlas of language structures*. Oxford: Oxford University Press.

Haspelmath, Martin. 2008. Frequency vs. iconicity in explaining grammatical asymmetries *Cognitive Linguistics* 19. http://www.eva.mpg.de/lingua/staff/ haspelmath/pdf/Iconicity.pdf. (5 February, 2011.)

Heine, Bernd. 1999. *The Ani: Grammatical notes and texts, Working Paper* 11. Köln: Institut für Afrikanistik, Universität zu Köln.

Hurch, Bernhard. 2005. *Graz database on reduplication*. http://reduplication.uni-graz.at/redup/. (6 July, 2010.)

Iwasaki, Shoichi. 2002. *Japanese*. Amsterdam: John Benjamins.

Jagger, Philip. 2001. *Hausa*. Amsterdam & Philadelphia: John Benjamins.

Jung, Wang & Guoqiao Zheng. 1993. *An outline grammar of Mulao*. Canberra: Australian National University, National Thai Studies Center.

Kajitani, Motomi. 2005. Semantic properties of reduplication among the world's languages. *LSO Working Papers in Linguistics* 5: *Proceedings of WIGL 2005*. http://ling.wisc.edu/lso/wpl/5.1/LSOWP5.1-08-Kajitani.pdf. (March 23, 2010.)

Klamer, Marian A. F. 1998. *A grammar of Kambera*. Berlin: Mouton de Gruyter.

Kornfilt, Jaklin. 1997. *Turkish*. London: Routledge.

Kouwenberg, Silvia. 2003. Reduplication in Berbice Dutch Creole. In Silvia Kouwenberg (ed.), *Twice as meaningful: Reduplication in Pidgins, Creoles and other contact languages*, 255–263. London: Battlebridge.

Kouwenberg, Silvia, Darlene LaCharité & Shelome Gooden. 2003. An overview of Jamaican Creole reduplication. In Silvia Kouwenberg (ed.), *Twice as meaningful: Reduplication in Pidgins, Creoles and other contact languages*, 105–110. London: Battlebridge.

Kruspe, Nicole. 2004. *A grammar of Semelai*. Cambridge: Cambridge University Press.

Lin, Hua. 2001. *A grammar of Mandarin Chinese*. München: Lincom Europa.

Mahootian, Shahrzad, & Lewis Gebhardt. 1997. *Persian*. London: Routledge.

Moravcsik, Edith. 1978. Reduplicative constructions. In Joseph H. Greenberg (ed.), *Universals of human language: Word structure*, vol. 3, 297–334. Stanford: Stanford University Press.

Nordlinger, Rachel. 1998. *A grammar of Wambaya, Northern Australia*. Canberra: Pacific Linguistics.

Okell, John. 1969. *A reference grammar of colloquial Burmese*. London: Oxford University Press.

Rau, Der-Hwa V. 1992. *A grammar of Atayal*. New York: Cornell University dissertation

Rubino, Carl. 2005. Reduplication. In Martin Haspelmath, Matthew S. Dryer, David Gil & Bernard Comrie (eds), *The world atlas of language structures*, 114–117. Oxford: Oxford University Press.

Rumsey, Alan. 2000. Bunuba. In Robert M. W. Dixon & Barry J. Blake (eds), *The handbook of Australian languages*, 34–152. Oxford: Oxford University Press.

Sakel, Jeanette. 2004. *A grammar of Moseten*. Nijmegen: Katholieke Universiteit Nijmegen dissertation.

Senft, Gunter. 1996. *Classificatory particles in Kilivila*. Oxford: Oxford University Press.

Spaulding, Craig & Pat Spaulding. 1994. *Phonology and grammar of Nankina. Data papers on New Guinea languages* 41. Ukarumpa, Papua New Guinea: Summer Institute of Linguistics.

Vamarasi, Marit K. 2002. *Rotuman*. München: Lincom Europa.

Chapter 5

On the distinction between transitive and intransitive verbs in Thai

Kingkarn Thepkanjana

1. Introduction

Verbs in any language are traditionally classified into transitive verbs (henceforth TVs) and intransitive verbs (henceforth IVs). The word "transitive" is derived from a Latin verb *transeo*, which means 'to go over or across'. The definition of the Latin verb implies a movement from one place to another. A remnant of this meaning is still present in the word "transitive" used as a grammatical term. The definitions of the TV are traditionally provided in two ways: syntactic and semantic. The TV is syntactically defined as a verb which requires a direct object (henceforth DO) while the IV has no DO (Jespersen 1969; Chomsky 1965). Semantically, the TV is defined as a verb which expresses an activity which is "carried over" or "transferred" from one participant to another, or a verb that expresses the effects of an action which pass over from the agent to the patient (Lyons 1968). The IV, in contrast, denotes an action which is not transferred between two participants or which does not have an effect on another participant. The semantic definition presupposes that the TV has two arguments denoting two participants whereas the IV has but one. However, the English verbs 'to leave', 'to hear', 'to reach' and 'to suffer' as in *He left Bangkok, I heard a noise, He reached Bangkok*, and *He suffered a stroke*, are considered TVs by the syntactic definition but, by the semantic criteria, are not considered TVs. This is because there is no transfer of an activity from one participant to another in the actions indicated by the four verbs above. The direct object arguments of the four sentences above are not the participants which "receive" the actions expressed by the verbs. It is apparent that some syntactically defined TVs are in conflict with the semantic definition of TVs as illustrated in the English examples above. TVs and IVs in Thai are defined along the same line. Panupong (1962), Warotamasikkhadit (1963) and Kullavanijaya (1974) propose a syntactic definition of TVs whereas Phraya Uppakitsilapasarn (1918), a traditional Thai grammarian, postulates a semantic definition, i.e. a TV is a verb that is not complete in meaning without an object.

However, to determine whether a given verb in Thai is a TV or an IV is not simple because of the following reasons. The semantic criteria for identifying both types of verb are vague and elusive. It is not easy to prove that a verb is complete or incomplete in meaning. Nor is it easy to say with certainty whether a verb expresses an activity which is carried over or transferred to another participant. Therefore, the semantic criteria cannot be completely relied upon. As for the syntactic criteria, a verb is identified as a TV if it can be followed by a noun. However, omitting linguistic elements including DOs is prevalent in Thai. Some linguists have observed that the DOs of TVs in Thai can be omitted. Kullavanijaya states that DOs in Thai can be omitted on two conditions, that is, (1) in certain contexts subject to recoverability (where omitted DOs are easily understood), (2) when the DOs are either indefinite or cognate.[1] Noss (1964) even claims that DOs in Thai can be freely omitted. The question is how we know whether or not a particular verb which appears in a sentence without a DO is actually followed by a DO at any level of representation. In other words, how do we know if the DO is merely omitted but in fact understood in a given context, or, if there is no DO present at any level of understanding? One of the tests is to try to put a noun after the verb. If the verb allows the occurrence of a noun to follow, it can be considered a TV. Another test is to put the interrogatives àray 'what' and khray 'who' after the verb. If a meaningful question can be formulated or if it is possible to think of an answer to that question, it means that the verb does have a DO. For example, verbs such as wítòk 'worry', khít 'think', nâŋ 'sit', dâyyin 'hear', kròot 'be angry', nɔɔn 'lie, sleep' and dəən 'walk', are identified as TVs on syntactic grounds since they can be followed by nouns or the interrogative words. In contrast, the verbs rɔ́ɔŋhây 'cry', yɯɯn 'stand' and lúk 'rise', are syntactically identified as IVs since they cannot be followed by either nouns or interrogative words. The fact that a verb allows the presence of a DO naturally leads one to believe that the verb is in itself semantically incomplete and so needs a DO to complete its meaning. However, this does not always hold true in Thai. The problem is that our intuition sometimes suggests that some verbs which occur with DOs, such as pràmàa 'be nervous', sŏŋ sǎy 'be suspicious', dəən 'walk', thûam 'flood', pìak 'be wet', com 'sink', are not semantically incomplete when occurring without a DO. Some people categorize these verbs as intransitive verbs because they feel that these verbs are semantically complete without a DO. We can see that there are two kinds of transitivity emerging from the discussion above, namely, syntactic and semantic transitivity. It is apparent that the two kinds of transitivity do not always coincide with each other in Thai. It has been noted that there are some cases in which Thai speakers are of the same opinion and other cases in which they are not as to the type of a given verb. For example, Thai speakers consider the following verbs TVs: tii 'hit', lây 'expel', tàt 'cut' and láaŋ 'wash', whereas the following verbs are IVs: rîip 'hurry', rɔ́ɔŋhây 'cry', yím 'smile', and tòk 'fall'. However, there is some disagreement over the verbs kròot 'be angry', kèŋ 'be skilful', phɔɔcay 'be satisfied', thûam 'flood' and chanàʔ 'win'. This paper will investigate what semantic underpinnings may lie behind such intuitive judgments. To be precise, this paper will analyze the semantic properties of the groups of verbs that are uniformly and not uniformly agreed upon as TVs and IVs. The data analyzed in this paper is drawn from the appendices in two theses, namely, *Intransitives in Thai* (Phancharoen 1967) and *Transitive verbs in the Thai language* (Kanchanawan 1969). These appendices contain lists of three groups of verbs, namely, TVs, IVs and ambivalent verbs or AVs. TVs are syntactically defined in these theses as verbs that inherently require DOs. However, the DOs can be omitted in appropriate contexts. IVs are defined as verbs that do not allow the presence of a DO. AVs are defined as verbs that have DOs which are optional even out of context; therefore, they may occur both with and without DOs. The DOs of AVs are thus regarded as extra arguments of the verbs.

2. The prototype approach to transitivity

There are two "theories" which can be classified as the prototype approach to the concept of transitivity. The first one is set forth by Hopper and Thompson (1980). According to Hopper and Thompson, transitivity is a property of a clause, not a verb. It involves a number of components, one of which is the presence of a direct object. Clauses can be more or less transitive depending on the features of the parameters of transitivity. Hopper and Thompson identify ten components or parameters of transitivity and study the ways in which they are typically encoded by languages. Each parameter suggests a scale according to which clauses can be ranked. The ten parameters are listed below.

	High Transitivity	**Low Transitivity**
a. Participants	2 or more participants, A (agent) and O (object)	1 participant
b. Kinesis	action	non-action
c. Aspect	telic	atelic
d. Punctuality	punctual	non-punctual
e. Volitionality	volitional	non-volitional
f. Affirmation	affirmative	negative
g. Mode	realis	irrealis
h. Agency	A high in potency	A low in potency
i. Affectedness of O	O totally affected	O not affected
j. Individuation of O	O highly individuated	O non-individuated

Of all the ten parameters of transitivity listed above, three are concerned with the lexical semantics of verbs, namely, kinesis, aspect and punctuality; two with the properties of the entities denoted by the subject arguments, namely, volitionality and agency; and the other two with those denoted by the direct object arguments, namely, affectedness of O and individuation of O. The word "kinesis" refers to the movement of an organism in response to a stimulus such as light. In the context of transitivity, kinesis refers to the transfer of energy from one participant to another. Actions involve the transfer of energy between participants whereas states do not. Aspect is the viewing of the temporal structure of an action. A telic action, which has an endpoint or conceptual boundary, is more effectively transferred to a patient than one without an endpoint. Punctuality is concerned with the suddenness of an action, i.e. whether or not there is a transitional phase between inception and completion. Actions carried out with no obvious transitional phase between inception and completion have a more marked effect on the patients than those with transitional phases. Volitionality is concerned with the agent's purpose in carrying out an action. A volitional action has more effect on the patient than a non-volitional one. Agency is concerned with the semantic properties of the agentive subject on the Agency Hierarchy (Silverstein 1976) shown below. The left end of the cline represents the highest agency or potency whereas the right end represents the lowest.

> 1st Person > 2nd Person > 3rd Person > Proper Name > Human > Animate > Inanimate

Volitionality and agency concern the degree of planned involvement of an agent in the activity expressed by the verb. The affectedness of O, which refers to the change-of-state of O as a result of the action denoted by a transitive verb, suggests the degree to which an action is transferred to a patient, and, consequently, suggests how effectively the action is done. The individuation of O refers to both the distinctness of the patient from the agent and to its distinctness from its own background. Transitivity seen in this light can be broken down into the ten components listed above, each of which focuses on a different facet of the transferring of an action in a different part of the clause. These ten parameters allow clauses to be characterized as more or less transitive. The more features a clause has in the high transitivity column, the more transitive it is. In short, the notion of transitivity in Hopper and Thompson's account is not a clear-cut category but rather a continuum.

The other theory which belongs to the prototype approach is that of proto-roles put forth by Dowty (1991). Dowty argues that thematic roles are not discrete categories but rather cluster concepts. He postulates two cluster concepts, which are called proto-roles in his theory, namely, Proto-Agent or Agent Proto-Role, and Proto-Patient or Patient Proto-Role. Only these two role types are needed to describe argument selection. Arguments in a sentence are posited to have different degrees of membership in a role type. He postulates the following contributing properties for the Proto-Agent and Proto-Patient (Dowty 1991: 572).

(i) Contributing properties for the Proto-Agent:
    a. volitional involvement in the event or state
    b. sentience (and/or perception)
    c. causing an event or change of state in another participant
    d. movement
    (e. exists independently of the event named by the verb)

(ii) Contributing properties for the Proto-Patient:
   a. undergoes change of state
   b. incremental theme
   c. causally affected by another participant
   d. stationary
   (e. does not exist independently of the event, or not at all)[2]

In this paper, I will draw on insights from the prototype approach, especially the parameters which are relevant to the lexical semantics of the verbs and the semantic properties of the direct object arguments, in analyzing the three groups of verbs.

3. Transitive verbs (TVs)

The verbs that are listed under the TV list in the appendix in *Transitive Verbs in the Thai Language* (Kanchanawan 1969) are volitional, action verbs, i.e. verbs which denote activities performed with volition on the part of the agent. The TVs in this appendix may be classified into three subclasses according to the semantic roles of DOs.

3.1 TVs with created DOs

The TVs of this type are creation verbs such as sâaŋ 'build', tɛ̀ɛŋ 'compose' and kɔ̀ɔ 'build'. The entities referred to by the DO arguments of these verbs do not exist before the performance of the actions. However, these entities represent the goals that the agents have in mind while performing the actions. The verbs of this type are volitional, actional, telic, non-punctual and take a subject noun phrase which is high in potency. In addition, the created entities resulting from performing the actions denoted by these verbs are highly individuated because they are highly distinct from the agents and from their own background. However, the parameter of affectedness of O is not applicable to this type of verb because O does not exist before the performance of the action. The parameter of "createdness of O" is thus postulated for this type of TV only.

The semantic features of this type of TV are as follows:

[+actional]
[+telic]

[+volitional]
[−punctual]
[+Agent high in potency]
[+createdness of O]
[+DO highly individuated]

3.2 TVs with target DOs

The target refers to an entity which "receives" a volitional action carried out by an agent in some way. The target is the entity which an action is directed at. This group of TVs is subclassified according to whether the DO is affected or not and according to the degree of affectedness of O as below.

3.2.1 TVs with highly affected DOs

This group of verbs may be used as answers to the question: What does someone do to an entity? The entities which receive the actions denoted by these verbs have a high degree of physical and conceptual distinctness from the agents and from their own background. In other words, the agents are physically distinct from the patients in that they are highly individuated participants which interact with each other. The agents are conceptually distinct from the patients in that they are characterized by opposing semantic properties in terms of their involvement with the events in question. In addition, they are highly and physically affected by the actions. The affectedness can be in the form of a change of state or a change of location. Some examples of these verbs are tàt 'cut', tɔ̀y 'punch', yók 'lift' and sùup 'pump'. These verbs are semantically actional, telic and usually volitional. Some verbs of this type, such as tàt 'cut' and tɔ̀y 'punch', are punctual, whereas others are not. The semantic features of the verbs of this type are shown below.

[+actional]
[+telic]
[+volitional]
[±punctual]
[+Agent high in potency]
[+DO highly affected]
[+DO highly individuated]

3.2.2 TVs with moderately affected DOs

This group of verbs have all of the same set of semantic features as those in the first group but one, i.e. the DOs of this group of TVs are moderately affected, or in other words, less highly affected than those in the first group. Some examples of this group of verbs include kòtkhìi 'oppress', khúkkhaam 'threaten', kooŋ 'deceive', ùppathăm 'support', tômtŭn 'fool', raŋkhwaan 'annoy' and chûay 'help'. The symbol ~ is used in front of the feature [DO highly affected] to indicate that the DO is moderately affected or less highly affected than in the first group. In addition, the DOs of these verbs can be individuals, collective groups of people, or even organizations. Therefore, the referents denoted by the DO noun phrases are less individuated than those in the first group, henceforth marked by the symbol ~.

[+actional]
[+telic]
[+volitional]
[-punctual]
[+Agent high in potency]
[~DO highly affected]
[~DO highly individuated]

3.2.3 TVs with non-affected DOs

The verbs of this type are characterized by the fact that they express actions which are directed at some entities but do not affect or produce any perceptible change in the entities denoted by the DO arguments. Unlike TVs with affected DOs, TVs with non-affected DOs do not constitute appropriate answers to the question: What does someone do to an entity? However, the DOs still represent targets of actions but receive no effect from them. These verbs can be characterized as actional, nontelic, usually volitional and nonpunctual. It is not necessary for the actor to be high in potency. However, the DOs are physically and conceptually distinct from the agents and from their own background. Some examples of these verbs include dàa 'scold', piin 'climb', klàp 'return', pay 'go', hàw 'bark', thákthaay 'greet', khɔ̀ɔpkhun 'thank', sɔ̌ɔn 'teach', phàan 'pass', chom 'praise' and tamniʔ 'reprimand'. Notice that the examples of this type of verb are of two types, i.e. communicative and motional. The communicative verbs express verbal actions which target somebody. On the other hand, the motional verbs express motions or actions of traveling across, over, through, or to a locational entity, which can be perceived as a target of a motional action. However, the DO entities which are targets of the actions denoted by the TVs are not necessarily affected by the actions. The semantic features of these verbs are spelled out below.

[+actional]
[-telic]
[+volitional]
[-punctual]
[±Agent high in potency]
[-DO highly affected]
[-DO highly individuated]

3.3 TVs with non-target DOs

Verbs of this type express non-translational body motions. In this kind of motion, the agent moves a body part without changing the overall position. The agent's motion may result in a certain body posture. The DOs of these verbs typically refer to body parts. Some examples of this type of verb are bòok (mɯɯ) 'wave hand', phayák (nâa) 'nod (face)', ŋəəy (nâa) 'lift (face)', kôm (nâa) 'lower (face)', khɔ́ɔm (tua) 'bend (body)'. It is obvious that the body parts realized by the DO arguments are the entities that are actually in motion. They are therefore the entities that "act", not the entities that are "acted upon". The entities indicated by the subject noun phrases represent the human beings that are in possession of the relevant body parts and are in control of those body motions. We can see that the body parts expressed by the DO arguments represent the "immediate" actors of the motions whereas the human beings expressed by the subject noun phrases represent the more "remote" actors of the motions. Since the body parts are considered to be "active" entities rather than "passive" ones in the actions, they are considered non-target entities. This is the case of DOs with low individuation since the DO argument represents the affected entity that is not physically and conceptually distinct from the agent. The affected entity, which is in this case a body part, is physically a part of the agent and also contributes to the performance of the action. The semantic features of this group of verbs are shown below.

[+actional]
[−telic]
[+volitional]
[−punctual]
[+Agent high in potency]
[+DO highly affected]
[−DO highly individuated]

Among the various groups of TVs discussed above, the group of TVs that has the highest degree of transitivity is TVs with highly affected target DOs, which have only one transitivity feature represented as the plus/minus sign, namely, [±punctual]. The groups of TVs that have lower degrees of transitivity are TVs with created entity DOs, TVs with less highly affected target DOs, TVs with non-affected target DOs and TVs with non-target DOs, respectively. We can see that the TVs with non-target DOs have the lowest degree of transitivity since they have three low-transitivity features. The types of TVs discussed above are diagrammatically represented in Figure 1.

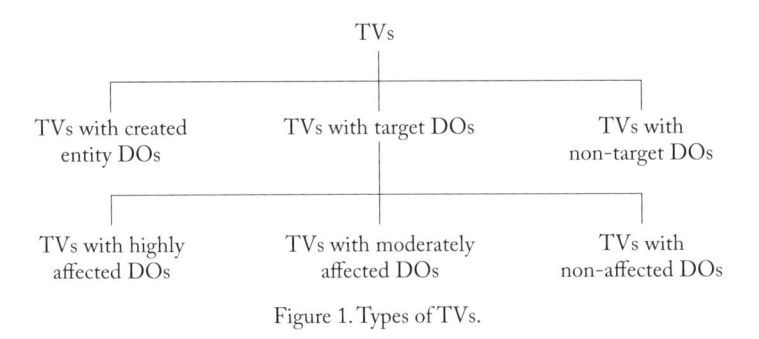

Figure 1. Types of TVs.

The semantic features of all of the types of TVs described above are summarized in Table 1.

Table 1. Semantic Features of All Types of TVs

	TVs with created entity DOs	TVs with target DOs (highly affected)	TVs with target DOs (moderately affected)	TVs with target DOs (non-affected)	TVs with non-target DOs
Actional	+	+	+	+	+
Telic	+	+	+	−	−
Volitional	+	+	+	+	+
Agent high in potency	+	+	+	±	+
DO created or highly affected	+	+	~	−	+
DO highly individuated	+	+	~	+	−
Punctual	−	±	−	−	−

4. Intransitive verbs (IVs)

The verbs listed under the IV list of the appendix in *Intransitives in Thai* (Phancharoen 1967) may be classified into three subclasses on the basis of whether the IVs are actional or not. The first subclass consists of [+actional] IVs, the second one [±actional], and the third one [−actional]. The semantic features of the IVs are described formally in terms of five semantic features, i.e. [actional], [telic], [volitional], [punctual] and [Agent high in potency]. Since these verbs are intransitive, the two semantic features describing the properties of the DO, namely, [DO highly affected] and [DO highly individuated], are not relevant.

4.1 [+Actional] IVs

4.1.1 IVs indicating unspecified body actions without external control

The verbs in this group express unspecified body actions which are initiated by the agents and are not transferred to any other participants. They are semantically vague in that we do not know exactly how the actions expressed by these verbs are performed. Some examples of verbs in this group are phákphɔ̌ɔn 'rest', nɔɔn 'lie, sleep', rîip 'hurry' and thalǎy 'dawdle'. These verbs typically take human subjects and express volitional actions. The semantic features are described below.

[+actional]
[–telic]
[+volitional]
[–punctual]
[+Agent high in potency]

4.1.2 IVs indicating translational motions and vocal actions

The verbs in this group express two types of actions: translational motions and vocal actions. The former express motions of the body in specific manners with change in overall position such as rûaŋ 'fall', pliw 'drift', lǎy 'flow', khlaan 'crawl', wîŋ 'run' and tên 'dance'. These verbs are characterized by the fact that we can visualize clearly how the motions expressed by these verbs are realized. The vocal action verbs express actions of making speech as well as nonspeech sounds such as phɯmpham 'murmur', phûut 'say', hàw 'bark', kriìtróɔŋ 'scream', móo 'boast' and rɔ́ɔŋhây 'cry.' Some of these verbs take human while others take nonhuman subjects. In the former case, the actions can be carried out volitionally as well as nonvolitionally. The semantic features of these verbs are shown below.

[+actional]
[–telic]
[±volitional]
[–punctual]
[±Agent high in potency]

4.2 [±Actional] IVs : IVs indicating actions resulting in body postures

Verbs which can be actional or nonactional IVs are those which express actions which result in body postures, such as nâŋ 'sit', yɯɯn 'stand' and nɔɔn 'lie, sleep'. These verbs are ambiguous between (a) actions which change body postures, and (b) stationary body postures resulting from actions in (a). Therefore, the feature [actional] is marked by the plus/minus sign. Note that the subjects of these verbs can be both human and nonhuman; thus the feature [Agent high in potency] must be marked also by the plus/minus sign. If the IVs are actional verbs which take human subjects, the actions are volitional. The semantic features of these verbs are shown below.

[±actional]
[-telic]
[±volitional]
[-punctual]
[±Agent high in potency]

4.3 [-Actional] IVs
4.3.1 IVs indicating physical sensations and symptoms

The verbs in this group express physical sensations and symptoms of animate entities including human beings and animals such as sadûŋ 'be startled', ay 'cough', khan 'itch', khlûɯnsây 'nauseous' and caam 'sneeze'. Some of these verbs express telic and punctual actions such as sadûŋ 'be startled', ay 'cough' and caam 'sneeze'. It can be said that telicity is subsumed by punctuality. Therefore, the features of telicity and punctuality are not really independent of each other. The semantic features of this group of verbs are described as follows:

[-actional]
[±telic]
[-volitional]
[±punctual]
[±Agent high in potency]

4.3.2 IVs indicating processes, states, attributes, feelings and emotions

The IVs of this type express processes, states, attributes, feelings and emotions which may occur independently, i.e. without external control. It is noted that stative verbs in Thai are ambiguous between stative and inchoative readings (Thepkanjana 2003). The context of situation and some co-occurring aspect markers help disambiguate the two meanings. Stative verbs of this type can express external or physical states, internal states, attributes, feelings and emotions. The IVs which express states are buam 'swollen', yûɯt 'stretched', bìt 'wiggled', hòt 'shrunk', ŋɔ́ɔm 'ripe', nâw 'rotten', caaŋ 'fade', rɔ́ɔn 'hot', tûɯn 'shallow', yaaw 'long', krɔ̀ɔp 'crispy' and yàap 'rough'. Notice that the verbs buam 'swollen', yûɯt 'stretched', bìt 'wiggled' and hòt 'shrunk' express resulting states of non-translational motions. Non-translational motion verbs are defined by Kemmer (1993) as verbs which move the body without change in overall position. Some examples of verbs which express attributes and qualities are chalàat 'clever', phǽæŋ 'expensive', rîapróɔy 'well-mannered', suphâap 'polite' and kèŋ 'competent'. Some examples which express feelings and emotions are tòkcay 'frightened', kròot 'angry', diicay 'glad', kaŋwon 'worry', tùɯɯntên 'excited' and ŋǎw 'lonely'. Subjects of verbs in this group can be human as well as nonhuman. Some can take inanimate subjects. Therefore, the feature [Agent high in potency] is marked by the plus/minus sign. The semantic features of this group of verbs are as below.

[-actional]
[-telic]
[-volitional]
[-punctual]
[±Agent high in potency]

It is apparent that the groups of IVs discussed above have varying degrees of transitivity based on their semantic features. They are ordered according to their degree of transitivity. If we look at Figure 2 below, the type of IV on the top has the highest degree of transitivity and the type at the bottom has the lowest degree. The others in between have progressively lower degrees of transitivity. Notice that the IVs in (4.2), which indicate actions resulting in body postures, and those in (4.3.1), which indicate physical sensations and symptoms, are similar in that they do not have any plus features and have the same number of minus ones. However, they differ in the features which are marked by the plus/minus signs. It is rather hard to determine which type of verb is more transitive. Therefore, they are considered as having the same degree of transitivity. The types of IVs are shown in Figure 2.

Chapter 5 On the distinction between transitive and intransitive verbs in Thai

```
                    ┌─ [+Actional] IVs ─┬─ IVs indicating unspecified body actions
                    │                   │   without external control
                    │                   └─ IVs indicating translational motions and
                    │                      vocal actions
        IVs ────────┼─ [±Actional] IVs ──── IVs indicating actions resulting in body
                    │                       postures
                    │                   ┌─ IVs indicating physical sensations and
                    └─ [-Actional] IVs ─┤   symptoms
                                        └─ IVs indicating processes, states, attributes,
                                           feelings and emotions
```

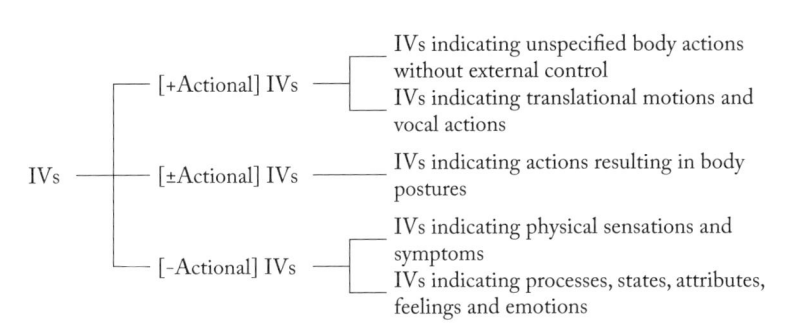

Figure 2. Types of IVs.

The semantic features of all types of IVs can be shown in Table 2.

Table 2. Semantic Features of All Types of IVs

Types of IVs / Semantic features	+[Actional] IVs — indicating unspecified body actions without an external control	+[Actional] IVs — indicating translational motions and vocal actions	±[Actional] IVs — indicating actions resulting in body postures	-[Actional] IVs — indicating physical sensations and symptoms	-[Actional] IVs — indicating processes, states, attributes, feelings and emotions
Actional	+	+	±	−	−
Telic	−	−	−	±	−
Volitional	+	±	±	−	−
Agent high in potency	+	±	±	±	±
Punctual	−	−	−	±	−

5. Ambivalent (AVs)

There is a group of verbs listed in the appendices of Phancharoen (1967) and Kanchanawan (1969) as being both TVs and IVs at the same time. That is, these verbs are claimed to appear both with and without DOs out of context. They are termed in this paper "ambivalent" verbs. Ambivalent verbs are usually defined as verbs which have both a monadic and dyadic argument structure. Given this definition, there are two types of ambivalent verbs. The first type refers to causative transitive verbs which have homophonous inchoative intransitive forms such as *break, melt* and *bounce* in English (Thepkanjana 2000). The second type refers to transitive verbs which can appear with and without their direct object arguments out of context, i.e. when no context is involved. In other words, the direct object arguments of the second type of ambivalent verbs are optional. This paper discusses only the second type of ambivalent verbs, the list of which appears in the appendices of Phancharoen (1967) and Kanchanawan (1969). Therefore, I use the term "ambivalent verb" in the narrow sense in this paper, i.e. to refer to a Thai transitive verb which can appear with or without an object out of context.

Ambivalent verbs as used in the narrow sense in this paper consist of two subclasses of verbs. The first subclass consists of verbs which are claimed to be either TVs or IVs in the appendices in Kanchanawan (1969) and Phancharoen (1967), respectively. In the former case, they are the verbs which are claimed by Kanchanawan to be TVs with optional absence of DOs out of context. In the latter case, they are claimed by Phancharoen to be IVs with optional presence of DOs. In other words, the former normally appear with DOs which are optionally absent out of context. Even though they appear objectless in sentences, they are intuitively felt and considered to be TVs with omitted DOs rather than IVs. The latter normally appear without DOs but can optionally take DOs in some cases. Even though they appear with DOs in sentences, they are intuitively felt to be IVs rather than TVs on semantic grounds. The second subclass of ambivalent verbs as used in this paper consists of verbs which do not appear in either the TV list in Kanchanawan (1969) or the IV list in Phancharoen (1967). These verbs constitute another class of verbs which are different from the ones on the TV and IV lists in Kanchanawan (1969) and Phancharoen (1967). They are claimed to be able to occur with or without DOs out of context. In other words, they are neither TVs nor IVs according to Kanchanawan (1969) or Phancharoen (1967). Since they are not parts of the TV or IV groups as claimed by Kanchanawan (1969) and Phancharoen (1967) respectively, they are considered *real* ambivalent verbs, which are called "genuine" ambivalent verbs in this paper. The first subclass of ambivalent verbs, which is a part of either the IV or TV classes as claimed by Kanchanawan (1969) and Phancharoen (1967) respectively, is called "non-genuine" ambivalent verbs. The two subclasses of ambivalent verbs are examined in detail below.

5.1 Non-genuine ambivalent verbs

As mentioned above, non-genuine ambivalent verbs consist of verbs of two types, namely, (a) verbs which are claimed to be TVs with optional absence of DOs out of context, and (b) verbs which are claimed to be IVs with optional presence of DOs. The two classes of verbs are examined below.

5.1.1 Non-genuine ambivalent verbs of the TV type

Non-genuine ambivalent verbs of the TV type consist of three subtypes of verbs as below.

5.1.1.1 *TVs with less highly affected target DOs*

The TVs with less highly affected target DOs can appear objectless out of context. These verbs are semantically vague in such a way that the means and manner by which the actions named by the verbs are performed are not specified. In addition, these actions may consist of several more specific "subactions". The entities indicated by the DOs of these verbs are not necessarily physically affected. Rather, they may be psychologically affected. Some examples of these verbs are kòtkhìi 'oppress', khúkkhaam 'threaten', kooŋ 'cheat', ùppathǎm 'support', tômtǔn 'cheat, deceive' and raŋkwaan 'annoy'. Notice that the TVs with highly affected DOs, such as tàt 'cut', rin 'pour', tɔ̀y 'punch', yók 'lift', tii 'hit' and sùup 'pump', are *not* non-genuine ambivalent verbs. In other words, these verbs just mentioned are felt to always require DOs; otherwise, they will be perceived to be semantically incomplete without DOs.

5.1.1.2 *TVs with non-affected target DOs*

Some of the TVs with non-affected target DOs appear on the list of non-genuine ambivalent TVs. These verbs express actions which are directed at some entities but do not affect or produce any perceptible change in the entities denoted by the DO arguments. Some examples of the non-genuine ambivalent verbs of this type include maa (rooŋrian) 'come (school)', meaning 'come to school', khóoŋ (khonduu) 'bow (audience)', meaning 'bow to the audience' and faŋ (khǎw) 'listen (him)', meaning 'listening to him'. These verbs are felt to be semantically complete without DOs in some cases.

5.1.1.3 *TVs with non-target DOs*

These verbs express body motions which take body part noun phrases as DOs. Some examples of the non-genuine ambivalent verbs of this type are: bòok (mɯɯ) 'wave (hand)', phayák (nâa) 'nod (face)', ŋɤɤy (nâa) 'lift (face)', kôm (nâa) 'lower (face)' and khɔ́ɔm (tua) 'bend (body)'.

In summary, it is found that the two most highly transitive groups of TVs, which are TVs with created entity DOs and TVs with highly affected DOs, *cannot* be non-genuine ambivalent verbs. That means these TVs are *not* felt to be semantically complete if they are objectless. In contrast, the less transitive or non-prototypical TVs, i.e. the TVs with less highly affected DOs, TVs with non-affected DOs, and TVs with non-target DOs, *can* be non-genuine ambivalent verbs because they are felt to be semantically complete to a certain extent even if they are objectless. In other words, DOs are always required if the actions are of the creation type, and if the actions are carried out by means of physical and direct contact with some perceptible changes in the affected entities. In contrast, the TVs which allow DOs to be optionally absent express nonphysical actions as well as actions which do not necessarily produce any effects in the target entities. In the case that the actions produce some effects, the effects are neither obvious nor concrete.

5.1.2 Non-genuine ambivalent verbs of the IV type

It is found that all of the classes of IVs optionally allow the presence of DOs although not all IVs in each class do. IVs which optionally allow the presence of DOs and therefore become non-genuine ambivalent verbs express states of affairs which need co-participants that are salient in the realization of the states of affairs to a certain degree as described below.

5.1.2.1 *IVs expressing psychological processes and states which require stimulators*

A stimulator is an entity which triggers or stimulates a certain feeling in a human being. The feelings denoted by this type of IV do not come about without cause. The stimulator can be considered the target of a feeling at the same time. That means the stimulator triggers some feeling in a human being, and the feeling is in turn projected towards the stimulator. Some of these IVs are as follows.

(1) ìtchǎa   (chǎn)
     be.jealous (me)
     'be jealous of me'

(2) sŏŋsăy   (kháw)
    be.suspicious (he)
    'be suspicious of him'

(3) khlâŋ   (thəə)
    be.crazy (you)
    'be crazy about you'

5.1.2.2 *IVs expressing physical processes and states of inanimate entities which require "co-participants"*

The IVs in this group require co-participants which play a crucial role and are therefore cognitively salient in the realization of the state of affairs denoted by this type of IV. Some co-participating entities can represent locations while others can function as modifiers. Some examples of the former are as follows.

(4) (nam)   thûam (thanŏn)
    (water) flood (road)
    "The road is flooded with water."

(5) (sèetkràdàat)   klùɯan   (bâan)
    (pieces of water)   be.scattered (house)
    "The house is scattered with pieces of paper."

In (4) and (5), in order for the states of affairs to take place, the entities expressed by the subject and object noun phrases of the IVs of this type must be in contact with each other. The entities indicated by the object noun phrases can express locations where the states of affairs take place. As for the latter case, the object noun phrases express co-participants which are not affected by the states of affairs denoted by the verbs, but are practically "necessary" and cognitively salient in their realization. Some examples of this type of IV are as below.

(6) (rɔɔŋtháw) lɔ́ʔ   (khloon)
    (shoes)   be.dirty (mud)
    "The shoes are dirty with mud."

(7) (kaaŋkeeŋ) pìak   (nám)

(pants)   be.wet   (water)
"The pants are wet with water."

(8) (sûɪa)   chûm   (ŋɯ̀ɪa)
     (shirt) be.drenched (sweat)
     "The shirt is drenched with sweat."

(9) khan   (khǎa)
     itch   (leg)
     'itch at the leg'

(10) pùat   (lǎŋ)
     ache   (back)
     'have a backache'

(11) krahǎay   (nám)
     be thirsty (water)
     'be thirsty'

(12) samrɔ̂ɔk (aahǎan)
     vomit   (food)
     'vomit'

(13) maw   (rɯa)
     be.intoxicated (ship)
     'feel seasick'

(14) nâŋ   (kâwʔii)
     sit   (chair)
     'sit on a chair'

(15) dəən (thanǒn)
     walk (road)
     'walk on the road'

It is found that IVs which never require DOs or, in other words, which can never be non-genuine ambivalent verbs of the IV type, are verbs which express actions, processes, states and properties that *can* independently take place. They do not need salient co-participating entities other than the actors, the experiencers and the themes in their actualization. These "non-alternating" IVs, or IVs which are not ambivalent verbs, are as follows.

5.1.2.3 *IVs expressing translational motions of animate and inanimate entities, and symptoms and physical sensations of animate entities*

Some examples of this type of verb include chalɛ̀ɛp 'dash', yòt '(water) drop', krasen 'splash', kradɔɔn 'bounce', bin 'fly', lúk 'rise, get up', yɯɯn 'stand', phàʔŋàʔ 'stop moving abruptly', sadûŋ 'become startled', hòklóm 'fall' and ay 'cough'.

5.1.2.4 *IVs expressing physical and psychological processes, and states of animate entities which can occur without stimulators*

Some examples of this type of verb include kràtûɯ aŋ 'recuperate', làp 'fall asleep', sòtchûɯ ɯn 'fresh', ŋăw 'lonely' and kràsàpkràsàay 'restless'.

5.1.2.5 *IVs expressing inherent qualities and attributes of animate and inanimate entities*

Some examples of this type of verb include ŋôo 'stupid', dûɯ 'stubborn', sûɯ 'honest', talòk 'funny', sân 'short', yaaw 'long', sàʔaat 'clean' and săy 'transparent'.

5.2 Genuine ambivalent verbs

Genuine ambivalent verbs are verbs which are neither listed as TVs nor IVs in the appendices of the theses under investigation. The optional DO arguments of these verbs do not represent created entities nor targets of actions. They have a variety of semantic roles which are hard to identify. They represent what Halliday (1985) calls "range". The range element is defined by Halliday as the element that specifies the range, domain or scope of the states of affairs. The range is an indirect, not inherent, participant in a state of affairs. It is usually an optional extra. Some examples of verbs of this type are khrâykhruan (khamtɔ̀ɔp) 'figure out (answer)', thútcarìt (ŋən) 'cheat (money)' and tên (caŋwàʔrew) 'dance (a quick rhythm)'.

In summary, non-alternating or non-ambivalent TVs, i.e. TVs which do not allow DOs to be optionally absent out of context, are TVs with highly affected target DOs and TVs with created entity DOs. These two types of TVs are considered prototypical TVs because they consist of the largest number of high transitivity features. Non-genuine ambivalent TVs, i.e. TVs which allow DOs to be optionally absent out of context, are TVs with moderately affected target DOs, TVs with non-affected target DOs and TVs with non-target DOs. These TVs are non-prototypical TVs because they have fewer high transitivity features. Genuine ambivalent verbs, i.e. verbs which are not categorized as TVs nor IVs and which have optional DOs, are verbs whose DOs have a variety of semantic roles called "range". If we consider these verbs TVs, they have the fewest high transitivity features. It is apparent that prototypical TVs do not allow DOs to be absent out of context and that non-prototypical TVs allow them to be absent. Verbs with range objects, which are not even considered TVs in normal cases, also allow the DOs to be absent. We can conclude that (a) TVs with the highest semantic transitivity coincide with those with the highest syntactic transitivity, (i.e. the case of non-alternating TVs or non-ambivalent TVs), and (b) verbs with the lowest semantic transitivity coincide with those with the lowest syntactic transitivity, (i.e. the case of genuine ambivalent verbs, which are not even considered TVs in the first place in the appendices of the theses investigated.) The figure below illustrates correspondences between semantic and syntactic transitivity.

While there are neat correspondences between semantic and syntactic transitivity in the case of TVs, we cannot find such correspondences in the case of IVs. Entities which may appear as optional DOs of IVs are "circumstantial" participants whose presence is verb-specific. Therefore, we cannot provide an account of the (in)ability of IVs to take optional DOs in terms of varying degrees of transitivity.

highest semantic transitivity	highest syntactic transitivity
TVs with created entity DOs (prototypical TVs)	non-ambivalent (non-alternating) verbs (obligatory presence of DOs)
TVs with highly affected DOs (prototypical TVs)	non-ambivalent (non-alternating) verbs (obligatory presence of DOs)
TVs with moderately affected DOs (nonprototypical TVs)	non-genuine ambivalent verbs (optional absence of DOs)
TVs with non-affected DOs (nonprototypical TVs)	non-genuine ambivalent verbs (optional absence of DOs)
TVs with non-target DOs (nonprototypical TVs)	non-genuine ambivalent verbs (optional absence of DOs)
TVs with range DOs	genuine ambivalent verbs
lowest semantic transitivity	**lowest syntactic transitivity**

Figure 3. Correspondences between semantic and syntactic transitivity of TVs.

6. Conclusion

This paper has analyzed the intuition behind the categorization of verbs into transitive, intransitive and ambivalent verbs in the appendices of two theses on transitive and intransitive verbs in Thai. It was pointed out that the notion of a transitivity continuum can be applied to Thai verbs, especially transitive verbs. The transitivity continuum shows correspondences between the syntactic and semantic (in)transitivity of transitive verbs. The transitivity continuum can be used to account for the obligatory nature as well as the optionality of direct objects. The optional absence and presence of direct objects is also accounted for in a cognitive linguistic framework. It can be concluded that there is no clear-cut distinction between transitive and intransitive verbs in Thai.

Acknowledgements

This paper is a substantially revised version of the paper entitled "Transitivity continuum in Thai," in Sudaporn Luksaneeyanawin et al. (eds), (1992). Pan-Asiatic linguistics: Proceedings of the Third International Symposium on Language and Linguistics, Chulalongkorn University, Bangkok, Thailand. January 8–10. Vol. I. 308–323. This research was supported by the Center of Excellence Program on Language, Linguistics and Literature (Chulalongkorn University Centenary Academic Development Project), Faculty of Arts, Chulalongkorn University, and the Higher Education Research Promotion and National Research University Project of Thailand (HS1231A), Office of the Higher Education Commission, Ministry of Education, Thailand. I would like to thank the two reviewers for their comments and suggestions.

Notes

1   A cognate object is an object that can be predicted by the selectional requirement of the verb (Kullavanijaya 1974: 119).
2   Dowty puts the (e)'s in (i) and (ii) in parentheses because he is not sure to what extent they should be attributed to the discourse associations of subjecthood rather than proto-role definition (Dowty 1991: 572).

References

Chomsky, Noam. 1965. *Aspects of the theory of syntax*. Cambridge: MIT Press.
Dowty, David. 1991. Thematic proto-roles and argument selection. *Language* 67(3). 547–619.
Halliday, Michael A. K. 1985. *An introduction to Functional Grammar*. London: Edward Arnold.
Hopper, Paul J. & Sandra A. Thompson. 1980. Transitivity in grammar and discourse. *Language* 56(2). 251–299.
Jespersen, Otto. 1969. *Essentials of English grammar*. Tuscaloosa: University of Alabama Press.
Kanchanawan, Nittaya. 1969. *Transitive verbs in the Thai language*. Bangkok: Chulalongkorn University MA Thesis.
Kemmer, Suzanne. 1993. *The middle voice*. Amsterdam & Philadelphia: John Benjamins.
Kullavanijaya, Pranee. 1974. *Transitive verbs in Thai*. Honolulu: University of Hawai'i dissertation.
Lyons, John. 1968. *Introduction to theoretical linguistics*. Cambridge: Cambridge University Press.
Noss, Richard B. 1964. *Thai reference grammar*. Washington DC: Foreign Service Institute.
Panupong, Vichin. 1962. *Inter-sentence relations in modern conversational Thai*. London: University of London dissertation.
Phancharoen, Suree. 1967. *Intransitives in Thai*. Bangkok: Chulalongkorn University MA thesis.
Silverstein, Michael. 1976. Hierarchy of features and ergativity. In Robert M. W. Dixon (ed.), *Grammatical categories in Australian languages*, 112–171. Canberra: Australian Institute of Aboriginal Studies.
Thepkanjana, Kingkarn. 2000. Lexical causatives in Thai. In Ad Foolen & Frederike van der Leek (eds), *Constructions in cognitive linguistics,* 259–282. Amsterdam & Philadelphia: John Benjamins.
Thepkanjana, Kingkarn. 2003. A cognitive account of the causative/inchoative alternation in Thai. In Eugene H. Casad & Gary B. Palmer (eds), *Cognitive linguistics and Non-Indo*

European languages, 247–274. Berlin & New York: Mouton de Gruyter.
Uppakitsilapasarn, Phraya. 1918. *Lak phasaa Thai*. Bangkok: Thai Wattanaphanit.
Warotamasikkhadit, Udom. 1963. *Thai syntax: An outline*. Austin: University of Texas dissertation.

Chapter 6

Parallels between motion and resultative constructions

Naoyuki Ono

1. Talmy's typology of event framing

No one would deny that one of the most intriguing proposals in cognitive approaches to linguistic typology is Talmy's idea that languages fall into two categories according to how they encode primary semantic components of motion events in verbs and satellites (Talmy 2000). In so-called satellite-framed languages like English, motion events are typically expressed in terms of MANNER verbs combined with PATH denoting satellites. (1a) shows this framing pattern: the verb *walk* denotes the MANNER component of an event frame and the PP satellite *to school* denotes the PATH component. In verb-framed languages like Japanese, the same motion event may only be expressed via verbs denoting both MOTION and PATH (e.g. *iku* 'go' in 1b) with the MANNER component encoded in subsidiary verbs in participial form (e.g. *hasiru* 'run' in 1b):[1]

(1) a. John walked to school. [Satellite-framed language]
          ↑   ↑
       MANNER   PATH

 b. *Taroo-wa gakko-ni   hasitte   it-ta.* [Verb-framed language]
    Taro-TOP school-DAT run-TE   go-PAST[2]
                            ↑   ↑
                         MANNER MOTION+PATH

"Lit. Taro went to school by running."

Talmy's typology of event-framing patterns has been studied mostly in terms of motion events in previous literature. However, Talmy's original idea was that this cross-linguistic typology is assumed to cover the other conceptual domains of event framing (Talmy 2000: 214). According to him, it is relevant to five categories of "macro-events": MOTION, TEMPORAL CONTOURING, STATE CHANGE, ACTION CORRELATION and REALIZATION. If so, they should exhibit the same typological patterns in the encoding of basic conceptual components as those in the encoding of motion events. However, to the best of my knowledge, very little research has been conducted to assess the validity of this typology in the other domains of event frames.

The present study aims to examine the typology of event-encoding patterns in terms of resultative constructions. Resultative constructions are particularly important in this respect because they represent a macro-event (STATE CHANGE or REALIZATION),[3] where the primary conceptual component (i.e. what Talmy calls the "schematic core") of an event is expressed by a verb or a satellite in parallel with a motion event. In the following section, I will explicate parallelisms between motion and resultative constructions in more detail. In section 3, a recent view of Talmy's typology is introduced. Under this view, the typological variations are assumed to follow from a particular set of lexical resources of a given language. With these assumptions at hand, I will show that there is a crucial difference between motion and resultative constructions.

2. The motion and resultative parallelisms

Many researchers take for granted the fact that there are obvious parallelisms between the motion construction and the resultative construction (Aske 1989; Goldberg 1995; Goldberg & Jackendoff 2004, among others). Satellite-framed languages encode MANNER into verbs and RESULT (PATH) into satellites resultative event expressions. The semantic component encoding into verbs and satellites in resultative event expressions is thus parallel with the motion construction. Thus, in English, a resultative event may be expressed with a MANNER verb and a satellite phrase such as an AP (*flat*) or PP (*into a flat, pizza-like form*) as in (2a). In verb-framed languages, on the other hand, the same event must be expressed in terms of a combination of a MANNER verb and a RE-

SULT verb as shown in the Japanese example in (2b).

(2) a. John pounded the dough flat/into a flat, pizza-like form.
                  ↑   ↑
            MANNER   RESULT (PATH)

   b. *Taroo-ga   pankizi-o   taira-ni   tataki   -nobasi-ta.*
      Taro-NOM   dough-ACC   flat-DAT   pound   -flatten-PAST
                                                  ↑   ↑
                                        MANNER RESULT (PATH)
      "Lit. Taro flattened the dough by pounding it."

The parallelism between the two constructions is further supported by the observation that verb-framed languages show a systematic correlation between the lack of the satellite-framed pattern of motion constructions and the lack of the satellite-framed pattern of resultative constructions. The satellite-framed patterns corresponding to the English sentences in (1a) and (2a) are generally ruled out in Japanese, as shown in (3a) (a satellite-framed pattern of motion construction) and (3b) (a satellite-framed pattern of resultative construction):

(3) a. **Taroo-ga   eki-ni   hasit-ta.*
     Taro-NOM   station-DAT   run-PAST
     "Taro ran to the station."

   b. **Taroo-ga   pankizi-o   taira-ni   tatai-ta.*
     Taro-NOM   dough-ACC   flat-DAT   pound-PAST
     "Taro pounded the dough flat."

Given the assumption that there are strong parallelisms between motion and resultative constructions in terms of event-framing patterns, it seems self-evident that the dichotomy between verb-framed and satellite-framed languages can be extended to resultative constructions. If this assumption is correct, the fact that languages exhibit the relevant typological differences not only in expressing motion events but also in expressing change-of-state (resultative) events will serve as a strong piece of evidence in favor of Talmy's typology.

3. Language types or lexical resources?

Before entering into a substantial discussion about resultatives, I will argue that there are some empirical problems if we maintain that Talmy's cross-linguistic typology follows from two distinct language types across the world. The problems are centered on the fact that verb-framed and satellite-framed encoding patterns often co-exist in a given language. As an ideal picture of this typology, one language may be either the satellite-framed type or the verb-framed type but cannot be both types. However, as Talmy himself notes (Talmy 2000: 240–41), the encoding of STATE CHANGE tends to exhibit what he calls a "parallel system of conflation", which means languages tend to exhibit both of satellite-framed patterns and verb-framed patterns in expressing change-of-state events. Thus, English makes use of the satellite-framed encoding pattern as in (4a), as well as the verb-framed one as in (4b).

(4) a. He choked to death on a bone. (Satellite-framed pattern)

    b. He died from choking. (Verb-framed pattern)

This is seen as evidence that the typological distinction is somewhat blurred in the domains other than the motion macro-event.

The same problem arises if we take a closer look at resultative constructions in light of the verb-framed vs. satellite-framed dichotomy. We see that resultatives actually comprise the verb-framed and satellite-framed patterns of event-framing. As is discussed in the literature, resultative constructions fall into two categories. The resultative sentence in (5a) is what Washio (1997) calls a "strong" resultative, where the verb denotes MANNER and the resultative satellite (flat) expresses RESULT. The resultant state is not inherently involved in the verb's meaning. The resultative construction in (5b), on the other hand, is called a "weak" resultative, where both STATE CHANGE and RESULT are encoded in a single verb (for this reason, these types of verbs are dubbed "change of state" or "result" verbs). The resultative phrase only serves to specify the resultant state which is part of the verb meaning.

(5) a. John pounded the dough flat.

b. John broke the vase into pieces.

Notice that the former is by definition a satellite-framed pattern, and the latter a verb-framed pattern. In (5a) the RESULT component of a change-of-state event frame is encoded as the satellite to the MANNER verb. In (5b) it is the verb that denotes the RESULT component. The resultative phrase in (5b), unlike the one in (5a), may or may not be present in expressing a change-of-state event. Thus, if we look at resultative sentences in English, we see that there is a "parallel conflation" problem in linguistically expressing state change events.

Another empirical problem is that verb-framed languages sometimes exhibit satellite-framing options. In many verb-framed languages, there is an S-framed encoding option where a main verb encodes the manner component and an ad-position, which is roughly equivalent to *until* in English, expresses the PATH component. In fact, Japanese has this option (Beavers et al. 2010). The *made* 'until' phrase can be used to encode a path of motion as shown in (6b):

(6) a. **Taroo-ga   eki-ni   hasit-ta.*
         Taro-NOM   station-DAT   run-PAST
         "Taro ran to the station."

      b. *Taroo-ga   eki-made   hasit-ta.*
         Taro-NOM   station-until   run-PAST
         "Taro ran to the station."

Given that the *made* phrase denotes a path in (6b), it is a satellite-framing device used in a verb-framed language. This again amounts to saying that the verb-framed and satellite-framed distinction is not made at the level of grammatical language variations.

A word of caution is in order here. I am not saying that any satellite-framing option is possible in verb-framed languages. In particular, it is important to notice that satellite-framing options in resultatives are not licensed in Japanese. While English resultatives comprise both verb-framed and satellite-framed options as shown in (5), Japanese only licenses the verb-framed option of resultatives, rejecting the satellite-framed resultatives, as shown in the contrast in (7a) and (7b).

(7) a. *Taroo-ga   pankizi-o   taira-ni   tatai-ta.
       Taro-NOM   dough-ACC   flat-DAT   pound-PAST
       "Taro pounded the dough flat."

   b. Taroo-ga   kabin-o   konagona-ni wat-ta.
      Taro-NOM   vase-ACC   pieces-DAT break-PAST
      "Taro broke the vase into pieces."

To avoid the above-mentioned "parallel conflation" problem, I adopt the idea that Talmy's typology arises not from distinct language types, but from the inventory of lexical resources for encoding different lexicalization patterns (Beavers et al. 2010). In this view, verb-framing and satellite-framing are alternative encoding strategies which are made available if a given language can make use of appropriate resources for those encoding options. What I am assuming here is that Japanese and English, for example, exhibit distinct conflation patterns not because they belong to distinct language types, but because they exploit different encoding strategies. Given that the two conflation patterns introduced by Talmy are treated not as variations in language types but rather as descriptions of alternative encoding strategies, it is not unreasonable to assume that the two options may, and often do, co-exist within a single language if the language makes use of appropriate lexical resources for encoding. For the sake of the discussion to follow, I will call this idea a "lexical resource view" of the event-framing typology. In the lexical resource view, the question arises as to what lexical resources comprise different encoding strategies. We will turn to this question in the next section.

4. Lexical resources for satellite-framed encoding

As for the question mentioned in the previous section, a number of researchers have independently proposed a similar solution. The distinction between verb-framed and satellite-framed languages lies in the inventory of prepositions that are specifically made to lexicalize a semantic distinction between a (bounded) path and a location. (Asbury et al. 2008; Folli & Ramchand 2005; Kageyama 2003; Mateu 2002). English has prepositions specialized for encoding a bounded path (goal), in contrast with prepositions which are used to mark a static location of an individual or an event. See the examples in (8):

(8) a. John walked to/into the store.
   b. John walked in the store.

To/into lexically expresses a directional meaning, whereas *in* denotes a static location where no translational motion is involved.[4]

The relevant distinction available in the lexical inventory of prepositions in English is not available in the Japanese lexicon. We have seen that the *ni* phrase denotes a goal in (1b) and a resultant-state in (2b), both of which are conceptually identified as a bounded path (Ashbury et al. 2008; Talmy 2000). However, it should be noted that the *ni* phrase is not specifically designed to mark a bounded path. It denotes a bounded path or a static location, depending on the verb. When it appears with a verb that entails translational motion (e.g. *iku* 'go' in (9b)), the *ni* phrase serves as a goal marker denoting a bounded path. The same phrase, however, has an alternative use as a location marker if the verb entails a static location of entities or events as in (9b). The "goal" phrase with such a marker is in fact more like a locative phrase.

(9) a. *Kare-wa   eki-ni   iku.*   (goal)
       he-TOP   station-DAT   go-PRES
       "He goes to the station."

   b. *Kare-wa   eki-ni   iru.*   (location)
       he-TOP   station-DAT   be-PRES
       "He is at the station."

Whether a *ni* phrase is interpreted as a goal or a location depends crucially on the verb semantics. In this view, the difference between the languages in question comes from the different nature of the particular prepositions involved rather than the different nature of manner-of-motion verbs. This means that the source of the framing typology lies in a lexical inventory of a given language, not in language variation.

5. Lexical resources for resultatives

Under the assumption that particular linguistic resources are responsible for the distinction between verb-framing and satellite-framing in a given language, the question arises as to whether or not the resources for encoding motion events are available in encoding other event types. If it turns out that resultative constructions are in parallel with motion constructions with respect to lexical resources, this will support the lexical resource view of event-framing typology.

As discussed earlier, English allows two types of resultatives: "strong" resultatives, which include a verb denoting a manner or means of activity with a result-denoting satellite, and "weak" resultatives, which cosist of a change-of-state (or result) verb along with a result phrase which gives a further specification of the resultant state denoted by the verb. We have seen that lexical resources that render the satellite-framing option available in English are path-denoting prepositions such as *to* and *into* (see (8)). Similarly, in encoding a resultative event, manner verbs must be combined with the path-denoting prepositions to make use of the satellite-framing option. In (10a), this option is implemented using the manner verb *pound* and the path-denoting satellite *into pieces*. In (10b) the stative PP *in pieces* cannot be used in the satellite framing option since the stative PP does not encode a transition.

(10) a. She pounded the metal into pieces.

b. *John pounded the metal in pieces.

As it turns out, the lexical resources that make available the satellite-framing option in encoding motion events are also used to implement the satellite-framing option in expressing resultative events in English.

In the other type of resultatives, where the verb lexically implies a resultant state, there is no restriction on the selection of prepositions because the encoding of a resultant state is conducted by the verb, not by the satellite. Thus, both the transitional and the stative PPs can co-occur with the result verb.

(11) a. John broke the stick into pieces.[5]

b. John broke the stick in pieces.

We have discussed that resultative constructions such as those in (11) are a verb-framed option because the RESULT component is encoded in the verb. Thus, the resultative phrase serves to provide a further specification of the lexical entailment of the verb. Thus, the PPs denote the same meaning despite the difference in their surface forms.

More evidence is provided in the following examples. (12) shows that *to/into/in exhaustion* exhibits the same restriction on the choice of prepositions in the satellite-framing option. In (12), where the manner verb *run* is used in a resultative sentence, only (bounded) path-denoting PPs can serve as a viable satellite.

(12) a. Children ran themselves to/into exhaustion.

b. *Children ran themselves in exhaustion.

It is also the case in (13). The stative PP *in sleep* is rejected from the satellite-framing of a resulatative event.

(13) a. She talked herself to/into sleep.

b. *She talked herself in sleep.

If we look at the verb-framing option in (14), where the result-denoting verb *fall* is used, both types of prepositions are allowed.

(14) She fell to/into/in sleep.

Why, then, is it the case that (unbounded) location markers are not available for the satellite-framing option in resultatives? To answer this question, we need to look at the difference in the lexical resources in more detail.

6. Path compensation in motion constructions

It is often pointed out that under certain circumstances, the static location PP in a sentence like (15b) can be interpreted in the same way as the bounded path PPs in (15a).

(15) a. John walked to/into the store.

b.　John walked in the store.

In other words, the sentence in (15b) is ambiguous: it denotes an event that takes place in a certain location, or a translational motion that ends up at a certain place. There are some pragmatic factors that trigger the motion reading of the sentence. Nikitina (2008: 180) notes, "[i]f *into* can be treated as a lexical marker of goals, *in* is ambiguous and can only be used to mark a goal of motion when the meaning of change of location is encoded by some other element in the sentence, or, alternatively, if it can be inferred from context."

　　We do not enter into a discussion of what factors are at work in the directional motion reading of the *in*-phrase in (15b); instead, we assume that English has a linguistic strategy that extends a static place into a bounded path. In fact, a similar idea is proposed in Yoneyama (2009: 104) to explain the well-known ambiguity of a sentence like (16a). This ambiguity is accounted for if we assume a conversion from the place function [_{Place} IN ([_{Thing}　])] in a Jackendovian semantic structure into the path function [_{Path} TO ([_{Place} IN ([_{Thing}　])])]:

(16)　a.　The bottle floated under the bridge.

　　　b.　[_{Path} TO ([_{Place} IN ([_{Thing}　])])]

This ambiguity is not due to the typological generalization of the language per se, but derives from the lexical property of the preposition.

　　Whatever the nature of the path compensation strategy may be, it makes the goal of-motion reading in (15b) and (16a) available. With that linguistic device, be it lexical, semantic or pragmatic, we need to assume that the notion of path is somehow appended to the PP which otherwise allows only a static location meaning.

7.　The motion-resultative parallelism revisited

We have thus far argued that satellite-framing and verb-framing are different encoding strategies. Any language can make use of them if it has appropriate lexical resources. Also, we have assumed that what we call the path compensation applies under certain conditions to the static location PP.

　　In light of the path compensation discussed in the previous section, it is important to note that that strategy does not work in resultatives. Thus, the resultative sentence in (17a) will never be interpreted in the same way as the sentence in (17b).

(17) a. *John pounded the metal in pieces.

   b. She pounded the metal to/into pieces.

Why does the path compensation not work in resultatives? Why is it that the same strategy does not fit into the two constructions that utilize parallel lexical resources? Note that in this way, a parallel is lost between the motion and the resultative constructions in this respect.

Turning to motion constructions in Japanese, we see that path compensation fails to apply. If it is applied to a sentence like (18), it would be acceptable in parallel with the English sentence in (15b):

(18) *Taroo-ga   eki-ni   hasit-ta.
     Taro-NOM   station-DAT run-PAST
     "Taro ran to the station."

But under certain conditions, manner-of-motion verbs combined with the locational ad-position can denote goal-of-motion. In (19), manner verbs such as 'walk' and 'fly' are used with the *ni* phrase:

(19) a. *Nobita-wa*   *Takeshi-o*   *ichirui-ni*   *aruk-ase-ta.*
        Nobita-TOP   Takeshi-ACC   first-base-DAT   walk-CAUSE-PAST
        "Nobita walked Takeshi to the first base."

   b. *Suneo-wa*   *nyuuyooku-ni*   *ton-da.*
      Suneo-TOP   New York-DAT   fly-PAST
      "Suneo flew to New York."

The difference between (18) and (19) is that the manner verbs in the latter are somehow conventionalized to mean a translational motion. In (19a), *walk to the first base* is a baseball term which conventionally means that a person moves to the first base. In (19b) *fly to New York* means "go to New York by plane". It does not mean that a person literally flies. Similar examples are found in French, another allegedly verb-framed language.[6] The sentences in (20) do not mean that someone actually ran or jumped; hence, the meaning is somehow weakened in idiomatic use of the expressions.

(20) a. *Elle a1uru   chez   le médecin.*
       she has run   at-the-place-of the doctor
       "She ran to the doctor."

   b. *Il a   sauté   dans un taxi.*
      he has jumped in   a   taxi
      "He jumped/leaped into a taxi."

So, in motion constructions, path compensation works at times even in languages where the satellite-framing option is generally rejected because of the lack of appropriate resources for that purpose.

However, the point is that the path compensation has no effect on resultatives. That is why satellite-framing options like the following examples are rejected even in satellite-framed languages like English, as well as in verb-framed languages like Japanese.

(21) a. *John pounded the metal in pieces.

   b. *John-ga   kinzoku-o   konagona-ni   tatai-ta.*
      John-NOM   metal-ACC   pieces-DAT   pound-PAST
      "John pounded the metal into pieces."

(21a) is rejected in English for the same reason that (21b) is rejected in Japanese. The reason is that the ad-positions *in* and *ni* are not qualified as lexical resources for satellite framing.

To close the discussion here, I would like to point out another piece of evidence that path compensation works in motion expressions but not in resultatives. It has to do with the *made* path expression we mentioned earlier. *Made* is used in a wide range of adverbial expressions, such as temporal limitation, degree, spatial domain. The goal-like behavior in (22b) is one of those various usages.

(22) a. *Taroo-ga   eki-ni   hasit-ta.
       Taro-NOM   station-DAT   run-PAST
       "Taroo ran to the station."

   b. Taroo-ga   eki-made   hasit-ta.
      Taro-NOM   station-until   run-PAST
      "Taro ran to the station."

As discussed earlier, *made* serves as a lexical resource that renders a satellite-framing option available in Japanese.

If so, then we would expect the same lexical resource to be used in resultative constructions as well. This prediction is only partially born out. As shown in (23a), a bi-clausal resultative expression (Wechsler & Noh 2001) is possible in parallel with the bi-clausal motion construction in (23b):

(23) a. Taroo-ga   [chokkaku-ni naru] made kinzokuboo-o   tatai-ta.
       Taro-NOM [right-angle-DAT be] until metal bar-ACC pound-PAST
       "Taro pounded the metal bar right angle (lit. until it is right angle)."

   b. Taroo-ga   [eki-ni tuku]-made   hasit-ta.
      Taro-NOM [station-DAT arrive]-until   run-PAST
      "Taro ran until he reached the station."

But this parallelism is lost in mono-clausal constructions, as shown in the contrast in (24):

(24) a. *Taroo-ga   chokaku-made   kinzokuboo-o   tatai-ta.
       Taro-NOM   right angle-until   metal bar-ACC   pound-PAST
       "Taro pounded the metal bar right angle (lit. until it is right angle)."

   b. Taroo-ga   eki-made   hasit-ta.
      Taro-NOM   station-until   run-PAST
      "Taro ran to the station."

The *made* satellite is ruled out in resultatives, such as in (24a), while it is ruled in in the motion construction in (24b). This is another piece of evidence that motion constructions are not completely parallel with resultative constructions. The resultative sentence in (24a) is rejected because path compensation does not apply in resultatives. This means that the verbal expression is necessary to encode a transitional path in resultatives, as shown by the bi-clausal resultative sentence in (23a). Why is this so? Since path compensation works only to append an intermediate path to the motion event encoding, there is no way to provide a conceptual ground on which you can infer the presence of the path in resultatives. Thus, it is necessary to lexicalize the path in a verb form. In other words, you need to resort to a verb-framed strategy of encoding a state-change in the case of resultatives.

This account is borne out by the fact that if we replace the manner verb in (24a) with a result verb, the sentence is acceptable as shown below.

(25) a. *Taroo-ga chokkaku-made kinzoku-o mage-ta.*
Taro-NOM right-angle-until metal-ACC bend-PAST
"Taro bent the metal at (lit. 'until') right angle."
b. *Taroo-ga [chokkaku-ni naru] made kinzoku-o mage-ta.*
Taro-NOM [right-angle-DAT be] until metal-ACC bend-PAST
"Taro bent the metal (lit. until it is right angle)."

This is because, with result verbs, the sentences (both mono-clausal and bi-clausal resultatives) implement the verb-framed option; hence, they do not resort to the satellite-framing option.

8. Conclusion

In this paper I have approached the problem of encoding event frames from a slightly different perspective, treating the verb-framed and satellite-framed patterns introduced by Talmy not as language types but rather as descriptions of alternative encoding strategies. I have shown that motion constructions parallel resultative constructions in terms of lexical resources that make available the encoding strategies, but that they have crucial differences between them, such as the fact that path compensation works under certain conditions in motion constructions, but not in resultative constructions.

Acknowledgements

I am grateful to Tadao Miyamoto and an anonymous reviewer for their helpful comments on a draft of this chapter. Thanks to Ryan Spring for his help with stylistic improvement. This work was supported by Grants-in-Aid for Scientific Research from the Japan Society for the Promotion of Science (#20320068).

Notes

1. Verb-framed motion constructions can be found in English. Verbs such as *enter* and *exit* denote a motion event where the MOTION+PATH component is embedded solely in the verb meaning. Thus, the following English sentence is by definition an instance of verb-framed encoding of a motion event.
    (i) John entered/exited the room.
2. The following abbreviations are used the in the glosses: TOP=topic marker (case), NOM=nominative case, ACC=accusative case, DAT=dative case, PAST=the past form of the verb.
3. Resultative constructions denote macro-events ranging from STATE CHANGE (*The candle blew out./He choked to death on a bone.*) to REALIZATION (*I kicked the hubcap flat./I washed the shirt clean.*), depending on the meaning of verbs used in the construction.
4. Translation motion here means movement that changes the position of an object, as opposed to rotational motion. Note that, under certain circumstances, the sentence in (8b) expresses the same situation as the sentence in (8a) denotes. Native-speaker judgments vary as to whether a static locational meaning has priority over a translational motion meaning in examples such as (8b). We will return to the source of this discrepancy in a later section.
5. The data in (11) and the subsequent examples in (12)–(14) are drawn from the British National Corpus and via a Google search on the internet.
6. I owe the examples in (20) to Takeshi Nakamoto (Tohoku University).

References

Ashbury, Anna, Jakub Dotlacil, Berit Gehrke & Rick Nouwen. 2008. *Syntax and semantics of spatial P*. Amsterdam: John Benjamins.
Aske, J. 1989. Path predicates in English and Spanish: A closer look. In Proceedings of the Fifteenth Anual Meeting of the Berkeley Linguistic Society, 1–14.
Beavers, John, Beavers, John, Beth Levin & Shiao Wei Tham. 2010. The typology of motion expressions revisited. *Journal of Linguistics* 46, 1–58.
Folli, Raffaella & Gillian Ramchand. 2005. Prepositions and results in Italian and English: An analysis from event decomposition. In H. Verkuyl, A. van Hout & H. de Swart (eds), *Perspectives on aspect*, 1–20. Berlin: Springer.

Goldberg, Adele. 1995. *Constructions: A construction grammar approach to argument structure*. Chicago: The University of Chicago Press.
Goldberg, Adele E. & Ray Jackendoff. 2004. The English Resultative as a Family of Constructions. *Language* 80. 532–568.
Kageyama, Taro. 2003. Why English motion verbs are special. *Korean Journal of English language and Linguistics* 3(3). 341–373.
Mateu, Jaume. 2002. *Argument structure: Relational construal at the syntax-semantics interface*. PhD dissertation, Universitat Autònoma de Barcelona.
Nikitina, Tatiana. 2008. Pragmatic factors and variation in the expression of spatical goals: The case of *into* and *in*. In Asbury, A., J. Dotlacil, B. Gehrke & R. Nouwen (eds), *Syntax and semantics of spatial P.*, 175–195. Amsterdam: John Benjamins.
Talmy, Leonard. 2000. *Toward a cognitive semantics*. Cambridge, Massachusetts: MIT Press.
Washio, Ryuichi 1997. Resultatives, compositionality and language variation. *Journal of East Asian Linguistics* 6. 1–49.
Wechsler, Sephen & Bokyung Noh. 2001. On Resultative predicates and clauses: Parallels between Korean and English. *Language Sciences* 23. 391–423.
Yoneyama, Mitsuaki. 2009. *Imiron-kara miru eigo-no koozoo* (*The structure of English from a semantic perspective*). Tokyo: Kaitakusha.

Chapter 7

The cognitive theory of subjectivity in a cross-linguistic perspective: Zero 1st person pronouns in English, Thai and Japanese

Satoshi Uehara

1. Introduction

Langacker's (1985) seminal work on subjectivity, "Observations and speculations on subjectivity", has set a framework for, and has had great influence on, all research works on subjectivity that followed. Most notably, a voluminous amount of work has developed in the direction of subjectification, i.e. subjectivity in its diachronic dimension in the context of grammaticalization (e.g. his own subsequent work and Traugott's (1989, 1995) work, among others).

The semantic extension observed in a verb of seeing in Thai /hĕn/ 'see' exemplifies such a fact in the process of subjectification. Rattanaphanusorn and Thepkanjana (2008) and Wongtawan (2010), among others, argue that the verb of seeing /hĕn/ has grammaticalized into the evidential marker /hĕn/, where the speaker's role is "subjectified" from the "syntactic" subject of the verb hĕn on stage, as in (1a), into the "speaking" subject of the whole event, as in (1b) (i.e. from the <u>object</u> of conception to the <u>subject</u> of conception).

(1) a. phǒm **hĕn** khăw thiînii.
      I   see   him here
      "I <u>saw</u> him here."

   b. kaanbaân mây **hĕn** cà yâak ləəy.
      homework not see will difficult particle
      "The homework doesn't <u>look</u> difficult at all."

The cognitive theory of subjectivity has, however, had a potential to develop in a cross-linguistic dimension as well. This synchronic, rather than diachronic, aspect of subjectivity relates itself to the use of deixis and the so-called "dropping" or omission of the first person pronouns in contemporary languages. The current paper discusses this synchronic aspect of linguistic subjectivity and attempts to attain the following two goals: i) to develop the cognitive theory of subjectivity in its cross-linguistic dimension, and ii) to provide a cognitive account of implicit reference phenomena for a possible typology of linguistic subjectivity.

The outline of the paper is as follows. Section 2 discusses Langacker's theory of subjectivity in terms of its distinction between implicit and explicit reference to the speaker. It proposes to make some modifications to it for its typological applications. Section 3 applies it and examines some cross-linguistic differences in terms of omissibility of the experiencer subject referents of internal state predicates in English, Thai and Japanese. Section 4 summarizes the findings and concludes the paper.

2. Cognitive theory of subjectivity and implicit reference

2.1 Different ways of expressing/construing an event involving the speaker

The kinds of subjectivity phenomena that we are examining in this paper are those in a synchronic domain. In other words, they do not necessarily involve any diachronic change, unlike the "subjectification" phenomena observed in the process of grammaticalization. The difference, rather than the change, in the subjectivity level in a synchronic domain is illustrated by what I call a 'minimal pair of subjectivity', exemplified in (2) below, where the two sentences describe the objectively same spatial configuration of the two people, Vanessa and the speaker, sitting across a table from each other. The two sentences, however, differ in that the expression of explicit reference to the speaker in (2a), *from me*, is "dropped" in (2b).

(2) a. *Vanessa is sitting across the table from me!* (Langacker 1991: 328)
    b. *Vanessa is sitting across the table!*

A typical context for (2b) is where the speaker finds and sits on a seat during a meeting and looks up to find Vanessa sitting across the same table, while that for (2a) is where the speaker shows his friend a photo of the above situation, i.e. he and Vanessa are sitting across the table from each other. Langacker (1985: 141) claims that "the speaker is construed more subjectively" in (b) than in (a).

Notice here that the linguistic expressions in contrast dealt with in the current research have two characteristics: i) they have the same propositional content, and ii) the speaker is involved as a participant in the event denoted by the proposition. These two characteristics exemplified in (2) exactly differentiate the subjectivity phenomena we are dealing with in this paper from the subjectification phenomena exemplified in (1) above. In (1), the two sentences differ drastically in their propositional content, and the speaker in (1b) is outside the event denoted by the proposition and conceives the event, rather than participates in it.

Since the two sentences in (2) are both used to express the objectively same event, it follows that the difference between the two expressions lies not in the situation or event in the objective reality, but in the construal of it. In other words, the two expressions in (2) represent different ways of construing an event/situation that involves the speaker. Between the two expressions, the one with the first person pronoun, as in (2a), represents the objective construal, while the implicit reference to the speaker, as in (2b), corresponds to the subjective construal.

Examples of this kind can be easily multiplied in English. Langacker introduces another pair, as in (3), where the structural difference lies in the presence/absence of the first person pronoun *me*, providing a contextual difference similar to the one for the pair in (2) above. He adds that in (a) "the speaker is simply describing an aspect of his immediate physical environment," but in (b) "the speaker is describing what he actually sees" (Langacker 1985: 138).

(3) a. *There is snow all around me!*
    b. *There is snow all around!*

In the examples in (2) and (3) (and all other similar examples) in English, the expressions representing the objective construal in (a) include the first person pronoun, while those representing the subjective construal in (b) have implicit reference to the speaker. This is why he states "[i]mplicit reference to the speaker correlates with the speaker being construed more subjectively" (Langacker 1985: 140).

Let us examine more closely the crucial distinction in terms of subjectivity between the two types of sentences in (a) and (b). Prompted by Langacker's descriptions of the expressions in (b) representing the subjective construal, such as "(b) portrays the situation as seen 'through the eyes of' the speaker" (p.141), Uehara (1998, 2006a) has pictographically represented what the two types of sentences in (a) and (b) depict, using the pair of examples in (2). His figures are reproduced in Figure 1 below:

a. *"Vanessa is sitting across the table from me!"*   b. *"Vanessa is sitting across the table!"*

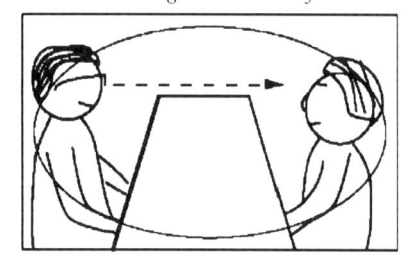

Figure 1. Pictographic representations of the visual images that the speaker has in uttering the two sentences in (2) [Reproduced from Uehara (2006a: 277)].

Figure 1a represents a rather objective construal, where not only Vanessa on the right in the figure, but also the speaker himself on the left, appears in the visual image depicted by the sentence in (2a). It is just as though the speaker utilizes the perspective of some other person who is outside the event, to observe Vanessa and the speaker himself from outside. In contrast, Figure 1b represents the subjective construal, where Vanessa alone resides as the object of perception by the speaker, who participates in, and is experiencing live, the event. It is exactly like an image captured from the camera angle of the speaker himself.

It should be noted here for our later discussion that the two images in Figure 1 nicely account for the iconic motivation for explicit and implicit references to the speaker corresponding to objective and subjective construals, respectively. The first person pronoun is overt in (2a) because the speaker himself is overt and observed in the image from the perspective of the outsider in Figure 1a. In contrast, the first person pronoun is covert in (2b) because the speaker himself appears nowhere in the image in Figure 1b. The camera cannot normally capture any image of the camera holder himself, who is the speaker in this case.

Langacker talks about another level of subjectivity or objectivity using the sentences below in (4) (Langacker 1985: 126).

(4) a. <u>The person uttering this sentence</u> doesn't really know.
  b. <u>I</u> don't really know.
  c. Don't really know.

Notice here that all three sentences in (4) describe the objectively same event involving the speaker, the difference being in the expressions referring to the speaker. The speaker is represented by the first person pronoun *I* in (4b), while the same person is represented by a descriptive phrase *the person uttering this sentence* in (4a) and by zero in (4c). Langacker, in discussing on the difference in the degree of subjectivity, notes that "a pronoun portrays the speaker (or another ground element) more subjectively than a descriptive phrase, and zero more subjectively than a pronoun" (pp. 126–127). Here again, the implicit reference to the speaker is equated with the (most) subjective construal of the same situation.

However, there arise some questions: how can we apply this surface distinction of subjectivity to zero pronominal languages like Thai and Japanese, where first person pronouns (as well as other personal pronouns) are very frequently "dropped" and almost done so "freely"? Does this mean that Thai and Japanese are both "subjective" languages, compared to "objective" English? Or, if these implicit first person pronouns in English differ from the cases of zero pronominals in Asian languages, do we know how to differentiate them?

2.2 A proposal

To answer these questions, this paper proposes two points of modification to Langacker's theory of subjectivity:

1. The subjectivity of a sentence is not indicated by the referring expression to the speaker alone, but rather by <u>the whole construction</u> that it appears in.
2. That subjectivity is not a matter of how <u>the speaker</u> is construed, but rather how <u>the situation</u>/<u>event</u> that involves the speaker is construed by him.

Point 1 suggests that we pay more attention to the part of the sentence other than the expression referring to the speaker, more specifically to its predicate. To see the case in point, it should be noted that in (4a) above, where a descriptive phrase is used as the expression that refers to the speaker, its predicate is marked with *does*, a marker of the third person, not the first person.

Point 2 follows from Point 1. As is clear from his expressions such as "the speaker is construed [...] subjectively" for (2a) and "a pronoun portrays the speaker [...] more subjectively than a descriptive phrase, and zero more subjectively than a pronoun" for (4), Langacker emphasizes how the speaker as an entity is construed. The current research, on the other hand, takes into consideration how the event is construed by the speaker participating in it. The proposed approach to linguistic subjectivity is well captured by the two images in Figure 1. They both depict the situation represented by the whole sentence, not by the explicit or implicit expression referring to the speaker; and Figure 1b, in particular, depicts the image of the event entertained by the speaker, not of the speaker by another person.

The proposed modification leads us to take a constructional approach and to call and characterize the two types of constructions exemplified in (2) as follows:

a. The "self-monitoring speaker" constructions (as in (2a) *Vanessa is sitting across the table from me!*) depict the events involving the speaker as though he is monitoring them from the perspective of the third person (as in Figure 1a).

b. The "experiencing speaker" constructions (as in (2b) *Vanessa is sitting across the table!*) depict the events involving the speaker as though he is experiencing it at that moment (as in Figure 1b).

This approach to the contrast in subjectivity in question does not stand alone in the current research, but has affinity with some previous analyses on linguistic subjectivity such as Iwasaki (1993), Ikegami (2003) and Nakamura (2004), in terms of perspectives, construals and cognitive modes, respectively. Table 1 below summarizes the related concepts in their analyses.

Table 1. Related Previous Analyses on Subjectivity and Their Key Concepts

	Experiencing speaker	Self-monitoring speaker
Iwasaki (1993: 30)	**S-perspective:** the perspective that the speaker takes for situations in which his own experience is involved	**O-perspective:** the perspective that the speaker takes for the situation in which another sentient being's experience is involved
Ikegami (2003)	**subjective construal:** The cognizer, who is the speaker, directly involves himself in the event and construes it as experiencing it himself.	**objective construal:** The cognizer, who is the speaker, does not directly involves in the event, and construes it as placing himself outside of it
Nakamura (2003)	**I(=Internactional) mode:** Cognizers, with physical entities, are interacting with some entities and constructing the cognitive images of them.	**D(=Displaced) mode:** Cognizers, displacing themselves from the locus of cognition, are observing the cognitive images of some entities as objective truths.

Nakamura's (2003) figures representing his I-mode and D-mode are reproduced here to give another illustration of the distinction between constructions of the experiencing speaker type and the self-monitoring speaker type, respectively.

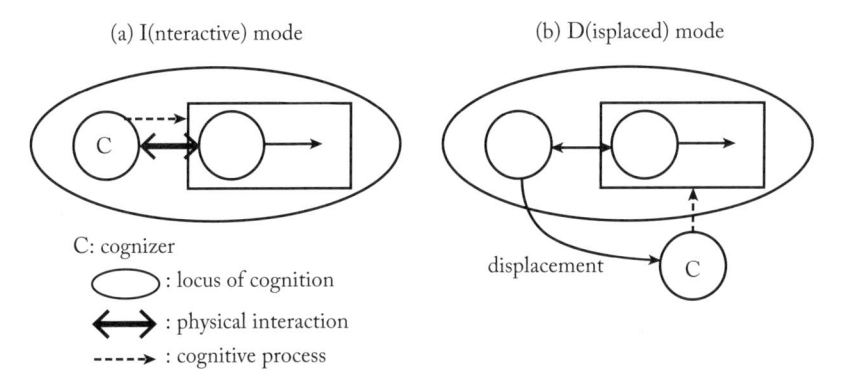

Figure 2. "Cognitive modes" (I-mode vs. D-mode) [Reproduced from Nakamura (2003)].

2.3 Lexicalization of the "experiencing speaker" construction

The examples of the "experiencing speaker" constructions discussed so far are of a compositional nature, i.e. they are composed to represent the subjective construal as a whole. No element in such examples alone (e.g. neither *sitting* nor *across* in (2b) alone) lexically indicates the subjective construal of the whole construction. Natural language, however, sometimes lexicalizes the "experiencing speaker" pattern and forms what I call "deictic predicates". The motion verb *come* is one such example.

The verb *come* is a "deictic predicate" of the "experiencing speaker" pattern, because it, in its basic motion sense, presupposes the existence of the speaker (or another ground element) at the end of the motion path, differing from a verb like *move*.[1] The speaker is always present in the event denoted by the verb *come* even without the use of a deictic locative *here* or the first person pronoun *me* in the sentence. In uttering the sentence in (5), for instance, the speaker talks of his 'experience' as a participant in the event where the person by the name of *Taro* approached/moved toward him.

(5) *Taro <u>came</u> (here/to me).*

What this sentence depicts can be pictographically represented as shown in Figure 3 below.

Figure 3. Pictographic representation of *TARO <u>came</u>*.[2]

Notice here the commonalities between the representations in Figure 3 and Figure 1b, which indicate that the two are both of the 'experiencing speaker' pattern. In both images, the speaker appears nowhere, but simply provides the vantage point for the observed scene, in which the object of his perception, Taro and Vanessa, respectively, alone appears. The two differ only in the type of event they represent. The event of coming in Figure 3 is a motion event, which is indicated by the arrow pointing toward the vantage point of the speaker, while the event of sitting in Figure 1b is a stative event. It should be noted again that there is a difference in compositionality. The subjective construal in (5) is lexical and inherent to the verb *come*, which is a deictic predicate, while that in (2b) is compositional.

Let us here examine the grammatical role of the constituent referring to the speaker (*to me* or *here* in (5)) for deictic predicates like *come*. The argument/adjunct distinction for verbal predicates is theoretically important, but apparently the referring expression to the speaker in question is neither an argument nor an adjunct of the verb *come*. It is not an argument because it can be omitted in English (cf. arguments cannot be omitted in English: *He handed it *(to me)*.). It also differs from an adjunct in that its denotation, i.e. the speaker or his location, is inherent to the predicate and present in the event denoted by the predicate whether formally absent or not (cf. an adjunct's denotation is not implicated by the predicate: *He kissed her here*. ≠ *He kissed her*.). Therefore, let us coin terms and call the expression in a deictic predicate that refers to the speaker as the "deictic argument" and its implicit occurrence as the "deictic zero". (The deictic argument occurs as the deictic zero by default.) Accordingly, the implicit reference to the speaker for predicates like *come* represents not a dropped pronoun/zero pronominal, but the deictic zero.

The function of deictic zero is to represent in general the speaker in the experiencing speaker construction. Table 2 characterizes the two types of expressions denoting an event involving the speaker.

Table 2. Expressions of an Event Involving the Speaker

Construction type	Zero expression referring to the speaker	Lexicalized predicates
self-monitoring speaker	zero in general† (incl. zero pronominal)	predicates in general†
experiencing speaker	deictic zero	deictic predicates

Note. † 'in general' here means 'not specific to the first person'.

3. Cross-linguistic differences in the lexicalization patterns

3.1 Linguistic typology

Linguistic typology, the study of world languages, demonstrates that languages can vary a great deal in their lexicalization patterns, and the lexicalization patterns of expressions of events involving the speaker are no exception. Even such a basic verb as the deictic motion verb 'come' is missing from the lexical inventories of some languages.

DeLancey (1985: 367), in his discussion of "directive" verb systems in Tibeto-Burman, notes: "In a language with an extreme version of the directive system, there are not two deictically specified lexical items 'go' and 'come', but a single unspecified motion verb [...]" and mentions Jinghpaw and Rawang. In Jinghpaw, for example, "where the deictically neutral motion verb string *sa wa*, which we can gloss for the present purposes as 'go', can be deictically specified (like any other motion verb) by means of the postverbal particles *r-* 'hither' and *s-* 'hence'" (DeLancey 1985: 370):

(6) MaGam gat deʔ **sa wa** [r-aʔ ai/s-ai].³
    market to go here-3rd DEC/from.here-DEC
    "MaGam [came/went off] to market."

In the following, we will examine internal state predicates to see whether there is any cross-linguistic variation in their lexicalization.

3.2 Cross-linguistic differences in the lexicalization patterns of internal state predicates

Internal state predicates (ISPs, henceforth) are those predicates denoting emotions, sensations, thought processes, etc. of sentient beings (Iwasaki 1993). Let us examine ISPs in English, Thai and Japanese, which exhibit different behavior in terms of omissibility of the experiencer-role nominals denoting the speaker, and find out whether or not the "experiencing speaker" pattern is lexicalized for them.

First of all, as we have noted earlier, there is a well-known typological distinction between English on the one hand and Thai and Japanese on the other. In the former type, pronouns cannot be omitted, while pronouns are omitted rather freely in the latter, which are thus called zero pronominal languages. This typology holds for the experiencer-role pronouns for ISPs in the languages in question as well, as illustrated with an emotion predicate meaning 'to be glad' in (7).

(7) English: *(I) am glad.
    Thai: (phǒm)   dii-cai.
              I   be.glad
    Japanese: *(watasi wa)   uresii.*
              I   TOP be.glad

ISPs in English are out of the question. Just like other pronouns in English, the experiencer-role nouns for the ISPs, in the first person or not, always have to be present, and they do not constitute a zero pronominal or deictic zero. The English ISPs, thus, are not of the "experiencing speaker" type; they are of the "self-monitoring speaker" type.

The question remains, then, as to the classification of ISPs in Thai and Japanese, both of which are zero pronominal languages. Therefore, we will focus on, and compare, the ISPs in the two languages.

3.3   Thai and Japanese internal state predicates in contrast

ISPs in the two languages are contrastively examined in this section, and it is demonstrated that ISPs in Thai are of the "self-monitoring speaker" type while those in Japanese are of the "experiencing speaker" type. Three pieces of evidence are provided.

3.3.1   First person restriction in Japanese

It is well known that ISPs in Japanese exhibit first person restriction on their experiencer subject, unlike those in other languages like English (Kuroda 1973; Kuno 1973; Iwasaki 1993; Uehara 1998). In other words, ISPs in Japanese can take only the first person pronoun for their subjects, and to be used with third person subjects they have to co-occur with some evidential markers such as *souda* 'appear' and *garu* 'show the signs of being' (as illustrated in (8b) below). Surprisingly, such personal restriction does not exist for ISPs in Thai, a zero pronominal language like Japanese, and they rather resemble those in English except for their omissibility. This is illustrated with the following examples of ISPs: emotion predicates ('be glad/sad') in (8); predicates of desire ('want/feel like') in (9); markers of intention ('will/intend to') in (10); and predicates of thought processes ('think') in (11). In the example sentences, the parentheses indicate the omissibility of the subject nominals.

Emotion predicates ('be glad/sad'):

(8) Thai: (phǒm/khǎw)　　dii-cai/sǐa-cai.
　　　　　I/he　　　　　　be.glad/be.sad
　　　　　"I am/He is glad/sad."

　　Jpns: a. (watasi/*kare wa)　uresii./kanasii.
　　　　　　 I/he　　　　　　　TOP　be.glad/be.sad
　　　　　　 "I am glad/sad."

　　　　　b. (kare　wa)　uresi-/kanasi-**souda**.
　　　　　　　he　　TOP　be.glad/be.sad-appear
　　　　　　　"He looks glad/sad."

Predicates of desire ('want/feel like'):

(9) Thai: (phǒm/khǎw)　yàak　dɯ̀ɯm　bia.
　　　　　I/he　　　　　want　drink　beer
　　　　　"I/he want(s) to drink beer."

　　Jpns: (watasi/*kare wa)　sake　ga　hosii/nomi-tai.
　　　　　 I/he　　　　　　　TOP　sake　NOM　want/drink-want.to
　　　　　 "I want/want to drink sake."

Markers of intention ('will/intend to'):

(10) Thai: (phǒm/khǎw)　tâŋcay　rian　phɛ̂ɛt.
　　　　　 I/he　　　　　intend　study　medicine
　　　　　 "I/he will/intend(s) to study medicine."

　　 Jpns: (watasi/*kare wa)　igaku　o　manab-oo.
　　　　　 I/he　　　　　　　TOP　medicine　ACC　learn-will
　　　　　 "I will learn medicine."

Predicates of thought processes ('think'):

(11) Thai: (phǒm/khǎw)　khít　wâa　fǒn càʔ　tòk　phrûŋníi.
　　　　　 I/he　　　　　think　that　rain will　fall　tomorrow
　　　　　 "I/he think(s) that it will rain tomorrow."

Jpns: (*watasi/*kare   wa)   asu   ame ga   huru   to   omou.
      I/he   TOP   tomorrow   rain NOM   fall   that   think
      "I think that it will rain tomorrow."

The data above indicates that the first person experiencer nominal is inherent and lexicalized in the meaning of ISPs in Japanese and constitutes a deictic zero when it is covert, while in Thai the experiencer nominal has no such person constraint for ISPs and counts as a zero pronominal when it is covert.

3.3.2   First person restriction in Thai – marked or basic

One might wonder if Thai predicates exhibit any degree of the person restriction that we see for ISPs in Japanese. The Thai constructional pattern, with an exclamatory particle /can/ 'really', is interesting in this regard. (12) illustrates the use of /can/ with emotion predicates (cf. (8) above).

Exclamatory expressions of one's emotions in Thai ('be REALLY glad/sad'):
(12) (phǒm/*khǎw)   dii-cai/sǐa-cai   **can**.
     I/he   be.glad/be.sad   really
     "I am REALLY glad/sad."

The grammatical pattern with /can/ 'really' in Thai above in (12), i.e. the inability to take the third person subject, parallels the patterns observed with ISPs in Japanese and indicates that the former in Thai exhibits the same person restriction as the latter in Japanese. Notice a difference, however, that the person restriction for Thai is compositional and not inherent to emotion predicates, while that in Japanese is lexical and inherent to the lexicon of internal states.

3.3.3   Sensation predicates

There seem to be at least two modes of expressing sensations like pain: i) the descriptive mode, in which the speaker describes his sensation rather objectively in order to convey it to another person (e.g. 'It hurts!'), and ii) the exclamatory mode, in which he makes an exclamatory expression of his sensation as he experiences it (e.g. 'Ouch!'). English has undergone lexicalization for those descriptive mode sensation predicates distinct from the simple exclamation. Consider the lexicalization patterns in Thai and Japanese in the descriptive mode in (13) and in the exclamatory mode in (14).

Descriptive mode: A beginner nurse gave you a medical injection, with her hand trembling. You felt pain on the arm and say "It hurts!":
(13)   Thai: (Óoy) cèp!   Jpns: *Itai!*
          ouch hurt   hurt

Exclamatory mode: Walking alone on the street, you tripped over something, fell and hurt your knee. You cry out "Ouch!":
(14)   Thai: Óoy! (*cèp.)   Jpns: *Ita(i)!*
          ouch hurt   ouch

The Thai pattern parallels that of English and has lexicalized a descriptive predicate of sensation distinct from exclamatory outcry, and the Thai sensation predicate /cèp/ can be used only when there exists an interlocutor, to whom the speaker objectively describes and conveys his sensation of pain, as in (13). It cannot be used when the speaker is alone with no one else around—the most subjective context—as in (14). In contrast, the Japanese sensation predicate *itai* is formally, and thus arguably functionally as well, indistinct from the outcry of pain.

3.4   Summary

This section has contrastively examined ISPs in Thai and Japanese, both of which are classified as a zero pronominal language, and demonstrated that ISPs in Thai resemble English ISPs and represent the "self-monitoring speaker" type, while those in Japanese represent the "experiencing speaker" type and are lexicalized as those providing the speaker's speech-time experience. Thus, Japanese ISPs are deictic predicates while Thai ISPs are not. The three pieces of evidence provided are summarized in Table 3 below.

Table 3. Thai and Japanese Internal State Predicates in Contrast

	ISPs in Thai	ISPs in Japanese
1. person restriction of the experiencer subject	no restriction	limited to the first person
2. default mode of the predicate lexicon	descriptive	exclamatory
3. [sensation predicates] distinction from the outcry of sensation	distinct	indistinct

What this difference in lexicalization patterns between the ISPs of the two languages means is that sentences with ISPs in the two languages that correspond to the same English translation by default represent two different construals. Of the two sentences with an implicit experiencer subject and a predicate of desire 'want' in (15), for example, the Thai sentence represents an objective construal of the "self-monitoring speaker" type, pictographically represented in Figure 3a, while the Japanese version represents the subjective construal of the "experiencing speaker" type, pictographically represented in Figure 3b.

(15) Thai: yàak dùɯm bia.   Jpns: *sake ga*   *hosii*.
     want drink beer   *sake* NOM want
     "(I) want to drink beer."   "(I) want *sake*."

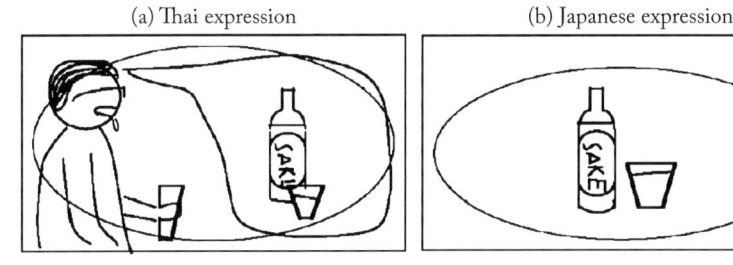

(a) Thai expression   (b) Japanese expression

Figure 4. Pictographic representations of sentences in (15) [reproduced from Uehara (2006a: 281)].

4. Conclusion

This paper has re-examined the cognitive linguistic theory of subjectivity (Langacker 1985 and others), more specifically, the overt/covert distinction of the first person pronouns relative to the degree of subjectivity in certain English constructions, and proposed some modifications on it for its wider cross-linguistic application. It has been shown in the paper that the implicit first person pronouns in the 'experiencing speaker' construction differ from zero pronominals and instead represent cases of "deictic zero", and that languages vary in conventionalizing/lexicalizing the experiencing speaker pattern into "deictic predicates", such as the verb of coming. Deictic predicates conceptually entail the existence of the speaker in the denoted events, which is termed the 'deictic argument', whose implicit instance constitutes a deictic zero. Thai and Japanese are both classified as zero pronominal languages, while English is not. With this new sub-typology of zero pronouns, as far as the experiencer subject pronoun of ISPs is concerned, its covert instantiation in Thai represents a zero pronominal, while that in Japanese represents a deictic zero. Table 4 summarizes this new typology.[4]

Table 4. A New Typology of Languages with respect to the ISPs

	English	Thai	Japanese
zero pronominal language?	no	yes	yes
covert subjects of ISPs	N/A	zero pronominal	deictic zero

Acknowledgements

I would like to thank Kingkarn Thepkanjana and Kanokwan Laohaburanakit Katagiri for providing and checking the Thai data in the paper. I am also grateful to Tadao Miyamoto and Bob Sanders for their suggestions on textual improvements. Needless to say, all remaining errors are mine. This work was supported in part by a Grant-in-Aid for Scientific Research from the Japan Society for the Promotion of Science (No. 20520347).

Notes

1. Langacker (1985) calls the verb *come* in English a "deictic verb". The term "predicate" is employed here instead of "verb" because, as we see below, lexicons with similar grammatical features are not limited to verbal predicates alone, but are found in adjectival predicates as well in other languages.
2. This figure is originally adopted and slightly modified from a picture for the verb *come*, a visual aide to be used in foreign language classrooms, in Hatasa, et al. (www.sla.purdue.edu/fll/JapanProj/FLClipart/).
3. The following abbreviations are used in glosses: ACC = accusative; DEC = declarative; NOM = nominative; TOP = topic.
4. Although this is out of the scope of the current study, it should be noted that this new sub-typology of zero anaphora can be extended to cover ISPs in other zero pronominal languages of Asia. The data on Mandarin Chinese and Korean ISPs in Uehara (2006b, 2011) suggest that the former should be classified together with the Thai type, while the latter should be classified together with the Japanese type.

References

DeLancey, Scott. 1985. The analysis-synthesis-lexis cycle in Tibeto-Burman: A case study in motivated change. In John Haiman (ed.), *Iconicity in syntax*, 367–389. Amsterdam: John Benjamins.

Ikegami, Yoshihiko. 2003. Gengo niokeru 'shukansei' to 'shukansei' no gengo-teki shihyô ('Subjectivity' in language and its linguistic indicators), (1). *Studies in Cognitive Linguistics* 3. 1–40.

Iwasaki, Shoichi. 1993. *Subjectivity in grammar and discourse: Theoretical considerations and a case study of Japanese spoken discourse.* Amsterdam: John Benjamins.

Kuno, Susumu. 1973. *The structure of the Japanese language.* Cambridge: MIT Press.

Kuroda, S.-Y. 1973. Where epistemology, style, and grammar meet: A case study from Japanese. In Stephen Anderson & Paul Kiparsky (eds), *A Festschrift for Morris Halle*, 377–391. New York: Holt, Rinehart and Winston, Inc.

Langacker, Ronald W. 1985. Observations and speculations on subjectivity. In John Haiman (ed.), *Iconicity in syntax*, 109–150. Amsterdam: John Benjamins.

Langacker, Ronald W. 1991. *Concept, image, and symbol: The cognitive basis of grammar.* Berlin: Mouton de Gruyter.

Nakamura, Yoshihisa. 2003. Gengo sôtairon kara ninchi sôtairon e: Datsu-syutaika to 2-tu no ninchi mode (From linguistic relativity to cognitive relativity: Desubjectification and the two modes of cognition). *Kenkyû Nenpô (Annual Research Bulletin)* No.7, 77–93. Edward Sapir Society of Japan.

Rattanaphanusorn, Rungthip & Kingkarn Thepkanjana. 2008. Grammaticalization of the verb of seeing as an evidential marker in Thai. *Studies in Cognitive Linguistics* 7. 273–301.

Uehara, Satoshi. 1998. Subjective predicates in Japanese: A cognitive approach. Paper presented at the 4th Australian Linguistic Institute Workshop: Cognitive Research Issues in Cognitive Linguistics. (published as Uehara 2006a)

Uehara, Satoshi. 2006a. Internal state predicates in Japanese: A cognitive approach. In June Luchjenbroers (ed.), *Cognitive linguistics investigations across languages, fields, and philosophical boundaries*, 271–291. Amsterdam: John Benjamins.

Uehara, Satoshi. 2006b. Toward a typology of linguistic subjectivity: A cognitive and cross-linguistic approach to grammaticalized deixis. In Angeliki Athanasiadou, Costas Canakis & Bert Cornillie (eds), *Subjectification: Various paths to subjectivity*, 75–117. Berlin: Mouton de Gruyter.

Uehara, Satoshi. 2011. Syukansei ni kansuru gengo no taisyô to ruikei (Cross-linguistic comparison and linguistic typology in terms of subjectivity). In Harumi Sawada (ed.), *Hituzi imiron kouza 5: Shukansei to shutaisei (Hituzi Studies on Semantics 5: Subjectivity)*, 69–91. Tokyo: Hituzi Shobo.

Traugott, Elizabeth C. 1989. On the rise of epistemic meanings in English: An example of subjectification in semantic change. *Language* 65. 31–55.

Traugott, Elizabeth C. 1995. Subjectification in grammaticalization. In Dieter Stein & Susan Write (eds), *Subjectivity and subjectivisation: Linguistic perspectives*, 31–35. Cambridge: Cambridge University Press.

Wongtawan, Parinya. 2010. Subjectification in grammaticalization of the verb of 'seeing' in Thai: The emergence of pragmatic meaning through subjective construal. Paper presented at The 2010 Seoul International Conference on Linguistics, Korea University, Seoul, Korea, June 24, 2010.

Chapter 8

A contrastive case study of pronominal forms in English, Japanese and Thai: A parallel corpus approach

Theeraporn Ratitamkul and Satoshi Uehara

1. Introduction

It is widely acknowledged that the languages of East and Southeast Asia differ from Western languages like English in terms of referential expressions. Referents in East and Southeast Asian languages, such as Chinese, Japanese, Korean, Lao, Thai and Vietnamese, can be left unexpressed when they can be recovered from context.[1] Referential forms in these languages can be categorized into three main types, i.e. the lexical form, the pronominal form and the null form. Thus, there arises an interesting question as to how these forms get chosen in discourse and, more specifically, how they differ from one another with regard to their frequency of occurrence, their distribution as well as their semantic and pragmatic properties.

There exist both general principles and language specific constraints on the selection of referential forms. At the global level, referential forms depend to a large extent on the status of the referents (e.g. Chafe 1976; Givón 1983; Gundel et al. 1993, among others). For example, Chafe (1976) states that referents that are not in the consciousness of the interlocutors are usually expressed in their full lexical form whereas referents that are already present in the consciousness of the interlocutors at the time of speaking are realized with attenuated forms. It can be predicted, therefore, that a speaker will choose a lexical NP when he introduces a new referent and a pronoun or a null form when mentioning a referent that has already been made prominent in the discourse. This generalization seems to hold across languages. However, variations in referential choices among languages are also conspicuous. Each language has its own preferred patterns of reference, notwithstanding the fact that the three possible referential forms are similarly available in the language. To illustrate this, referents in both Japanese and Thai can appear in lexical, pronominal and null forms. Nevertheless, how speakers of Japanese and Thai choose referential expressions in their speech can vary greatly. It has been documented that although Japanese has many pronouns that refer to first and second persons, third-person pronouns are rarely used (Clancy 1980; Uehara 1998, 2001). Thai also has a large number of terms used to refer to the first and second persons. In fact, Cooke (1968) claims that Thai has 27 terms for the first person, 22 terms for the second person and 8 for the third person. However, in contrast to Japanese, third-person pronouns are not infrequent in Thai (see Ratitamkul 2007 for pronominal use in Thai narratives and conversations). Another difference between Japanese and Thai lies in the nature of pronominal forms. Siewierska (2004), taking the view that the noun-pronoun distinction is scalar, proposes that personal pronouns in Thai exhibit less pronominal and more nominal properties than those in Japanese. In other words, personal pronouns in Thai are more noun-like than Japanese pronouns. The dissimilarities discussed certainly lead to different patterns of referential expression in the two languages.

The present study is interested in referential strategies in Thai, compared with those in English and Japanese, paying particular attention to pronominal forms. To observe the use of referential forms in a comparable context, we analyze a short story in English and its translations in Japanese and Thai, adopting the methodology used by Uehara (1998, 2001). The aim is to answer the following questions. Firstly, to what extent do pronominal forms vary in English, Japanese and Thai? And secondly, what are the factors that influence referential choices in Thai?

2. Uehara's (1998, 2001) studies on referential expressions in Japanese

The present study expands the research conducted by Uehara (1998, 2001), which examined the short story, *The Last Leaf*, by O. Henry and its Japanese translation by Yasuo Ohkubo. The researcher investigates how personal pronouns in English are translated into Japanese, based on the widely assumed view that English pronouns more or less correspond to zero pronouns in Japanese. He also asks what functions overt pronouns in Japanese have, considering the assumption that Japanese zero pronouns can be equated with English pronouns.

The story, *The Last Leaf,* is short and has four main characters: Johnsy, Sue, Behrman and the doctor, thus making it convenient to observe referential expressions and discourse situations. There follows the synopsis of the story taken from Uehara (2001): Johnsy and Sue are two of a number of poor artists who started to settle down in a particular area of New York. The two help each other to make their living and make their way to become artists, when one day Johnsy is smitten with pneumonia. The doctor says to Sue that Johnsy has only a one-tenth chance of recovery, and that depends on whether she can stop thinking of dying. So Sue tries to get Johnsy's mind off dying, but Johnsy has been counting the number of ivy leaves still clinging in the winter wind to the vines on the wall of the building they can see from their window, saying that when the last one falls, she will die too. For all Sue's begging and other efforts to stop Johnsy thinking about the leaves and her dying, Johnsy has made up her mind that she is not going to get well, and keeps getting weaker until there is only one leaf left to fall. The last leaf, however, stays there for several days until at last Johnsy gains the energy to live and is out of danger. Around the same time, their friend Behrman, an old painter who lives beneath them, dies from pneumonia.

Concentrating on pronouns in the subject position (i.e. personal pronouns in nominative cases) in the English original and their corresponding forms in the Japanese translation, Uehara finds that more than half of the English pronouns (54.2%) are left unexpressed in Japanese, 30.5% are realized with pronouns, and 15.3% are nouns. However, if only third-person pronouns are taken into consideration, nouns are more frequent than pronouns, while ellipses are still in the majority. Uehara suggests that the "coherent anaphor" context accounts for referential choices in the Japanese text. That is, when an anaphoric expression is structurally or semantically closely related to its antecedent, it tends to be in the form of a zero pronoun; otherwise, overt forms are used. This is in accordance with what is found in Mandarin Chinese (Li & Thompson 1979). Uehara further reveals that while the coherent anaphor factor can explain ellipses of third-person referents, the fact that the first-person referents are not realized in Japanese is due to the "subjectivity" factor. Differing from English, Japanese has a set of internal state predicates which convey the intention, desires and mental processes of the speaker. These predicates are morphologically distinguished and tied to the speaker's perspective. Since their occurrences are restricted to the first-person subject, these predicates render the dropping of the first-person pronoun.

Uehara also discusses in detail the use of Japanese third-person pronouns. It has been noted elsewhere that occurrences of these pronouns (*kare* 'he', *kanozyo* 'she' and *karera* 'they') are not frequent when compared with those of first and second-person pronominal forms (Clancy 1980). Data analysis shows that only nine third-person pronouns are present and, interestingly, all of them are used only by the narrator to refer to the story's characters and not by the characters themselves. Uehara argues that the use of these pronouns in the Japanese translation is functionally motivated. While nominal reference may appear with honorifics and demonstratives, hence implying the speaker's attitude as well as a physical and psychological distance from the referents, the Japanese third-person pronouns are said to be relatively neutral in respect of the speaker's relationship with the referents. As it is a conventional practice of Japanese speakers to convey their perspective in their language use, the pronouns *kare*, *kanozyo* and *karera* would not be appropriate if used by the characters to refer to third-person referents. The narrator, on the other hand, can take a more objective view of the situation, legitimizing the use of third-person pronouns.

Uehara concludes that Japanese is "a speaker's perspective-oriented language", and this is reflected in the use of referential forms. Similar to other languages, the coherent anaphor factor plays a role in how referents are realized. The Japanese text shows that when a close connection is established between an anaphor and its antecedent, that anaphoric expression can be left unexpressed. However, an important factor that influences referential forms in Japanese, distinguishing its pattern of argument realization from a language such as English, is subjectivity. Subjectivity accounts for the omission of first-person referents with internal state predicates and also for the selection of third-person pronouns in the Japanese text.

3. English pronouns and their counterparts in Thai and Japanese

3.1 Data

In accordance with Uehara (1998, 2001), we analyzed the English short story,

The Last Leaf, along with its Thai and Japanese translations. As far as we know, there are two versions of this short story existing in Thai. The older one was printed in 1965 and translated by Po Mahakhan, and the other can be found online at http://wanakam.com and has been translated by a translator with the pseudonym 9Eleven and edited by Wo Suphan. Only the latter will be considered in this study because of its adherence to the original text and the accuracy of its translation. As an online translation may be questioned regarding its credibility, we have also obtained a certified translation from the Chalermprakiat Centre of Translation and Interpretation, Faculty of Arts, Chulalongkorn University. The translator was unaware of the purpose of the study and was specifically asked not to consult other translations of the text. We will present analyses of the online version, henceforth Text 1, and the certified translation, henceforth Text 2, side by side. As for the Japanese text, data shown in this study is taken from Uehara's previous studies.

To compare the use of pronominal forms in English, Japanese and Thai, we have paid particular attention to English pronouns in the subject position and their counterparts in Thai and Japanese. Sharing the same exclusion criteria with previous studies, English pronouns that do not have counterparts in Thai have been excluded from the analysis, e.g. the situational *it* in *when it was light enough*. Also excluded are those pronouns that do not appear in the translated texts due to differences in sentence structure between the two languages. For instance, the underlined *I* in *And now I must see another case I have downstairs* is not included because the pronoun is absent in the Thai translations; the Thai equivalent of "another patient downstairs" is used.

Out of 132 English subject pronouns, there are 118 eligible pronouns in Japanese, 126 in the Thai Text 1 and 120 in the Thai Text 2.[2] Corresponding linguistic forms in the translated texts are classified into three main types: Pronouns, Nouns and Null forms. Although the distinction between pronouns and nouns in Thai is not clear-cut, as has been mentioned earlier Thai pronouns are rather noun-like in nature, we have differentiated between the two forms and treat only "personal pronouns proper" as pronouns. The term "personal pronoun proper" was used in Kullavanijaya (2000) to refer to non-derived personal pronouns as opposed to derived forms, which are, for example, kin terms and other common nouns used as personal pronouns. Detailed descriptions of specific referential forms are also provided in the next section.

3.2 Results of the analysis

The data reveals that English pronouns are not always translated into pronouns in Thai and Japanese. Table 1 shows the number of the three forms (Pronouns, Nouns and Null) in T1, T2 and Japanese. It can be observed that the Thai translations, T1 and T2 alike, contain a large proportion of overt pronouns (84.9% in T1 and 55% in T2). The forms that are of the second highest number are nouns (10.3% in T1 and 26.7% in T2), whereas zero pronouns are the fewest (4.8% in T1 18.3% in T2). The Japanese text, on the other hand, exhibits a different pattern. More than half of the forms used in the Japanese translation are ellipses, 30.5% are pronominal forms and 15.3% are nouns.

Table 1. Pronouns, Nouns and Null Forms in the Thai and Japanese Texts

	Pronouns		Nouns		Null		Total	
Thai T1	107	84.9%	13	10.3%	6	4.8%	126	100%
Thai T2	66	55%	32	26.7%	22	18.3%	120	100%
Japanese	36	30.5%	18	15.3%	64	54.2%	118	100%

Tables 2, 3 and 4 present the numbers of each referential form, grouped according to the English pronouns in the original, for T1, T2 and Japanese, respectively. Since the first and second-person reference seems to have a special status in discourse, distinguishing them from the third-person reference (Lyons 1977), we make a distinction between the two types of reference.

Table 2. Pronouns, Nouns and Null Forms in Thai T1

Thai T1

	Pronouns		Nouns		Null		Total	
1st and 2nd person								
I	39	93%	3	7%	0	0%	42	100%
we	1	50%	0	0%	1	50%	2	100%
you	14	82%	0	0%	3	18%	17	100%
3rd person								
he	16	84%	2	11%	1	5%	19	100%
she	22	88%	3	12%	0	0%	25	100%
it	11	92%	0	0%	1	8%	12	100%
they	4	44%	5	56%	0	0%	9	100%

Table 3. Pronouns, Nouns and Null Forms in Thai T2

Thai T2

	Pronouns		Nouns		Null		Total	
1st and 2nd person								
I	31	74%	5	12%	6	14%	42	100%
we	2	100%	0	0%	0	0%	2	100%
you	7	41%	4	24%	6	35%	17	100%
3rd person								
he	11	65%	5	29%	1	6%	17	100%
she	11	44%	8	32%	6	24%	25	100%
it	4	50%	3	38%	1	13%	8	100%
they	0	0%	7	78%	2	22%	9	100%

Table 4. Pronouns, Nouns and Null Forms in Japanese

Japanese

	Pronouns		Nouns		Null		Total	
1st and 2nd person								
I	21	50%	0	0%	21	50%	42	100%
we	0	0%	0	0%	3	100%	3	100%
you	6	40%	0	0%	9	60%	15	100%
3rd person								
he	3	17%	5	28%	10	56%	18	100%
she	4	17%	7	29%	13	54%	24	100%
it	1	13%	2	25%	5	63%	8	100%
they	1	13%	4	50%	3	38%	8	100%

Taking a closer look at the realization of each English pronoun, we notice a difference between Thai and Japanese. The first-person pronouns in English can appear in lexical forms in Thai, but not in Japanese. Moreover, T1 and T2 are different with regard to the proportion of referential forms. T1 has more pronouns than T2. Tables 2 and 3 reveal that if the first and second-person pronouns are set aside, approximately half of the original pronouns are expressed in pronouns in T2 (26 out of 59 instances or 44.7%), while a majority are realized as pronouns in T1 (53 out of 65 instances or 81.5%). This further contrasts with the Japanese text, in which pronominal use for third-person reference is rare (9 out of 58 instances or 15.5%). As for nouns and null forms in the Thai texts, they are infrequent in T1. Their proportion in T2 is clearly larger than that in T1.

4. Referential choices in Thai

Thai is well-known for its rich referential system. Many researchers have noted that the language has a large number of pronominal forms used to refer to first, second and third persons (Baron 2001; Cooke 1968; Palakornkul 1972; Ratitamkul 2007, among others). Moreover, one of the characteristics of Thai can be seen in the use of lexical items, such as nicknames, kin terms and occupation titles for self-reference.[3] These forms are different from pronouns in that they are not deictic in nature. The following examples show a nickname and an occupational title, which are used to refer to the speaker.[4]

(1) Nít   khít   wâa   Nít   ca   mây pay
    Nit   think Comp Nit   Mod   Neg go[5]
    "Nit (=I) thinks that Nit (=I) will not go."

(2) khruu   ca   maa   phrûŋníi
    teacher Mod   come   tomorrow
    "Teacher (=I) will come tomorrow."

The translated Thai texts show a variety of pronominal forms and lexical forms for person reference. In addition, zero pronouns are also possible. Table 5 displays corresponding linguistic forms for each English pronoun in T1 and T2. We propose that two factors influence referential selection in the Thai texts in 4.1 and 4.2.

Table 5. Corresponding Forms of the English Pronouns in the Thai Translations

	T1	T2
I	chăn '1st Pers', phŏm '1st Pers', mɔ̌ɔ 'doctor'	chăn '1st Pers', chăn.ʔeeŋ '1st Pers.Reflex', ʔây.raw 'Title.1st Pers', mɔ̌ɔ 'doctor', tuaʔeeŋ 'Reflex', ø
We	phûak.raw 'Pl.1st Pers', ø	raw '1st Pers', raw.thúk.khon '1st Pers. every.person'
You	khun '2nd Pers', raw '1st Pers', thəə '2nd Pers', ø	khun '2nd Pers', raw '1st Pers', thəə '2nd Pers', luŋ 'uncle', nŭu 'mouse (lit.)', ʔii.nŭu 'Title.mouse (lit.)', ø
He	kɛɛ '3rd Pers', khăw '3rd Pers', mɔ̌ɔ 'doctor', taa.bəəmɛɛn 'Title.Behrman', ø	kɛɛ '3rd Pers', luŋ.kɛɛ 'uncle.3rd Pers', mɔ̌ɔ 'doctor', ø
She	thəə '3rd Pers', cɔɔnsîi 'Johnsy', tuaʔeeŋ 'Reflex'	lɔ̂n '3rd Pers', thəə '3rd Pers', cɔɔnsîi 'Johnsy', khon.khăw 'person.3rd Pers', khonkhây 'patient', suudîi 'Sudie', yǐŋ.săaw 'young lady', ø
It	man '3rd Pers', ø	man '3rd Pers', baymáay 'leaf', khɔ̂ɔ.níi 'issue.Dem', nîi 'Dem', ø
They	phûak.khăw 'Pl.3rd Pers', phûak.man 'Pl.3rd Pers', khray 'someone', tháŋkhûu 'both', tháŋsɔ̌ɔŋ 'both'	tháŋkhûu 'both', tháŋsɔ̌ɔŋ 'both', khon 'person', khon.làw.níi 'person.Pl.Dem', khray 'someone', ø

4.1 Recoverability from context

A principle in Goldberg's Pragmatic Mapping Generalizations (2004), which concerns how referents are to be realized in utterances, stipulates that referents which are relevant and non-recoverable from a context must be overtly expressed. This leaves the possibility for those referents that can be recovered to be left unexpressed, which is apparently the case in the Thai translations at hand. Looking at null subjects in both of the Thai texts, we have discovered that referents designated by null forms can all be recovered from the context thus allowing them to be covert. However, not all context-recoverable referents are covertly expressed. Recoverability only offers leeway for prominent referents to be dropped; it does not compel argument omission.

A careful examination of the data reveals that there are two contexts which are likely to host zero forms. The first is the coherent anaphor context where a zero pronoun and its antecedent are closely related. Omission is facilitated by the ease of recoverability. As mentioned earlier, the coherent anaphor context can account for zero pronouns in Japanese as well. An example of a null form in the coherent anaphor context is manifested in (3), taken from T2. In the parentheses is the null form in the translated text, which can be straightforwardly linked back to the antecedent "Sue" in the preceding clause.

(3) After the doctor had gone Sue went into the workroom and cried a Japanese napkin to a pulp. Then <u>she</u> (ø) swaggered into Johnsy's room with her drawing board, whistling ragtime.

The second context is the one in which a request or command is directed toward the addressee. In such a context, the unexpressed subject, the second person "you", can be pragmatically inferred. This is the same in Japanese; Uehara (1998: n. 6) notes that most of the cases of omitted second-person pronouns occur in request or command patterns where the subjects are assumed to be the addressees. The following example is spoken by Sue to Johnsy; it shows a null form denoting the second person (Johnsy), which is found in both T1 and T2.

(4) Will <u>you</u> (ø) promise me to keep your eyes closed, and not look out the window until I am done working?

It is plausible that argument omission in Asian languages is driven by the recoverability of arguments from context. Data from Chinese, Japanese and Thai confirm that arguments are likely unexpressed and, when they are, can be easily identified from the context (e.g. Clancy 1980; Li & Thompson 1979; Ratitamkul 2007). Ease of recoverability depends on multiple factors, such as the prominence of the referent in question, its grammatical position in a clause as well as the existence of other competing referents. The Thai texts manifest two contexts which enhance recoverability, namely the coherent anaphor context and the directive speech act context.[6]

4.2 Attitude and relationship

The many forms of person-referring expressions in Thai carry different sociopragmatic meanings. Several sociolinguistic studies have listed a number of social dimensions associated with Thai referential terms (e.g. Cooke 1968; Iwasaki & Horie 2000; Palakornkul 1972). Cooke, for example, asserts that features, such as status, level of intimacy, deference, assertiveness, age, sex and kinship accompany person reference. Focusing on first and second-person reference, Iwasaki and Horie further suggest that referring expressions are one of the linguistic devices used to create speech register in Thai conversations and that the two important dimensions to be paid heed to are distance (social and psychological) and formality. In the following section, we will explore how overt referential forms in the two Thai texts reflect the speaker's attitude and relationship with the referent in focus, which can be, and most of the time is, the addressee.[7] We will begin with the first and second-person reference and then the third-person reference.

4.2.1 Pronominal and nominal forms designating the first and second persons
To begin with, the two Thai texts do not have exactly the same set of overt forms referring to the first and second-person referents. Table 5 shows that T2 contains a more varied set of referential terms than T1. The different forms for "I" and "you" are distinguished according to the gender of the speaker as well as the speaker's attitude to and relationship with the addressee. The following are descriptions of each pronoun taken from Iwasaki and Horie (2000: 527–529), in light of Cooke (1968). We include only those that are relevant to our discussion.

First-person pronouns
 a. chăn (male/female speakers): male speaking to inferior or female intimate; female speaking to an intimate equal or inferior.
 b. phŏm (male speaker): general polite term used by males speaking to equals and superiors.
 c. raw (male and female speakers): superior to inferior; between friends of the same sex; referring to oneself in soliloquy.

Second-person pronouns
 a. khun (male/female speakers): general polite term used to equals and superiors.
 b. thəə (male/female speakers): speaking to inferiors or intimate equals, especially by or to female.

The data reveals that the intimate chăn is chosen for self-reference by the female characters, namely Sue and Johnsy, when they talk to each other. The two use the intimate thəə for 'you', indicating their close relationship. The pronoun chăn is also seen when Sue talks to Behrman, as they are neighbors who know each other well.

Moreover, comparing T1 and T2, Thai readers can deduce from the use of referential forms the subtle difference in the relationship between Sue and Behrman. In T1, a conversation between Sue and Behrman shows that Behrman refers to himself with the general polite phǒm and to Sue with the general polite khun. Sue reciprocates by using the same general polite khun. In contrast, T2 has Behrman referring to himself with the more intimate chǎn and to Sue with the nominal (ʔii)nǔu, literally '(Title)mouse', an endearing term used with a young female interlocutor. Sue, in response, calls Behrman luŋ 'uncle', a kin term which can be used with an intimate. It can thus be observed that the relationship between Sue and Behrman is closer and more informal in T2 than in T1.

A unique property of Thai, that is the use of an occupational title for self-reference, is evident in the texts. The doctor almost always uses mɔ̌ɔ 'doctor' for 'I', as seen in Example (5). An occupational title signals the professional role of the speaker, in this case a doctor, and implies the doctor-patient relationship. Interestingly, in T1 the doctor switches to the general polite phǒm after his patient begins to get well perhaps with the effect of deemphasizing his professional role. This is shown in (6).

(5) But whenever my patient begins to count the carriages in her funeral procession I (mɔ̌ɔ 'doctor' in T1 and T2) subtract 50 per cent from the curative power of medicines.

(6) And now I (phǒm in T1; mɔ̌ɔ 'doctor' in T2) must see another case I have downstairs.

Likewise, a change in the second-person reference when the doctor is talking to Sue indicates a change in their relationship. The general polite khun referring to Sue is found at the beginning of the story in both texts but toward the end it is switched to the intimate thəə in T2, which is possible after the doctor and Sue have become close acquaintances. The use of thəə in contrast with khun is manifested in (7).

(7) She's out of danger. You (khun in T1; thəə in T2) won. Nutrition and care now — that's all.

Another pronoun for the first person which is present only in T2 is ʔây.raw used by Behrman to refer to himself. Switching from chăn, this usage makes it sound as if the character is making a self-directed speech. The pronoun raw is, in fact, ambiguous because it can refer to the first-person singular or plural, depending on the context. As can be seen, the English pronoun *we* can also be translated into raw and phûak.raw (phûak signifies plurality) in the Thai texts.

It is evident that the choices of referential expression reflect the speaker's relationship with the addressee and affect the reader's understanding of the relationship between the characters. The first-person reference is selected based on the speaker's perception of himself or herself with regard to the addressee, and the second-person reference depends on the speaker's attitude toward the addressee. As we have seen, there is no "neutral" person reference for the first and second persons in Thai. Each linguistic form, pronominal or nominal, communicates information about the speaker and addressee, which includes gender, attitude and relationship.

4.2.2 Pronominal and nominal forms designating the third person

Exhibiting the same pattern as the first and second-person reference, T2 shows a greater variety of third-person referential forms than T1 (See Table 5). A list of third-person pronouns we focus upon is given below, adapted from Cooke (1968).

Third-person pronouns
  a. kɛɛ: informal and familiar term referring to both superiors and inferiors, implying intimacy with the referent or is otherwise slightly disrespectful.
  b. khăw: general term referring to a male or female referent (both intimates and non-intimates) without particular respect or disrespect.
  c. lɔ̀n: form referring to females and used in written language especially in novels.
  d. thəə: elegant term referring to females.

The pronoun kɛɛ is used to refer to Behrman by the narrator and the story's characters except for the doctor in T1. The use of kɛɛ gives a hint that Behrman is an old familiar man to whom there is no need to show deference. To illustrate the point, one of the female characters, Sue, refers to Behrman with kɛɛ. This contrasts with the doctor's reference to Behrman with the general pronoun khǎw in T1. (See Examples (8) uttered by Sue and (9) uttered by the doctor.) These two pronouns lead to the interpretation that from Sue's point of view, Behrman is familiar to her; the doctor, on the other hand, does not have any particular relationship with Behrman in T1.

(8) Mr. Behrman died of pneumonia today in the hospital. <u>He</u> (kɛɛ in T1 and T2) was ill only two days.

(9) There is no hope for him; but <u>he</u> (khǎw in T1; kɛɛ in T2) goes to the hospital today to be made more comfortable.

In fact, the general khǎw occurs only in T1. This pronoun is somewhat neutral; it does not imply any particular attitude of the speaker toward the referent. In addition to its reference to Behrman by the doctor, it is used by Sue when she mentions the doctor to Johnsy, and also by the narrator. Referring to the doctor with khǎw, Sue conveys an indifferent attitude toward him. Moreover, a narrator who holds a relatively objective view of characters can also use khǎw to express his indifference. It can be noticed that the narrator of T1 shows an indifferent feeling toward the doctor through the use of khǎw and, at the same time, a subjective perspective of Behrman by the use of kɛɛ.

There exists the occupational title mɔ̌ɔ 'doctor' in both T1 and T2, used by Sue when she talks about the doctor and by the narrator of T2. This is demonstrated in (10), in which the narrator refers to the doctor with mɔ̌ɔ 'doctor'. It can be noticed that while kɛɛ is used to refer to Behrman by Sue, the doctor and the narrator in T2, it never refers to the doctor. Instead, the term mɔ̌ɔ 'doctor' is constantly used by Sue and the narrator. Replacing the English he with mɔ̌ɔ 'doctor' is appropriate in the Thai language. As being a doctor is considered to be a respectable profession, it is felicitous to acknowledge his status even in a third-person reference. It should be noted here that the narrator of T1 and, for some of the time, Sue also use the general khǎw to refer to the doctor, which is not unacceptable.

(10) The doctor came in the afternoon, and Sue had an excuse to go into the hallway as <u>he</u> (khǎw in T1; mɔ̌ɔ 'doctor' in T2) left.

Other nominal forms in the texts are a kin term luŋ 'uncle' and taa. bɔɔmɛɛn 'Title.Behrman' (taa is a title used before a male name to indicate closeness), both referring to Behrman. The former is used by the doctor when he speaks to Sue in T2 and the latter is used by Sue when speaking to Johnsy in T1. These terms again serve to reveal the speakers' familiarity with Behrman. As an illustration, in Example (11), the doctor shows a feeling of intimacy toward Behrman by his use of luŋ 'uncle'. It is in fact accompanied by the intimate kɛɛ in a manner similar to a left dislocation: luŋ kɛɛ… 'the uncle, he …' Although it may not be the case that the characters have a close relationship, the kin term actually helps to create a sense of intimacy the speaker has toward the person referred to.

(11)   He (khǎw in T1; luŋ 'uncle' in T2) is an old, weak man, and the attack is acute.

As for the English pronoun *she*, there is only one pronominal form in T1, namely thəə, which is also a second-person pronoun. The third-person thəə is gender specific in that it is restrictively used with female referents. However, it appears more often in novels than in everyday conversation. In T1, thəə represents the female characters, Sue and Johnsy, and is used by both the characters and the narrator. On the other hand, T2 displays a distinctive pattern for the corresponding Thai pronouns for the English *she*. While thəə, as in T1, is used by the characters to refer to a female referent, the narrator exclusively uses lɔ̂n, not thəə, when referring to the female characters. The pronoun lɔ̂n is both gender specific and genre specific. Iwasaki & Horie (2005) have noted that lɔ̂n is a female third-person pronoun occurring only in novels. The pronoun lɔ̂n retains a distance between the narrator and the characters, indicating the narrator's estranged relationship with the referent. An example is to be found in (12).

(12)   An hour later she (thəə in T1; lɔ̂n in T2) said: "Sudie, some day I hope to paint the Bay of Naples."

As well as pronominal forms, overt realization of the English *she* is carried out in nominal forms, such as khonkhâi 'patient' and yǐŋsǎaw 'young lady' in T2. An example is in (13); the doctor uses khonkhâi 'patient' for the corresponding English *she* (Johnsy), indicating the doctor-patient relationship.

(13) "She (thəə in T1; khonkhâay 'patient' in T2) has one chance in – let us say, ten," he said, as he shook down the mercury in his clinical thermometer.

Another example is in (14), where the corresponding form of *she* referring to Sue is the nominal yǐŋsǎaw "young lady" in T2. Like lɔ̂n, yǐŋsǎaw is only seen being used by the narrator.

(14) She (thəə in T1; yǐŋsǎaw 'young lady' in T2) arranged her board and began a pen-and-ink drawing to illustrate a magazine story.

An interesting observation is that occurrences of the same pronominal form denoting different referents in a single sentence are not preferable in Thai. Hence, when the original English text has two identical pronominal forms that do not refer to the same referent in the same sentence, the Thai texts have two different forms for them. To illustrate the point, Example (15) displays different forms that correspond to Sue (she) and Johnsy (**she**). It is preferable for the pronoun *she* for Johnsy to be explicitly realized in a full form, rather than adopting the same pronoun that is used to refer to Sue.[8]

(15) She (thəə in T1; lɔ̂n in T2) told him of Johnsy's fancy, and how she (thəə in T1; ø in T2) feared **she** (cɔɔnsîi 'Johnsy' in T1 and T2) would, indeed, light and fragile as a leaf herself, float away, when her slight hold upon the world grew weaker.

After examining pronominal and nominal referential forms for person reference, we can see that one of the factors underlying the selection of overt referential forms in Thai is the speaker's attitude to and relationship with the addressee and the person referred to in the discourse. Referential expressions are a linguistic tool utilized by translators to indicate social relationships between the characters as well as to express the attitude of the narrator toward the story's characters. Obviously, the translators of the two Thai texts have chosen to elucidate such information in their own way. For example, both similarly describe a close friendship between Sue and Johnsy through the intimate first and second-person pronouns chǎn and thəə, respectively. The narrator in both texts also shares the same attitude toward Behrman, that is, he is an old familiar man, by the use of kɛɛ. Nonetheless, the narrator of T1 retains a somewhat neutral attitude toward the doctor in the story as can be seen in the general third-person pronoun khǎw while the narrator of T2 acknowledges his professional status by referring to the doctor with the occupational title mɔ̌ɔ 'doctor'. Dissimilarity also lies in the use of female third-person pronouns thəə and lɔ̂n. The translator of T1 does not distinguish between the narrator and the character's view of the referent, as the third-person thəə is used by both. In T2, however, there exists a distinction between the narrator's view as indicated by lɔ̂n and that of the character signaled by thəə. Moreover, a closer and more informal relationship between Sue and Behrman in T2, as compared with T1, is also expressed through different referential terms for "I" and "you". To sum up, the data analysis has confirmed that differences in the use of referential terms affect understanding pertaining to the narrator's viewpoint and the characters' attitudes and social relationships.

5. Comparing referential forms in the Thai and Japanese texts

Although both Thai and Japanese allow nominal forms, pronouns and zero pronouns to occur in discourse, examination of the data affirms that each language has its own pattern of argument realization. There seems to be a general principle underlying argument omission in both languages, namely recoverability from context. The fact that a referent can easily be retrieved from the context makes it possible for it to be omitted. In both the Thai and Japanese texts, zero pronouns occur in the coherent anaphor context and the directive speech act context, which are the contexts where referents are easy to recover. Nevertheless, omission in Japanese also results from the subjectivity factor observed in internal state predicates and this does not exist in Thai.

An intriguing characteristic of the Thai language can be observed in the variety of nominal and pronominal forms for person reference. The many forms referring to oneself reveal the speaker's perspective of himself with regard to the person spoken to. The different second-person referential terms likewise reflect the speaker's attitude and relationship with the addressee. It should be noted that though different forms for the first and second persons do not appear in the Japanese text in this study, Japanese also has different overt forms denoting the speaker and addressee that are chosen based on the relationship of the interlocutors. However, these forms are more varied in Thai than in Japanese.

The two languages also differ in the use of occupational titles and nicknames for self-reference. While this is not common in Japanese, it is conventional in Thai. An example taken from the Thai Text 2 and the Japanese text is in (16). The doctor calls himself by his professional title in Thai and by a first-person pronoun *wasi* in Japanese. In the Japanese text, the pronoun *I* for the doctor is either omitted or translated into a first-person pronoun but never an occupational title (cf. n. 4).

(16) And now I (mɔ̌ɔ 'doctor' in T2; *wasi* in Japanese) must see another case I have downstairs.

For nominal forms used to refer to the second person, Thai and Japanese resemble each other in that kin terms, such as luŋ 'uncle' and *ozisan* 'uncle (honorific)' in Thai and Japanese respectively, can be used to refer to a middle-aged male addressee. Nonetheless, these terms seem to carry different information in Thai and Japanese. In Thai, kin terms when used for non-kin referents express the speaker's feeling of intimacy. To refer to a person who is not blood-related as if he were a member of the speaker's family helps to build up solidarity, making the interlocutors feel closer than when other pronominal forms are used. This also holds true for kin terms denoting the third person. However, unlike Thai, kin terms in Japanese are used without such constraints of intimacy and solidarity. The use of *ozisan* 'uncle (honorific)' here in Japanese would indicate that Behrman is Sue's uncle or else any middle-aged man with whom she does not have any particular intimacy. Example (17) from T2 shows the contrast in second-person reference between Thai and Japanese.

(17) But I think you (luŋ 'uncle' in T2; *anata* in Japanese) are a horrid old – old flibbertigibbet.

Furthermore, while third-person pronouns in Japanese are relatively neutral, those in Thai are somewhat semantically loaded. The pronoun khǎw in Thai can be considered the most neutral among the third-person referring forms. Other pronouns like kɛɛ, lɔ̂n and thəə as seen in the texts, are to a certain extent noun-like in that they express formality, familiarity and intimacy as well as genre-specific properties. This can be observed in (18), where the intimate pronoun kɛɛ is used in Thai by the narrator to refer to Behrman in contrast with the rather neutral *kare* in Japanese. Through the use of pronouns the narrators of the Thai texts reveal their perception of the character as an old familiar man.

(18) For the rest <u>he</u> (kɛɛ in T1 and T2; *kare* in Japanese) was a fierce little old man, [...]

Considering the great number of pronouns along with their socio-pragmatic meanings in Thai, it is not surprising that a large proportion of the English pronouns are realized with pronouns in Thai in comparison with the Japanese counterpart. Both pronominal and nominal forms in Thai, regardless of person, are a linguistic device to signal the speaker's attitude and social relationship with the referent in focus. The fact that the Thai pronouns function as such can be attributed to their noun-like properties. This is in accordance with the claim in Siewierska (2004) that personal pronouns in Thai are more like nouns than those in Japanese.

6. Conclusion

The present study investigates referential forms in English, Japanese and Thai in a comparable context and proposes two factors that affect referential choices in Thai. Concentrating on the English subject pronouns, we have discovered that the factors influencing referential forms in the Thai texts are recoverability from context and the speaker's attitude to and social relationship with the addressee and the referent mentioned in discourse. Compared with data from the Japanese text, the two Thai texts contain a large proportion of pronouns, which, together with nominal expressions, serve to convey information about attitudes and social relationships.

Admittedly, realization of referents with pronominal forms in Thai could have been influenced by the use of pronominal forms in the original English text. The translators of the two Thai texts might be attempting to adhere to referential use and the structure of the original text, resulting in a high percentage of pronouns in the translated texts. Analysis of a different type of text may yield a different result. Finally, we propose that a contrastive study of Japanese and Thai is necessary to obtain a complete picture of referential selection in the two languages.

Acknowledgments

We would like to thank Kanokwan Laohaburanakit Katagiri and the audience of the Chulalongkorn-Tohoku Cognitive and Typological Linguistics Symposium, held at Chulalongkorn University, for their helpful comments and suggestions. This work was partly supported by a grant from the Project on Language and Human Security in Thailand, within the Integrated Academic Innovation Initiative, Chulalongkorn University's Academic Development Plan (CU Centenary), and by the Higher Education Research Promotion and National Research University Project of Thailand, Office of the Higher Education Commission (HS1153A).

Notes

1. Unexpressed referents in East and Southeast Asian languages are different from the so-called pro-drop phenomenon present in languages such as Italian and Spanish, where subject arguments can be omitted and verbal inflections reflect person, number and gender of dropped arguments. Covert referents in East and Southeast Asian languages, on the other hand, can occupy various grammatical roles and can be identified through discourse-pragmatic inference rather than through verbal morphology.
2. The Thai Text 1 has more eligible pronouns than Text 2, which in turn has more eligible pronouns than the Japanese text, mainly because of the sentence structures chosen by each translator. As an example, the underlined you in the following exemple is included in the analysis of Text 1 and Text 2; it is replaced by a null form in both translations. However, this instance is excluded in the Japanese text analysis because it is translated into a different expression without the second-person subject, an equivalent of "that's fine" in English (*sore demo kekkou yo*):
   Very well, Mr. Behrman, if you do not care to pose for me, you (ø in T1 and T2; excluded in Japanese) needn't.
3. The use of these lexical expressions for self-reference is unique to Thai and also Lao, which is closely related to Thai.
4. Although names and occupational titles can be used for self-reference in Japanese, this usage is restricted to child speech and child-directed speech.
5. Abbreviations used in this work are as follows: Comp = Complementizer, Dem = Demonstrative, Mod = Modality marker, Neg = Negation marker, Pers = Person, Pl = Plural marker and Reflex = Reflexive.
6. As noted in Palakornkul (1972), omission of referential forms in Thai also results from the speaker's desire to avoid defining his attitude and relationship with the addressee or the third person referred to. This is in part due to the complexity of the referential system in the language which occasionally makes it difficult to decide which terms one should

use. (On a related note, it can be observed that at the initial introduction the parties may ask about the other's information, such as age and occupation, so that they can proceed with appropriate referential terms.) This type of ellipsis, however, does not concern us here.
7. We will not discuss the issue of formality in detail and leave it for future research as it seems irrelevant to the present data sets.
8. Japanese also shows the same preference. The following example is taken from the Japanese text, in which the reference to Johnsy is distinguished from the reference to Sue: She (*suu*) told him of Johnsy's fancy, and how she (ø) feared **she** (*kanozyo* 'Johnsy') would, indeed, light and fragile as a leaf herself, float away, when her slight hold upon the world grew weaker.

References

Baron, Amy M. 2001. *The interactive organization of reference to persons in Thai conversation*. Los Angeles: University of California dissertation.

Chafe, Wallace. 1976. Givenness, contrastiveness, definiteness, subjects, topics and point of view. In Charles N. Li (ed.), *Subject and topic*, 27–55. New York: Academic Press.

Clancy, Patricia M. 1980. Referential choice in English and Japanese narrative discourse. In Chafe Wallace (ed.), *The pear stories: Cognitive, cultural, and linguistic aspects of narrative production*, 127–202. Norwood, NJ: Ablex.

Cooke, Joseph R. 1968. *Pronominal reference in Thai, Burmese, and Vietnamese* (*University of California publications in linguistics*, 52). Berkeley: University of California Press.

Givón, Talmy. 1983. Topic continuity in spoken English. In Talmy Givón (ed.), *Topic continuity in discourse: A quantitative cross-language study*, 347–363. Amsterdam: John Benjamins.

Goldberg, Adele E. 2004. Pragmatics and argument structure. In Laurence R. Horn & Gregory L. Ward (eds), *Handbook of Pragmatics*, 427–441. Massachusetts: Wiley-Blackwell.

Gundel, Jeanette K., Nancy Hedberg & Ron Zacharski. 1993. Cognitive status and the form of referring expressions in discourse. *Language* 69. 274–307.

Iwasaki, Shoichi & Preeya Ingkaphirom Horie. 2000. Creating speech register in Thai conversation. *Language in Society* 29. 519–554.

Iwasaki, Shoichi & Preeya Ingkaphirom Horie. 2005. *A reference grammar of Thai*. Cambridge: Cambridge University Press.

Kullavanijaya, Pranee. 2000. Power and intimacy: A contradiction in a Thai personal pronoun. *Oceanic Linguistics Special Publications, No. 29, Grammatical Analysis: Morphology, Syntax, and Semantics*. 80–86.

Li, Charles N. & Sandra A. Thompson. 1979. Third-person pronouns and zero-anaphora in Chinese discourse. In Talmy Givón (ed.), *Syntax and semantics volume 12: Discourse and syntax*, 311–335. New York: Academic Press.

Lyons, John. 1977. *Semantics*, vols. 1–2. Cambridge: Cambridge University Press.

Palakornkul, Angkab. 1972. *A sociolinguistic study of pronominal strategy in spoken Bangkok Thai*. Austin: University of Texas dissertation.

Ratitamkul, Theeraporn. 2007. *Argument realization in Thai*. Urbana-Champaign: University of Illinois dissertation.

Siewierska, Anna. 2004. *Person*. Cambridge: Cambridge University Press.

Uehara, Satoshi. 1998. Pronoun drop and perspective in Japanese. In Noriko Akatsuka, Hajime Hoji, Shoichi Iwasaki, Sung-Ock Sohn & Susan Strauss (eds), *Japanese/Korean Linguistics 7*, 275–289. Stanford: CSLI at Stanford University.

Uehara, Satoshi. 2001. Anaphoric pronouns and perspective in Japanese: A text-based analysis. In Kaoru Horie & Shigeru Sato (eds), *Cognitive-functional linguistics in an East Asian context*, 35–53. Tokyo: Kurosio Publishers.

Chapter 9

Directives in Japanese and Thai group discussions: Communal versus individual

Ataya Aoki

1. Introduction

Group communication is a natural activity in any society and participation in discussions is regarded as a standard form of decision-making and equitable involvement in organizations. Communication in small groups can symbolize how group members define and enact their sense of self and their group (Lesch 1994). Group communication patterns can also be a reflection of the larger society. The present paper investigates how native groups of Japanese and Thai proceeded toward a set goal, and how their speech behavior revealed aspects of social relations in their respective groups by focusing on the directive speech acts that occurred during discussions.

Directives are defined as acts that have illocutionary force to stimulate the hearer(s) to respond (Bach & Harnish 1979). They express a desire by the speaker for the hearer(s) to perform a particular action, in accordance with the wishes of the speaker. In a discussion, these acts can be classified as asking for opinion/ confirmation/ clarification, giving orientation to members, suggesting ways to work out the problem, calling for attention, or designating the next turn. Not only do these acts play an important role in moving the task ahead, they also connote leadership performance.

Because directives commonly expect to elicit some response from the hearer(s), they constitute one unit of an adjacency pair (Schegloff & Sacks 1973), a discourse unit in which the first part of the pair acts as a force provoking the second part to follow. The speaker of the first part yields the turn to the next speaker to fulfill the pair with a response. Therefore, we can view directives as a turn-allocating process. Unlike dyads, turn-allocation in multi-party conversation can be problematic and involves relational management. How the current speaker transfers the turn, and the direction in which he or she focuses the message in a multi-party talk, can tell us about the speaker's perception of other members and about relationship management in the group.

From the perspective of Politeness Theory (Brown & Levinson 1987), directives can be a face-threatening act because the speaker risks intruding on a recipient's self-autonomy and freedom to act. Directives, therefore, often call for redressive action. However, Spencer-Oatey (2000) argues that directives can also be a sign of positive acknowledgement of a recipient in certain situations in some cultures. She views that not only face, but sociality right is also a motivation in social relationship management. She proposes the framework of Rapport Management Theory which suggests exploration other domains of language use besides the speech acts. Examples of these domains are participation, discourse, styles, and the non-verbal. This paper investigates some social relational aspects of the directive acts in Japanese and Thai discussions by taking a broader view of Rapport Management Theory.

2. The data

Six experimental discussion groups were assembled in order to attain comparable sets of data. Three were groups of Japanese speakers (Groups JA, JB and JC), and three were groups of Thai speakers (Groups TA, TB and TC). Each group was made up of five participants of mixed gender. The ratio of male and female members was either 2:3 or 3:2 in each group. Participants were undergraduate or graduate students between the ages of 19–35 who were members of some circles in their universities. In each group participants were close in age and academic background and were acquaintances. The discussions took place at campus facilities in Japan. The topic of discussion was a problem-solving situation that required the group to reach a consensus. The scenario was an accident scene in which the participants could only rescue seven people out of ten survivors. Participants discussed the scenario in their native language in a casual setting and the discussions were recorded and transcribed. All utterances were classified based on their communicative functions. The time spent for each group to reach a conclusion was as follows: JA-25 minutes, JB-53 minutes, JC-

37 minutes, TA-16 minutes, TB-41 minutes, and TC-41 minutes.

3. Analysis

The analysis reveals two distinctive and differing characteristics of Japanese and Thai groups. First, directives in Japanese groups were more likely aimed toward the group rather than at specific recipients, whereas the Thai groups showed the opposite tendency. Second, directives in Japanese groups tended to be responded to in closer sequence, making the structure of conversational exchanges solid and easily identifiable, while directives in Thai groups had more variations in sequential structures and did not always secure a response if a recipient was unspecified. The next section illustrates and discusses these findings.

4. Different directions of directives

In a conversation among three or more participants, the direction in which the current speaker aims his/her statement can be a crucial element in managing the course of interaction and rapport among members.

The directive statements in this experiment were classified into two categories based on whether they were addressed to an individual recipient - an "individual-focused directive", or to the group in general, a "communal-focused directive." Individual-focused directives can be achieved by calling out the recipient's name, gesturing and making eye contact. Examples are "Starting from you, Eri-chan", "Have you finished?" (a speaker looking at one particular participant) and "You chose the monk, didn't you?" On the other hand, communal-focused directives do not specify the recipient and any member can respond. Examples of communal-focused directives are "Have you guys finished?" "Let's start" and "How shall we work this out?" Analysis of results shows that Japanese group members tended to deliver directives towards the group as a whole rather than to individuals, whereas members of Thai groups preferred the opposite. The frequency of occurrences between communal-focused directives and individual-focused directives are compared within the same group, therefore, the differences in the discussion time among groups do not affect the result.

4.1 Japanese preference on the communal-focused directives

In all Japanese groups "communal-focused" directives occurred more frequently than "individual-focused" ones as shown in Table 1. It should be noted that group communication has a life and dynamic of its own, for it evolves in its own way depending on individual members, the situation, and the events that occur in that particular setting (Finley 1997). In this study, individual-focused directives in Group JC occurred less frequently than in the other groups. One explanation is of a synergetic effect among members when interacting in the group, which created a style particular to that group. However, this will not be the point of discussion in this paper. What is interesting here is that all three groups demonstrate the same pattern: i.e. "communal-focused" directives occurred more often than "individual-focused" ones.

Table 1. Summary of the Directions of the Directives in the Japanese Groups

Groups / Message types	Individual-focused directives	Communal-focused directives
Group JA	13	36
Group JB	26	46
Group JC	9	24

There are five possible reasons behind these findings. Firstly, they may represent the speakers' cognition that perceives the assembled group as being more prominent than separate individuals. A greater number of directives were directed toward the communal group rather than being issued to specific recipients. This resulted in more interactions at the group level than between any two individuals.

Secondly, a number of confirmations and consultations were repeated among group members concerning procedures and decisions in particular. Throughout the discussion, the speakers (especially the emerging leaders) made communal-focused directives such as what procedures should be carried out, whether everyone agreed and whether all were satisfied with the conclusion. A great number of communal-focused directives were produced around these types of confirmation questions. Excerpt 1 illustrates this point.

Excerpt 1 was taken from the final part of Group JA's discussion, illustrating how the participants debated the last choice, which was finally narrowed down to Choice E. The participants, including the male leader (JM3), confirmed each other's intention before finalizing their decision. The communal-focused directives are marked with arrows.

Excerpt 1 (Group JA)

→ 700 JM3: *E kana?*
         "Perhaps E?"
  701 JF1: *ja, yappari E no kana?*
         "So, after all, I'm thinking that perhaps E is the best choice?"
→ 702 JM3: *E de ii to omou?*
         "Are you all okay with E?"
  703 JM5: *E de..*
         "With E.."
→ 704 JM3: *daijoobu?*
         "Is it alright?"
→ 705 JF2: *E desu ka?*
         "E?"
  706 JF1: *soo da ne.*
         "Yes, I agree."
→ 707 JM3: *minna nani ka..hoka ni nani ka
         iinokoshita koto arun dattara.*
         "Does anyone have anything else?
         If you have something more to say."

The pattern in the above excerpt is in keeping with Watanabe's (2004) study on conflict management in Japanese group discussions. Watanabe found that at the end of the discussion, the leader sought confirmation from members as he/she felt it was the leaders' role to synchronize group members and manage conformity.

The third reason is that Japanese discussion groups conventionally employ a range of "speaking orders" to allow all group members to participate, reducing the need to prompt someone to express their opinion. These speaking orders are, for example, the seating order (starting with the person sitting on either the left or right-hand side of the facilitator, or the person sitting at the end of the front row, etc.), the seniority order (starting with the person who is most senior by age or by number of years associated with the organization), or the alphanumeric order of names on the roster. When the speaking turn is governed by a certain order, all members are guaranteed an equal chance to speak, and willing or not, they are automatically obliged to speak when their turn comes. In this study, the Japanese groups were observed using some of these conventions to set the speaking order. Members of Groups JA and JB started speaking in the order of their seating. In Group JC, members started speaking in order of seniority and degree of acquaintance with the organizer of the discussion. By using these conventional but unstated rules, the necessity of having to name the individual whose turn it is to speak is reduced.

Fourth, this result reflects the social relationship mechanism or rapport management in Japanese group interactions. Communally focused directives make the statements relevant to all participants. As anyone can take their speaking turn on a voluntary basis, the degree of imposition on any particular individual is reduced. Mitigation of face-threat is a preferred rapport management strategy in Japanese social interaction.

Finally, when posing a question to a group in a nonchalant style, the speaker can mollify his or her opinion that follows. In a discussion when participants are obliged to express personal opinions or to take the leadership roles, this can be seen as a softening technique. In the following examples, speakers make a communal-focused directive, pause for a moment and then continue with their opinion. In other examples (not shown here), the speaker asserted their opinions and intentions before continuing with a communal-focused directive. Either way, the speakers showed consideration for the group by suggesting their flexibility to take others' opinions into account, despite an intention to move on if no one responded. Below are two examples.

(1)   *takokuseki kigyoo, kono hito doo nan da? doo nan daroo?* .. (+ S's opinion)
       "What about this manager of the conglomerate business? How should we consider?"

(2)   *doo yatte ikoo kana.. ja, mazu tasuu ketsu de kime mashoo ka?*
       "How shall we go about this? Shall we decide by vote?"

In summary, Japanese preference for communal-focused directives underlines the strong influence of communal customs, a tendency to refrain from self-assertion and the intrusion of individual self-autonomy into a group setting, including their observation of conventions of interaction.

4.2   Thai preference for individual-focused directives

Unlike the Japanese groups, the Thai groups employed individual-focused directives more frequently than communal-focused directives. The frequency of individual-focused directives in comparison to communal-focused directives in the Thai group is summarized in Table 2.

Table 2. Summary of the Directions of the Directives in the Thai Groups

Groups / Message types	Individual-focused directives	Communal-focused directives
Group TA	25	9
Group TB	51	22
Group TC	41	40

In Groups TA and TB, individual-focused directives occurred more than communal-focused ones. Although Group TC shows marginal differences, their individual-focused orientation was characterized by the fact that more than half of individual-focused directives (28/41) and more than half of the communal-focused directives (28/40) came from the leader alone. There are five possible explanations as to why individual-focused directives occurred more than the communal-focused ones.

Firstly, the finding suggests that the cognition of Thai speakers perceived individual participants as more prominent than the collective. When the speaker issued a directive to a specified individual, the interaction at that point is exclusive to the two of them: the addresser and the addressee. Although gradually the verbal exchanges were intertwined and developed into group work, the dynamic force of interaction in Thai groups was essentially driven by personal exchanges and individual connection.

Secondly, it is a characteristic of Thai speech that speakers tend to form a statement by taking the hearer as the subject or topic. For example, such questions as "What did *you* choose?", "Did *you* choose…?", "Why did or didn't *you* choose?", or "What about *you*?" occurred more often than such questions as "What about *this choice*?", "How should *this choice* be considered?", "Isn't *this choice..*?", as is the case in Japanese groups where the concepts and choices were often made the themes of the statements. Thai groups were observed using these types of individual-focused directives in concluding their discussions, in contrast to how Japanese groups concluded theirs. To illustrate the point, Excerpt 2 was taken from the last part of Group TA's discussion. In this excerpt TF5 (the leader) was trying to conclude the discussion by confirming each member's decision.

Excerpt 2 (Group TA)

503. TF5 phîi (TF2) yàak.. phîi lɯ̂ ak phrà kɔ̀ɔn chây máy?
    "Sister (TF2) you want.. You chose the monk first, didn't you?"
504. TF2 ɯɯ.
    "Uh-huh."
505. TF5 wâa cà hây yùu chây máy? {pointing at TF2}
    "To leave him out, correct?"
506. TF5 â, phîi (TM3). {pointing at TM3}
    "(EXC), Brother (TM3)."
507. TF5 aw phrá dûay ìik khon nɯŋ ná.
    "You also chose the monk, didn't you?"
508. TF5 (TM4) aw khray?
    "(TM4) whom did you choose?"
    ……..
515. TF5 â, (TF1). {pointing at TF1}
    "(EXC), (TF1)."

In this excerpt, TF5, the youngest member of the group, conferred with TF2, TM3, TM4 and TF5 one-by-one regarding their choices. The use of fictive kin terms, nicknames, and the casual, light-hearted way of speaking created the ambience of a family circle throughout the discussion. TF5 addressed the members who were older than her, by using the title phîi or "older brother/sister". She also used exclamatives and hand movements to specify the recipients. Both types of directives in the Thai groups were delivered in a straightforward manner without hesitation.

The third reason is because discussions in the Thai groups proceeded in a free style format with no set speaking order. Specifying who the next responder should be was an effective means to control the process of group discussion, and also a crucial tactic to ensure a response to the question or the instruction. The next section illustrates that directives that were not aimed at a designated recipient did not always elicit a response.

Finally, a directive message such as asking for an opinion was not perceived as a face-threat to the Thai participants in this context. On the contrary, it could even be regarded as a show of attention and an acknowledgement of the importance of the recipient, which is one of the rapport management strategies in the Thai context.

In summary, the Thai preference for individual-focused directives implies their stronger cognition of individual members, and a style of rapport management which gives importance to personal quality and connection. The following section substantiates this claim.

5. Difference in participatory styles

This section illustrates the conversational sequences of directive statements at the beginning of the discussion in order to clarify the patterns and significance in the way speakers interacted in their group discussions. The beginning of the discussion is the crucial part where the leader usually emerges, relationships among members develops, and the style of discussion is established. Among three Thai groups, two groups had male leaders. Similarly, two Japanese groups among three had male leaders. To determine the leader of a group, the number of directive utterances each person made was calculated. The person who made the most directive statements was considered the group leader.

In this study, the discussion was considered to have started when one of the group members initiated a directive statement to the others in the group. This section gives examples to illustrate how Japanese and Thai participants are likely to respond to this act. The findings show that participants in Japanese groups tended to respond to the directives promptly or in close sequence, a style which I have labeled as "reciprocal style." In contrast, speakers in the Thai groups were slow to respond to directives that did not specify a recipient, i.e., communal-focused directives. They tended to participate in the event independently, a style which I have called an "independent style."

5.1 Japanese preference for reciprocal-style participation

The Japanese preferred a specific pattern of exchange: despite being in a multi-party situation, adjacency pairs were fulfilled in close sequence. Even communal directives which did not require an answer had sufficient weight to elicit a response from the group members. This characteristic demonstrates the reciprocal nature of the interaction. The exchange structure at the beginning of all Japanese groups can be identified as follows.

Initiation	<directive> (give orientation)
Response(s)	(answer)
Initiation	<directive> (give orientation)
Response(s)	(answer)

Excerpt 3 below shows an example of how Group JA started their discussion.

Excerpt 3 (Group JA)

1. JM3 *kimatta?* <directive> (give orientation)
   "Have you (all) decided?"
2. JF1 *kimat.. ja, kimatta.* (answer)
   "(I) have decided."
3. JM3 *ja. kimatta hito.* <directive> (give orientation)
   "Okay, (tell me) who has decided?"
4. JF1 [*hai.* (answer)
5. JF2 [*hai.* (answer)
6. JM4 [*hai.* (answer)
7. JM5 [*hai.* (answer)
   "Yes."
8. JM3 *yoshi. ja..* (give orientation)
   "Okay, then,"
9. JM3 *doo shiyoo ne?..* (directive)
   "How shall we proceed with this?"
10. JF2 (made a suggestion) (answer)

The discussions in every group began when one member took the initiative and began by asking if the others had finished selecting the choices. In all groups the directives were promptly answered in the following turns, demonstrating compliance. As members showed they were ready, the leaders issued a second directive to prompt the discussion, as seen in *yoshi, ja, dooshiyoo* (lines 8–9 in Group JA), and similarly in the other two groups, all of which can be roughly translated as "How shall we work this out?" Interestingly, these expressions were used identically in all three groups to launch the next part of the discussion and marked the point when one speaker emerged as the group leader.

Dooshiyoo "How shall (we) work this out?" may look like the act of asking for help, but it can also be perceived as a declaration that the speaker would take control of the situation. At the same time *dooshiyoo* works to soften any suggestion which the leader makes afterwards. Because *dooshiyoo* demonstrates (with modesty) that the speaker is as much lost as everyone else, a brief pause allows other members to interject if they want to (as in Group JA). If there was no interjection, the leader continued to assert his or her opinion (as in Group JB and JC), generally in an interrogative form, giving the impression that the speaker was asking for help.

5.2 Thai preference for the independent style of participation

Unlike the Japanese groups, no real pattern can be identified in the Thai groups, and the turn-taking system was not structured. Directives that did not specify a recipient (i.e., communal-focused directives) did not always secure a response. The beginning section of each group discussion can be summarized as follows.

In Group TA, the initial communal-focused directive was repeated, re-stated, or reformulated by several members with no replies. An answer finally appeared several responses later. In Group TB, the leader gave a communal-focused directive, but did not receive a prompt reply. He continued to give more directives. Again he did not receive any compliance from the members, but some confirmation questions instead. In the end, one member rejected his directives. Lastly in Group TC, the discussion was initiated by a directive specifying the recipient. This directive received a reply. A similar question was asked again of another member. However, this time it was replied to by a member to whom the question was not addressed. Moreover, when the discussion was about to start, it was diverted twice to other topics and finally the group broke into sub-group conversations. Excerpt 4 below shows an example of how a Thai group started the discussion.

Excerpt 4 (Group TA)
1. TM3 lâɯk khon năi kan mâŋ ŋâ?   <directive> (give orientation)
   "Who did you guys choose?"
2. TF1   tɛ̀ɛ lá khon lâɯk aray kan mâŋ nà <directive> (give orientation)
   "Who did each of you guys choose?"
3. TF2   aw thíŋ khray dii kwàa máy?   <directive> (give orientation)
   "Won't it be better to decide whom to leave out?"
4. TM4   khray thíŋ khray.   (repeat)

		"Who should choose to leave out whom?"	
5.	TF1	chây, khray thíŋ khray.	(repeat)
		"Right, who should leave out whom?"	
6.	TF1	phûut phìt. lûɯ ak thíŋ khray..	(repair directive)
		"I said it wrong. (Who) chooses to leave out whom?"	
7.	TF1	tɛ̀ɛ lá khon lɯ̂ɯ ak aray kan mân nà?	
			<directive> (give orientation)
		"Who did each of you guys choose?"	
8.	TF5	əə (TF5) kɔ̀ɔn lə́əy.	(answer)
		"O.K., I'll speak first."	

In the above excerpt, Group TA displays the Thai independent style of participation, where less reciprocity is observed in their conversational exchanges — a common characteristic in the three groups. The discussion of Group TA was initiated by TM3 in line 1, "Who did you guys choose?" Instead of receiving an answer, it was followed by similar statements, for example, "Who did each of you guys choose?" (line 2), "Won't it be better to decide whom to leave out?" (line 3), or "Who chose to leave out whom? " (line 4), until TF5 (line 8) volunteered to give an answer. These parallel statements pose the question as to whether the hearers perceived a directive as a directive or not. Observing conversational sequences in all Thai groups, I have made the assumption that directives that are not addressed to a particular recipient (i.e. communal-focused directives) usually do not have enough force to elicit a response. They are likely interpreted as general comments and may invite various kinds of reaction.

6. Summary

In this paper, I have presented the contrasting tendency of Japanese and Thai groups to target directive statements differently. I have also illustrated conversational sequences likely to occur in the adjacency pairs of directive statements.

It was found that the Japanese participants employed directives that were aimed at the communal group rather than at individuals, and their directives received a response in close sequence, even if the recipient of the directives was not specified (communal-focused directives). The study found that Japanese participants used this type of directive frequently at different stages of a discussion, making sure that all members agreed and came to a consensus.

Communal-focused directives in Japanese groups were also used as a device to mollify speakers' proposals, and as a rapport management tool. This is because in making statements relevant to all group members, the speaker could reduce the risk of imposing on any individual member. It also shows that attention is given to the benefits of collectivity. These behaviors are very much in keeping with Japanese social norms.

In the Japanese groups, a turn taking system and exchange pattern were clearly and easily identified. The adjacency pairs were fulfilled in close sequence, and participants played their assumed roles reciprocally, and were unlikely to compete. The speech behaviors found in the Japanese groups are the manifestation of speakers' cognition oriented to taking account of the group during social interaction.

On the other hand, Thai participants employed directives that were aimed more towards individuals than to the communal group. Directives that did not specify a recipient were not always interpreted as requiring a response or having enough force to elicit an answer. The use of more individual focused directives resulted in more interactions built on one-to-one connections between the addressor and addressee. Thai groups made more progress on the assigned task through the dynamism of exchanges at a personal level.

Personal connections in the Thai groups were reinforced by the participants' custom of calling each other by fictive kin terms and nick names. This contributed to the creation of a fictive family affection, where distance is minimized and a casual, independent interaction is preferred. Therefore, addressing a directive message to a recipient was not viewed as much of a face-threat to the listener, but rather as possibly welcome attention to an individual and his or her identity.

In the Thai groups, the system of turn taking was not clear and no similar exchange structure was identified. In a casual context, participants were seen cooperating in the event in parallel with some displaying contending roles. The speech behaviors found in the Thai groups can be interpreted as a manifestation of the speakers' cognition oriented towards the individual self of the participants in the interaction.

In conclusion, a group can manage its participants' interaction to work toward its goal in two dimensions: Communal and Individual. The degree and sensitivity of their usage differs from culture to culture based on the aspect each culture places importance on in social relations.

Transcription Conventions

.	=	intonation understood as final
..	=	pause longer than ,
?	=	intonation understood as question or confirmation request
{ }	=	comments on quality of speech, non-verbal behavior and context.
[	=	single bracket indicating overlapping speech
EXC	=	exclamation, words expressing a speaker's emotion

References

Bach, Kent & Robert M. Harnish. 1979. *Linguistic communication and speech acts*. Cambridge, MA: The MIT Press.

Brown, Penelope & Stephen C. Levinson. 1987. *Politeness: Some universals in language usage*. Cambridge: Cambridge University Press.

Finley, Linda. 1997. *Groupwork in occupational therapy*. Cheltenham: Nelson Thornes.

Lesch, Christee L. 1994. Observing theory in practice: sustaining consciousness in a coven. In Lawrence R. Frey (ed.), *Group communication in context: Studies of natural groups*, 57–82. Hillsdale, NJ: Lawrence Erlbaum Associates.

Schegloff, Emmanuel & Harvey Sacks. 1973. Opening up closings. *Semiotica* 7. 289–327.

Spencer-Oatey, Helen. 2000. Rapport management: A framework for analysis. In Helen Spencer-Oatey (ed.), *Culturally speaking: Managing rapport through talk across cultures*, 11–45. New York: Continuum.

Watanabe, Suwako. 2004. Conflict management strategies in Japanese group discussions. In Polly Szatrowski (ed.), *Hidden and open conflict in Japanese conversational interaction*, 65–93. Tokyo: Kurosio Publishers.

Chapter 10

The use of unconventional means of communication in Japanese and American blog comments

Barry Kavanagh

1. Introduction

Hall's (1976) cultural framework divides cultures according to context, the degree to which communication is explicit and verbal or implicit and non-verbal. Asian cultures such as Japan are placed high up on the high-low context continuum with western nations, such as America, being classified as having low context cultural variation (Hall & Hall 1990). Such cultures differ in their use of the amount of contextual information that is deemed necessary for the successful transaction of information. High context cultures are described as being more reliant on combining the verbal and non-verbal to convey the entire meaning of the message. In contrast low context cultures are said to rely on the explicit code, usually through verbal communication.

However, these distinctions were originally devised in a pre-internet period and were predominately applied to face to face interactions. With the advent of new technology that has led to the widespread use of online communication via the internet how applicable are these distinctions to this new medium of communication? This paper will aim to examine these contrasting types of communication styles specifically analyzing unconventional means of online computer mediated communication as demonstrated through a variety of unorthodox oral and visual depictions through Japanese and American personal weblog diaries. As online written communication is largely a low contextual form of communication how does a high context culture, such as Japan, communicate and express itself on the web that is high in text and content but low in context?

2. High and low context communication styles

Hall's (1976) high/low context distinction divides cultures according to their basic differences in cultural perspectives and communication style. High context cultures are typified as having indirect, ambiguous, understated, and reserved styles of communication that cater to and are sensitive to listeners. In contrast low context communication styles are described as being direct, explicit and precise paralleling the interlocutor's true feelings.

These patterns of communication are compatible with Hofstede's (1980, 1991) cultural dimension of individualism and collectivism respectively and were conveyed as an extension to Hall's cultural HC/LC framework. Kim (1994) writes that members of collective cultures are concerned with not hurting others or imposing on them, while their individualistic counterparts are more direct in their interactions. In Japanese culture collectivism involves a focus on the concepts of 和 *wa* (harmony) 甘え *amae* (dependency or interdependence) and 遠慮 *enryo* (reserve or restraint) and an emphasis on strong personal relationships (Gudykunst & Nishida 1994).

Communication within high context cultures places an emphasis and expectation on the listener's ability to be able to read between the lines or to read the context to grasp the unstated meaning. Yamada (1997: 38) supports this notion by suggesting "For the Japanese, the responsibility of communication rests with the audience, making listener interpretation not only the key but the main mode of communication". She labels Japan as utilizing a listener based mode of communication or 'listener talk'.

In contrast she states (Yamada 1997: 38) that "For the American responsibility of communication rests with the speaker". This parallels low context communication descriptions that suggest direct and explicit forms are used to ensure the listener receives the message precisely as it was sent, hence placing the responsibility on the shoulders of the speaker rather than the listener as in high context cultures.

Table 1. A Summary of High/Low Context Communication Styles

High context communication style	Low context communication style
• Indirect, implicit • Expect interlocutor to know what the message is without being specific, that is to read the signs/context • Responsibility of deciphering the message lies with the listener • Indirect verbal communication is valued and the listener is more able to read non-verbal expressions • Less reliant on words to express meaning • Ambiguous in nature • Harmonious • Values group sense and identity	• Direct, explicit • Verbal message is direct and an explicit approach is utilized to ensure that the listener receives the message exactly as it was sent • Responsibility of sending a clear message lies with the speaker • Direct verbal communication is valued and the listener is less able to read non-verbal communication • Reliant on words to express meaning • Precise and accurate • Open and direct with feelings • Values individualism

3. Computer mediated communication (CMC)

Computer Mediated Communication (CMC) is a process of human communication through the medium of connected computers. Herring (2002) states that CMC varies according to the technology on which it is based and to the context it is used in. Synchronous CMC, such as chat rooms and instant messaging, is carried out in real time with a physically present interlocutor and differs from asynchronous text based communication that takes place through weblogs, internet forums and e-mails where communication is not conducted in real time. These distinctions influence message length, complexity, language use, formality and interactivity as a result of time and temporal constraints on the processing and writing of the message (Ko 1996). Herring (2002) also claims that user demographics, such as age or gender, can influence the CMC technology used and the communication style employed.

Both modes of communication can be transmitted from one user to many or more personally as one user to another as in e-mails or blog comments. Common to all forms of CMC when visual equipment, such as webcams, are not present is that non-verbal communication or the expression of emotion and feeling are greatly limited in comparison to physical face to face communication.

Table 2. Types of CMC

	Asynchronous	Synchronous
1 to 1	E-mail Weblog comments	IM (Instant messaging) Chat rooms
1 to many	Bulletin boards, listservs, weblogs articles	Chat rooms Internet Relay Chat (IRC)

4. Unconventional means of communication (UMC) online

When compared to conventional written discourse as seen in academic papers, novels and newspapers, the internet offers a new system of writing that utilizes innovative yet unconventional means of communication. Crystal (2006) calls it 'Netspeak', which is neither spoken, nor written language but a new creative medium constructed through the computer. The language of weblogs he describes as 'naked' as it is without the interference of proofreaders or editors who aim to standardize its text. Matsuda (2008) suggests that the unorthodox use of orthography and language produced in Japanese blog articles is an attempt to create a form of cuteness and to solicit an interest in the blog creator's writings. For the purposes of this paper I would like to group these unorthodox representations as discussed in the next paragraph under the umbrella term of unconventional means of communication or UMC.

Online UMC is reflected in the attempt to convey orally or visually spoken and non-verbal language that indexes the writer's emotional stance and is sent and remains in the written form. Baron (2009) suggests CMC users add these elements in their written discourse in an attempt to avoid misunderstanding, and to convey their true stance with the aim of intensifying their shared and common ground. Harris and Paradice (2007) suggest recipients of messages will interpret the senders' emotional intentions using paralinguistic cues contained and sent within the message. Paralinguistic cues refer to message characteristics in text based CMC used to convey meanings normally achieved via tone of voice, body gestures, and other non-verbal communicative behaviors in face to face communication. Paralinguistic cues used in text based CMC according to Harris and Paradice (2007) and Carey (1980) can consist of vocal spellings, spatial arrays, and the manipulation of grammatical markers. Carey (1980: 67) suggests vocal spellings contain features that include "non-standard spellings" of words which bring attention to sound qualities. The spelling may serve to mark a regional accent or an idiosyncratic manner of speech". Such examples can be found in vocal spellings, such as Type back sooon!!!!! (Danet 2001) and in Japanese 終わりましたかぁ *Owarimashita kaa* 'Was it really over' (Nishimura 2003). Harris and Paradice (2007) suggest lexical surrogates such as 'yuk yuk' or the logographical lol (laugh out loud) or vocal spellings, such as "weeeeeell", are intended to imitate vocal sounds or provide a tone to the communication. Japanese examples include the use of logographical representations of laughter, such as the Chinese character 笑 *warau* 'to laugh', at the end of messages.

Spatial arrays are techniques often employed by CMC users to draw pictures using the features available on the keyboard that are often visual representations of emotion. Examples of this are emoticons such as :-) smile and :-(frown. The upright (^_^) is the basic smiley of Japan. Online emoticons, a phenomenon going back over 25 years, were also explicitly created with the goal of clarifying the writers intended meaning within their messages.

The manipulation of grammatical markers, such as the use of capital letters and exclamation marks used in CMC, are intended to express emphasis on lexical items as well as being a representation of tone of voice. Within online communication we often see punctuation marks for emphasis (??? or !!!), the use of capital letters as in GREAT or AWESOME, bold or italicized parts of the text, the repetition of words for emphasis as in '*really really cool*', and the deliberate use of different fonts within single messages.

It must be noted, however, that the use of these UMC's can be influenced by the mode of communication that they occur in. Real time synchronous communication, such as chat rooms or instant messaging, sees messages written at a pace similar to holding a conversation (Shea 1994). The effect of the synchronous environment on UMC usage invariably produces a larger occurrence of these unconventional online depictions (Werry 1996). Pull down graphic emoticon or smiley menus in some instant messaging clients may even promote their usage (Provine et al. 2007).

Asynchronous modes, such as weblogs which form the basis of this study, allow users to take time completing their written messages, editing if required and allowing time to consider how their text will be interpreted by the reader or readers. Therefore, the use of these UMC's is not necessarily time sensitive and their function may play a different role in comparison to synchronous online mediums of communication.

5. High and low context communication in CMC

At present there are very few studies that have explored the high and low context distinction within CMC but those that have investigated the relationship between auditory and visual cues and cultural background have found that these cues have more importance for members of collectivistic, high context, relationship orientated cultures than they do for members of individualistic, low context, task orientated cultures. Kayan, Fussel and Setlock (2006) found through a series of questionnaires to Instant Messaging users that North Americans rated emoticons and the use of audio and video chat significantly lower in importance than did Indians and East Asians. They conclude that these results are consistent with low and high context communication styles with the latter reliant on visual and oral channels for the successful transmission of information.

Other studies have suggested that greater usage of images in collectivist cultures is used to provide a context, with individualistic low context communicators more reliant on text to provide information. Würtz (2005) found that in her examination of McDonalds' websites, graphical design features and the visual effects offered by the internet are more likely to be adopted and used by high context cultures to convey their messages more effectively than their low context counterparts. Similarly, Kim and Papacharissi (2003) found in homepages of Korean and American users that the latter used far more textual representation, with the former more reliant on graphical images when conveying information. Kavanagh (2010) found that the use of non-verbal contextual cues as represented by emoticons are culturally grounded with high context cultures, such as Japan, relying heavily on these graphical accents in their blog entries. They were seen to play a part in the promotion of smooth communication across cyberspace to unknown recipients. In comparison, low context cultures as exemplified by American users, were found to use these emoticons sparingly. Although these studies point to the importance of oral, visual and nonverbal cues in a variety of online UMC's within written texts, their function in a comparative setting of asynchronous communication within Asian and western cultures has largely been under-represented.

6. CMC & Japanese and English scripts

Japanese uses both logographic *kanji* and phonographic *kana*. The logographic script represents the stems of words as seen in nouns and verbs, complimented with the syllabic script for grammatical inflexions and particles. Fouser et al. (2000) write that the inclusion of kanji enhances the visual nature of the language and that a purely phonographic system would complicate or slow down reading as the language has relatively few sounds and subsequently a large number of homophones. Nishimura et al. (2008) argue that this can actually make the language highly contextual as about 35% of words belong to one of the groups of homonyms, and that Japanese conversation cannot be understood without knowing the context as a result of these homophones. The most common method of imputing Japanese on a computer is through the FEP (Front End Processor) that converts *kana* into *kanji* directly. In other words, PC users can enter words via *romaji* or the English letter keyboard and the computer converts them automatically to a Chinese character or *kanji* with an optional dropdown bar in which the user can choose the appropriate *kanji* from the characters that have the same pronunciation.

English is based on the phonographic Roman alphabet; and as Sampson (1987) suggests English writing might be described as fundamentally phonemic but with some elements of logography. He gives the example of the spelling difference of rain and reign which have nothing to do with pronunciation but relate purely to word identity. Fouser et al. (2000) state that in CMC the use of acronyms that have become logographical representations of a string of words is often seen in internet communication with examples such as IMHO (In my humble opinion) and OMG (Oh my God).

7. Data and methods

The data on which this study is based came specifically from online personal weblogs or the online diary which forms the basis of the traditional and popular blog form. They can be categorized as an asynchronous mode of CMC derived from usually one writer. Their thoughts, opinions and description of events from the trivial to the dramatic, are written in diary-like entries to a broad audience without a specific reader in mind.

Entries on these blogs are usually posted in reverse chronological order on a daily or weekly basis and invite comments from their readership after each article or entry.

The author of the blog can respond to and interact with those who leave comments on their entries. Blogs can gain an extensive following of 'fans' who comment on each other's blogs, which can lead to the formation of a blog community. It is these written blog comments that are effectively communication between two people that the current paper will focus on.

Utilizing definitions of Hall's cultural framework it is hypothesized that these UMC's are used more by Japanese than American blog comment writers and that the use of these UMC's is to

a. create a human social presence, both visual and oral;
b. function as a tool to create solidarity;
c. express emotion or feeling more explicitly through both the tone and emotional or semantic content of the message.

Given that High Context Cultures place strong emphasis on the personal relationship and an emphasis on social harmony investigation of (a) and (b) above aims to examine how these UMC's play a role in this process examining the pragmatic function they play and how they may be used to create a human presence in cyberspace. However, (c) challenges the assumptions that high context Japanese communication is ambiguous and vague and that the use of these UMC's can promote a clearer message and emotional tone that can clarify the stance of the message.

A total of 100 blogs (50 from American blogs, 50 from Japanese blogs) were taken from a variety of blog trackers (Yahoo blogs, Blog catalogue, Blogumura) that contained blog directories of personal blogs, otherwise termed as online diaries, ranked according to popularity through the number of hits or readers the blog receives. An equal balance of female and male authored blogs were selected, 50 per gender, 25 in English and Japanese respectively, giving an even representative balance of weblog data. However, unlike the blogs themselves, the comments on these blogs could not be divided into gender as the sex of the comment author could not always be determined. Age was another variable that could also not be ascertained.

From each blog the comments of the 5 most recent blog entries were taken, giving a total of 500 entries (250 entries per language). As the counting of

UMC's formed the basis of this research the number of sentences per comment corpus was counted and the frequency of UMC usage also tallied and put into their percentage form. Each UMC category as illustrated in table 3 was counted per sentence. If the sentence had more than one particular category of UMC, for example two emoticons or a whole sentence in capitalized words it was still calculated as one. This allows for accurate figures on how many sentences had particular UMC's attached to them. The exception was in the counting of exclamation marks where all instances of sentences with 2 or more exclamation marks were counted.

Sentences counted included sentences or utterances conventionally thought of as major sentences, with minor sentences such as greeting expressions, emotional and onomatopoeic utterances and one-word sentences or utterances such as the use of adjectives such as 'great' or すごい *sugoi* also counted. Things not defined as sentences included lists such as one word only nouns and stand alone UMC's such as a series of emoticons with no text.

The Japanese wrote slightly more comments totaling 14691 sentences in comparison to the comments taken from American blogs registering 10347 sentences. Table 3 below shows the specific online UMC's that were analyzed. As the study aims to compare two very different language families which are written in different scripts efforts were made to compare like with like.

Table 3. UMC's Examined within the Japanese and English Data

	Emoticons (Text-based and graphical)	Representations of laughter	Unconventional phonetic spelling	Multiple exclamation mark use (!! or more)
Japanese	(^_^) (^o^;>) (^ ^;) (*^o^*) ☺	Logograhical 笑 *warau*, to laugh. The phonetical あはは ahaha and huhuhu ふふふ.	行きまーす *Ikima-su* (Will go). ありがとぅ *Arigatou* (Thank you).	彼女ができた！！！ *Kanojo ga dekita!!!* I got a girlfriend!!!
English	:-) :-(:-)) ☺	Logographical Lol (Laugh out loud). The phonetical Haha and hehe.	Greeeeeat! Sooooo Cooooool! Awwwesome!	That movie is cool !!!

The representations of laughter include one logographical representation from each language and two phonological ones. Emoticons are examples of semasiographs and Sampson (1987) writes that these semasiographic systems are independent graphic languages and therefore have no connection to any one spoken language. Exclamation marks or the multiple usages of them are not usually used in written Japanese although in informal writing they are not unusual.

The representations of laughter that were examined in both sets of data included extended versions of the phonetical spellings. Within the English data lengthened versions of haha and hehe as in hahahaha or hehehehe were counted. Similarly, extended versions of あはは (ahaha) or ふふふ (huhuhu) as well as their *katakana* versions as in アハハ (ahaha) were also tallied for the Japanese data.

Unconventional phonetic spellings in both the English and Japanese data included the unorthodox lengthening of vowel and consonant sounds as illustrated in the table below. The inclusion of the smaller hiragana vowel font in Japanese as in 終わりましたかぁ *owarimashitaa* (I finished) is an example of this. The wavy dash that signifies a long drawn out vowel as in そうですよね〜 *sou desu yo ne* (that's right) were also techniques employed to mimic vocal spellings.

8. Results

In every comparable category except multiple exclamation marks the Japanese data showed higher UMC frequency counts with all emoticon and unconventional spelling frequency totaling 21.7% and 16.4% respectively compared to the English data of 5.6% and 3.4%.

Table 4. Comment Data Results

	Japanese blog comments	English blog comments
Sentences	14691	10347
Text based emoticons	2937 (19.9%)	543 (5.2%)
Graphic emoticons	273 (1.8%)	42 (0.4%)
Unconventional spelling	2415 (16.4%)	361 (3.4%)
Multiple exclamation marks (2 or over)	746 (5%)	682 (6.5%)
Representations of laughter	562 (3.8%)	142 (1.3%)

Note. The figures in brackets denote the percentage of UMC per the number of sentences. Blog comments are treated as mixed in gender.

It must be noted, however, that the use of graphic emoticons is more common in synchronous chat rooms (Provine et al. 2007) and that these emoticons can be downloaded from online dictionaries or from drop down menus. These graphical emoticons were rarely used in both sets of data compared to the keyboard based text emoticons.

In total 47% of Japanese comment sentences had a UMC attached to them compared to 17% of English sentences. Japanese blog comment writers rely on these UMC's within their written communications more so than the American equivalent.

9. Un-comparable data categories

The use of acronyms in logographic representations, such as OMG (Oh my God), which are not found in Japanese totaled 104 (1%) excluding LOL frequencies which were tallied in the representations of laughter category. They were used to add emphasis or tone to their messages but were rarely used as the result suggests. Capitalized Roman alphabetical words are not common to Japanese writing; however, within the English data 792 or 7.6% of sentences used capitalization to express emphasis or vocalization on particular words. Notably those particular words consisted of mostly positive feelings towards their interlocutor such as LOVE your blog! GREAT idea! ABSOLUTELY AGREE with you! and adverbs of frequency such I ALWAYS do that too!

Within the Japanese data there were also un-comparable representations of UMC's. The ♪ symbol can represent the sound of bells often heard at the end of a comical stage performance (Nishimura 2003). The use of these ♪ symbols were often found at the end of sentences and often created a jovial sing-song intonation that is intended to create the mood and emotional tone of the communication. 1379 (9.3%) of sentences had ♪ attached to them as in the following example:

きっとルフィーくんにも、カワイイ彼女ができるよ〜♪
Kitto Rufee kun ni mo, kawaii kanojo ga dekiru yo ~♪
"Surely you too (Rufee) will get a cute girlfriend."

The use of 'w' at the end of sentences is a recent phenomenon whereby the conventional Chinese character (笑) spelt *warau* meaning to laugh is replaced by the 'w' of *warau* as in 面白いww, *omoshiroi ww* (funny ww). Multiple w usage signals a bigger reaction of laughter and 305 (2%) of sentences had one w or more attached to them. As the use of （笑） can be time consuming to input, this easier one key push representation of laughter seems to be gaining popularity as a more convenient and easier method to express laughter.

Results from the data sample here show that the use of these UMC's are implemented in greater numbers by Japanese blog users. The focus will now turn to examine the pragmatic function that these UMC's play and how they are used to create a social human presence, and function as a tool to create solidarity.

10. UMC's as pragmatic markers

10.1 Emoticons

Emoticons were constructed over 25 years ago; and they act as being representations of affective states conveying non-linguistic information that is found in non-verbal face to face interaction as seen in facial expressions or body language. While this is true of some uses of emoticons or the Japanese equivalent called *kaomoji* (facemarks), the use of these emoticons can be best understood as representing pragmatic meaning in addition to expressing emotion. The use of both positive and negative politeness strategies as described by Brown and Levinson (1987) was evident within the data here. This Japanese example below illustrates a *kaomoji* that reflects bowing with the visual representation of the hands by the face as if bowing on the floor. It is used as a negative politeness strategy indicating the minimizing of imposition of the request.

> ジャガイモの簡単レシピイタリア風…なにかありましたら
> *Jyagaimo no kantan reshipi itaria fu nanika arimashitara*
> おしえてくださいm(_ _)m
> *oshiete kudasai* m(_ _)m
> "If you know anything about simple Italian style potato recipes, please let me know m(_ _)m."

The *kaomoji* use here indicates a method to soften the illocutionary force of the written message and does not necessarily contribute to the propositional content of the language used nor indicate emotion, but acts as an aid in the meaning of the linguistic utterance and how the writer wishes to convey it.

Cases of requests which ended in ください *kudasai* (Please give me) within these comments were often accompanied with an emoticon to soften the utterance as was the use of the hedge *kamo* (might) or the sentence final particle ね *ne*. The former acts to indirectly give an opinion and soften the assertive force of the utterance which is further clarified with the use of an emoticon as in the following example.

> HACHIやっぱり泣けるんだぁ〜
> *HACHI yappari nakerun daa~*
> 私は南極物語の予告編で号泣したのでHACHIはやばいかも ^_^;
> *Watashi wa nankyoku monogatari no yokokuhen de goukyuu shita no de HACHI wa yabai kamo ^_^;*
> "As I thought I will cry at Hachi (I wailed at the South pole story (film) trailer so HACHI might be a bit risky ^_^;."

Hachi in the above example is a movie title. The use of ; on the side of the face of the ^_^; kaomoji represents sweat and is used when the writer feels what they are saying is perhaps too assertive (Sugimoto & Levin 2000).

The particle *ne* can also function as a tool to seek agreement, sometimes rhetorically as this example illustrates.

> さっぱり夏向きレシピですね^^
> *Sappari natsu muki reshipi desu ne*
> "A good recipe for summer, hey."

In contrast positive politeness strategies that notice or attend to the reader's need for support or approval were used as in the example below. The following Japanese comment was found attached to a blog article that focused on an 'original' crab brandy pasta recipe of the author's.

> おはようございます♪
> *Ohayou gozaimasu*
> カニとブランデーって聞いただけで・・・。ステキですよね〜＾＾。
> *Kani to burandi tte kiita dakede…suteki desuyone ~ ＾＾。*
> 香りもいいんでしょうね〜っ。(●´艸｀)
> *Kaori mo ii desyo ne*

ステキなブランチに(◎●‿●　□)ノ))凸ぽちッ♪
Suteki na buranchi ni pochi ♪
"Good morning."
"From just hearing crab and brandy it's wonderful."
"Bet it smells good too, hey."
"To a wonderful brunch pochi."

The comment expresses approval of the recipe punctuated with *kaomoji* that act as visual affirmation or endorsement of the recipe. This in turn can build a rapport with the blog author which is further supported by the comment closing which ends in *pochi* which is an onomatopoeic representation of the sound of a key being pushed on the keyboard. The use of the Chinese character 凸 (as in 凸凹 *dekoboko* meaning unevenness) is used creatively as a representation of the forefinger pressing the key. The pressing of this 傑作 *kessaku* or 'masterpiece' button within the blog interface helps raise the blog in popularity within the blog rankings (Kavanagh 2010). Interestingly, within the closing of English comments occasional examples found were often similar to those found in intimate letters such as 'Enjoy and big hugs to Ronaldo XXXX' or the innovative use of keyboard strokes to represent arms as in hugging: {{{{{{{{HUGS}}}}}}}}.

Positive politeness strategies were also evident within the English data with the example below showing the comment writer's admiration and interest in the blog author's entry commenting on the articles photos of the writer's child Charlie. It is a playful and lighthearted comment as reflected in its opening line and its concluding emoticon.

> Ca-UUUTE!
> Can Charlie be anymore adorable?
> Love those pics, and that outfit is so stinkin' cute! :)

In addition to the role these emoticons play, where and when they are deployed may influence their usage. Kavanagh (2010) found that the use of emoticons in Japanese and English weblogs may be related to the nature or the topic of the blog, gender may also play a part with females using emoticons more so than male CMC users (Kavanagh 2010; Wolf 2000). Their usage could even be related to the concept of T.P.O. (Time, place and objective) as the implementation of these emoticons are used in fun, playful and positive high tempo interactions rather than in formal or task focused CMC (Derks et al. 2007). These personal online weblog diaries are informal relationship orientated forms of writing whereby the blog users exchange everyday opinions about everyday topics.

10.2　Unconventional spelling

Unconventional spelling definitions within the Japanese and English data were analyzed as those with deliberate vowel or consonant lengthening to duplicate the sounds of vocal speech. Within the Japanese corpus 2415 or 16.4% of comment sentences were found to have unconventional spellings. This was in comparison to 361 or 3.4% of English comment sentences. This it would seem, parallels high context culture's need or reliance on auditory aids in the conveying of their message as if to share the same physical space with their reader. The examples below illustrate the use of these spellings that mimic the emotional responses from the blog comment writers in an attempt to give a voice to the text they type.

1) English examples:
   Doesn't it feel FAAAABULOUS to weed out stuff?
   You're right… it DOES make you feel lighter!!!
   "Thank you sooooooooooo much for sharing this post!"

2) Japanese examples:
   来週からは義理ママ、パパさんはホテル住まいですか？
   Raisyu kara wa giri mama, papa san wa hoteru zumai desu ka?
   少しはRoseさんもラクになるかなぁ〜？
   Sukoshi wa Rose san mo raku ni naru kanaa〜?
   Your mother-and father-in-law will stay in a hotel from next week? Perhaps that will be a bit easier for you?

   よく耐えたっ！！！！
   Yoku taeta!!!!
   You put up with it well!!!!" (A comment regarding boss harassment)

The small *tsu* っ in this last example indicates a final glottal stop, and is an example of the dialogue found in *manga* comics (Akizuki 2009).

10.3 Multiple exclamation use

Within the blog comments 5% of Japanese sentences and 6.5% of English sentences had multiple exclamation marks (defined as two or more) attached to them. As the comments are dialogues between 2 people this could perhaps suggest an increased level of excitability or interest in their dialogues within the blog community that they are writing in. English multiple !!! were usually preceded by CAPITALIZED words for emphasis as in the following examples.

I TOTALLY agree with you, buddy!!!!

ABOSOLUTELY AWESOME!!!! LOVE your blog!!!!!

The Japanese data showed similar results albeit on a slightly smaller scale. This is perhaps not surprising as the exclamation mark is not a commonly used grammatical marker. The use of Japanese multiple exclamation marks was usually preceded with unconventional vocal spelling as in the following examples.

めっちゃ食べたーーい！！！！！
meccha tabeta—i!!!!!
"I really wanna eat it !!!!!"
(A comment in response to a blog entry picture of a meal)

Bihandaさん すご〜〜〜い！！！
Bihanda san sugo〜〜〜i!!!
"You are great Bihanda !!!"

10.4 Laughter representations

When comparing the two sets of data the implementation of these representations of laughter are used in greater percentage (3.8% compared to the English 1.3%) by Japanese blog commentators. In addition to the Chinese character representations of logographical laughter (笑) and the phonological あはは and ふふふ Japanese blog users also employed emoticons to express written out laughter in a variety of ways and levels of laughter. In both sets of data these representations of laughter aimed to create a sense of solidarity and rapport within the blog user's social online interaction.

1) Japanese examples:
   やってくれるわ〜！！(≧▽≦)
   yatte kureru wa 〜！！(≧▽≦)
   "(He) did it!!"
   (^▽^)ｱﾊﾊﾊﾊ!笑わせていただきました〜！！
   (^▽^)*ahahahaha! Warawasete itadakimashita* 〜!!
   "That made me laugh."

2) English examples:
   hahahahahahahahaha! I just want you to know that I HOWLED when I read that!
   "all books buy one get one 50% off"? I've had my eye on a few things under ten bucks LOL.

11. Expressing yourself and the human social presence

Interaction between the comment author and blog writer is essentially communication between two people who have never met face to face and who, as with the majority of Japanese blog writers, assume anonymous handle names rather than revealing their own identity. Short et al.'s (1976) social presence theory, if applied to CMC, can clearly show that the level of social presence is lower in CMC than in face to face interaction. Nishimura (2003) writes that the inclusion of vocalized unconventional spelling gives the reader a more vivid picture of how this expression/phrase might be pronounced in face to face communication and the readers of these interactions or monologues can interpret the atmosphere of the dialogue in the nature it was intended to be sent in. She implies that the writer's intention is to convey the speakers' articulation as accurately as possible, and through this the writer or sender of the message can convey a high degree of affect and closeness, as if sharing the same physical space and time of conversation with the viewer. Katsuno and Yano (2007) suggest that *kaomoji* enacts a kind of intimacy that relies in part on their visual play.

These assertions can be linked to the high context framework of trying to establish a context of meaning to be read within this low context medium. Similarly these UMC's can play a similar role in English. Crystal (2006: 44) writes: "Addressing someone on the internet is a bit like having a telephone conversation in which the listener is giving you no reactions at all." Wallace

(2001) therefore recommends the use of these UMC's to improve rapport which can lead to warm and informal dialogue. Similarly, Walther (1996) suggests through his hyper-personal model that CMC message senders can depict themselves in a favorable light socially or otherwise in order to capture the attention of the person to whom the message is being relayed. This he argues can lead to friendly conversation that may surpass face to face conversation in terms of sociality. Message receivers may consequently enhance the image of the sender by overvaluing these text-based cues. In addition, the asynchronous nature of CMC gives the sender and the receiver enough time to edit their communication, making interactions in CMC more controllable and thoughtful in character.

From the results here, UMC's are employed in greater frequency by Japanese blog users to develop and promote this 'warm dialogue' in what are perhaps attempts to reach out to their reader, to add a visual and oral dimension to their communications as if duplicating a human presence in cyberspace. Derks et al. (2007) state that reduced visibility may have consequences for the decoding of sent text in CMC and that this generally results in a reduced social presence. They state, however, that this reduced visibility can strengthen the emotional style and content within CMC, and can consequently make it easier to express emotion. If emotion is conveyed explicitly in text-based messages the difficulty of interpreting the sent text may be reduced but they continue by suggesting that mere words alone may not be able to carry all the emotional information that someone wants to convey.

Crystal (2006: 41) agrees when he suggests that "written language has always been ambiguous, in its omission of facial expression, and in its inability to express all the intonational and other prosodic features of speech".

With reference to Hall's (1976) cultural framework the prominent use of words or lines of text as opposed to frequent UMC usage parallels Hall's low context descriptions of a communication style that is reliant merely on just words to express meaning. A faceless and impersonal CMC environment that lacks vocal or visual depictions can lead to misunderstandings and misinterpretation of written messages. The 'cues filtered out theory' states that people can become depersonalized within the online environment because the attention focuses on the written text, not the social context (Sproull & Kiesler 1986). It can therefore become the responsibility of the reader to decode and interpret the true intention of the message as opposed to low context communication descriptions which place that burden upon the speaker or writer to send a clear message. This concept can perhaps challenge Hall's low context communication framework in relation to this asynchronous written online communication.

Within the Japanese comments data, blog comment writers utilize these UMC's that reflect an explicit display of feeling, attitude and warmth. The same can be applied to the English data but in much less frequency. The majority of these UMC's were used in the promotion of positive feelings and solidarity. Pragmatically they aid in the complementing, strengthening and the clarifying of the illocutionary force of the utterance, and can be used as a vehicle for politeness strategies and to contribute to the playful nature of the interaction.

The explicit nature of the display of feeling and tone through these features is in contrast to Hall's descriptions of High Context Communication styles such as Japan as using a more ambiguous and vague language. Within the Japanese comments the writers' do not burden the reader to decipher the message but instead use these UMC's in an explicit way to convey the role and meaning of the utterance and how it should be interpreted. This explicit form of expressing themselves can act in the promotion of a harmonious online community.

The use of these UMC's may also be community linked, with those outside of the community perhaps unable to understand these UMC representations which would suggest differing online communities and online CMC mediums may promote differing uses and variations of UMC's. The Japanese internet forum *2 channel* would be an example of this. Nishimura (2008) states that community specific language or unconventional orthographic representations of lexical items are present in *2 channel* as in *otsu*, a shortened form of *otsukaresama* (thank you) written here in kanji with the same pronunciation of *otsu* but with a differing meaning: ありがたや 乙 *ari gata ya otsu*.

12. Conclusion

Results within this sample here have shown a larger reliance on UMC's by Japanese blog comment writers than their American equivalents. English blog comments can perhaps be described as being more formal and conventional in tone than their Japanese counterparts relying more on the written word to express meaning and emotion. The inclusion of these UMC's was found to be used in the same pragmatic sense of creating solidarity and harmony between the comment writers in addition to representing emotion, tone and attitude among the comment contributors. This was far more pronounced in the Japanese data which reflects high context cultural and linguistic descriptions of a communication style that is harmonious in nature. In addition these UMC's are used in an effort to bridge the gap between users and to create a human presence online as if talking to their reader face to face.

This paper has also attempted to examine how Hall's (1976) cultural frameworks are applicable to communication online. The communication style as employed by these Japanese comment contributors, with a high frequency use of UMC's, cannot be considered vague or implicit as typified in high context communication style descriptions. The expression of feeling and emotion, both positive and negative is more pronounced in the Japanese data allowing the reader to properly gauge the feelings and intention of their interlocutor.

It can be suggested that Japanese blog comment writers may feel it is their own responsibility as the writer to index their messages with the appropriate tones rather than giving such responsibility to the listener/reader to decipher their messages. However, a study into the motives and usages of these UMC's would need to be executed in order to validate this theory. Possible further questions also include how age and gender influence UMC usage across cultures. If the data targeted and specifically examined teenage blogs we could possibly see a higher frequency use and a larger variety of UMC depictions. It was not within the scope of this paper to examine such influential factors but these could be included in further research to give us a better understanding of how UMC usage is deployed cross culturally.

References

Akizuki, K. 2009. *Nihongo vijiuaru kei: Atarashi nihongo no kakikata* (*Visual extractions of Japanese: How to write new/neo Japanese*). Tokyo: Kadokawa.

Baron, N. S. 2009. The myth of impoverished signal: Dispelling the spoken language fallacy for emoticons in online communication. In J. Vincent & L. Fortunati (eds), Electronic Emotion: The mediation of emotion via Information and communication technology, 107–136. London: Peter Lang.

Brown, P. & S, C, Levinson. 1987. *Politeness: Some universals in language usage.* Cambridge: Cambridge University Press.

Carey, J. 1980. Paralanguage in computer mediated communication. In Norman K. Dondheimer (ed.), *Eighteenth annual meeting of the association for computational linguistics and parasession on topics in interactive discourse* 67–69.

Crystal, D. 2006. *Language and the internet,* 2nd edn. Cambridge: Cambridge University Press.
Danet, B. 2001. *Cyberpl@y: Communicating online.* Oxford & New York: Berg.
Derks, D., A. E. R. Bos & J. von Grumbkow. 2007. Emotions and social interaction on the internet: The importance of social context. *Computers in Human Behavior* 23(1). 842–849.
Fouser, R. J, N. Inoue & C. Lee. 2000. The pragmatics of orality in English, Japanese and Korean computer mediated communication In P. Pemberton & S. Shurville (eds), *Words on the web,* 52–62. Exeter, UK: Intellect Books.
Gudykunst, W. B. & T. Nishida, 1994. *Bridging Japanese/North American differences.* Thousand Oaks, CA: Sage.
Hall, E. 1976. *Beyond culture.* New York: Doubleday.
Hall, E. & M. Hall. 1990. *Understanding cultural differences: Germans, French and Americans.* Yarmouth, Maine: Intercultural Press.
Harris, R. B. & D. Paradice. 2007. An investigation of the computer-mediated communication of emotions. *Journal of Applied Sciences Research,* 3(12). 2081–2090.
Herring, S. C. 2002. Computer-mediated communication on the Internet. *Annual Review of Information Science and Technology* 36(1). 109–168.
Hofstede, G. 1980. *Culture's consequences: International differences in work-related values.* Beverly Hills, CA: Sage.
Hofstede, G. 1991. *Cultures and organizations*: Software of the mind. Berkshire, England: McGraw-Hill.
Katsuno, H. & C. R. Yano. 2007. *Kaomoji* and expressivity in a Japanese housewives' chatroom. In B. Danet & S. C. Herring (eds), *The multilingual internet: Language, culture, and communication online,* 278–300. New York: Oxford University Press.
Kavanagh, B. 2010. A Cross-cultural analysis of Japanese and English non-verbal online communication: The use of emoticons in weblogs. In *Journal of Intercultural Communication Studies* 19(3). 65–80.
Kayan, S., S. R. Fussell. & L. D. Setlock. 2006. Cultural differences in the use of instant messaging in Asia and North America. *Computer supported cooperative work (CSCW),* 525–528. NY: ACM Press.
Kim, M.S. 1994. Cross-cultural comparisons of the perceived importance of conversational constraints. *Human Communication Research* 21(1), 128–151.
Kim, H. & Z. Papacharissi. 2003. Cross-cultural differences in on-line self-presentation: A content analysis of personal Korean and US homepages. *Asian Journal of Communication* 13(1). 100–119.
Ko, K. K. 1996. Structural characteristics of computer-mediated language: A comparative analysis of InterChange discourse. *Electronic Journal of Communication* 6(3). http://www.cios.org/EJCPUBLIC/006/3/006315.HTML Accessed February 2011.
Matsuda, M. 2008. Keitai, web no hyogen sutairu. (Styles of expressions in mobile phone/web messages) *Gekkan gengo* (*Monthly language*) 37(1). 40–45.
Nishimura, S., A. Nevgi. & S. Tella. 2008. Communication style and cultural features in high/low context communication cultures: A case study of Finland, Japan and India. http://www.helsinki.fi/~tella/nishimuranevgitella299.pdf. Accessed February 2011.
Nishimura, Y. 2003. Linguistic innovations and interactional features of casual online com-

munication in Japanese. *Journal of Computer-Mediated Communication* 9 (1) http://jcmc.indiana.edu/vol9/issue1/nishimura.html. Accessed August 2011.

Nishimura, Y. 2008. Japanese BBS Websites as Online Communities:(Im)politeness Perspectives in *Language@internet*. Vol. 5. In J. Androutsopoulos & M. Beiswenger (eds), *Data and methods in computer-mediated discourse analysis: New approaches. Special Issue of Language@Internet.*

Provine, R. R., R.J. Spencer & D. L. Mandell. 2007. Emotional expression online: Emoticons punctuate website text messages. *Journal of Language and Social Psychology* 26(3). 299–307.

Sampson, G. R. 1987. *Writing systems* (revised edn). London: Hutchinson.

Shea, V. 1994. *Net etiquette*. San Francisco, USA: Albion Books.

Short, J. A., E. Williams & B. Christie. 1976. *The social psychology of telecommunication*. London: John Wiley & Sons.

Sproull, L. & S. Kiesler. 1986. Reducing social context cues: The case of electronic mail in organizational communication. *Management Science* 32 (11). 1492–1512.

Sugimoto, T. & J. A. Levin. 2000. Multiple literacies and multimedia: A comparison of Japanese and American uses of the internet. In G. E. Hawisher & C. L. Selfe (eds), *Global literacies and the world-wide web*, 133–153. London: Routledge.

Wallace, P. 2001. *The psychology of the internet*. Cambridge: Cambridge University Press.

Walther. J. 1996. Computer-mediated communication: Impersonal, interpersonal, and hyperpersonal interaction. *Communication Research* 23(1). 3–43.

Wolf, A. 2000. Emotional expression online: Gender differences in emoticon use. *CyberPsychology and Behaviour* 3(5). 827–833.

Werry, C. C. 1996. Linguistic and interactional features of internet relay chat. In S. C. Herring (ed.), *Computer mediated communication: Linguistic, social, and cross-cultural perspectives*, 47–63. Amsterdam: John Benjamins.

Würtz, E. 2005. A cross-cultural analysis of websites from high-context cultures and low-context cultures. *Journal of Computer-Mediated Communication*, 11(1). http://jcmc.indiana.edu/vol11/issue1/wuertz.html. Accessed February 2011.

Yamada, H. 1997. *Different games, different rules: Why Americans and Japanese misunderstand each other*. New York & Oxford: Oxford University Press.

Chapter 11

"Green stink" and "fragrant taste": Synaesthetic expressions in Thai

Naruadol Chancharu

1. Introduction

The term 'synaesthesia' is generally used to refer to a condition "in which the stimulation of one sensory modality is accompanied by one or more other modalities" (Howes 2005: 162).[1] Ramachandran and Hubbard (2001) characterise synaesthesia as involuntary, idiosyncratic, cross-modal associations that are individually stable and unidirectional. 'Synaesthetes,' as sufferers of synaesthesia are often called, are reported to hear colours, see sounds, feel tastes, etc. Although there has long been an interest in synaesthesia as a topic of psychological and neuroscientific research (cf. Baron-Cohen & Harrison 1997; Cytowic 1989; Marks 1978), it was not until recently that this neuropsychological phenomenon attracted the attention of the general public. More often than not, the phenomenon is deemed by non-synaesthetes as a rare, bizarre medical condition that has no or little relevance to them. Psychologists and neuroscientists, however, study synaesthesia not only for its inherent interest, but also for the insights it may give into the cognitive and perceptual processes that occur in both synaesthetes and non- synaesthetes.

Also, 'synaesthesia' is used in language studies, but with some differences in meaning. In this instance, the term refers to a linguistic phenomenon in which a linguistic expression encodes the perception of one sense modality through another, but without necessarily entailing a neuropsychological condition. For example, the expression *Mary has a sweet voice* is synaesthetic in that the adjective *sweet*, which is originally used to denote a quality of TASTE, is used here to denote a quality of SOUND. In other words, there is a 'synaesthetic transfer' from the gustatory sense to the auditory sense. There are two major traditions of language studies on synaesthesia. The first tradition deals primarily with how synaesthetic expressions are used as a figurative device in literature,[2] and the second with how those expressions used in everyday language reveal cognitive mechanisms within the conceptualisation of human experience. The two traditions are by no means mutually exclusive; however, their goals are generally distinct. While the work on literary synaesthesia seeks to learn how authors consciously employ synaesthetic expressions, often extensively and elaborately, to produce figurative effects, the work on everyday synaesthetic expressions concerns itself with synaesthetic expressions that have a relatively high frequency of occurrence in ordinary language and are unconsciously employed by the user.[3]

Transfers between sense modalities are often associated with metaphor, which can be simply explained as the understanding of one entity in terms of another. The study of metaphor has a very long tradition, dating back to as early as Aristotle's *Poetics* (circa 335 BC). Traditionally, metaphor is deemed as a figurative device used in poetic language to produce a rhetorical effect, generally by depicting or clarifying an image. An example is Shakespeare's metaphor *All the world's a stage* (*As You Like It* 2/7), in which particular properties of the stage can enhance the understanding of the world, e.g. players who have different parts to perform on the stage are compared to people who have different fates to meet and experience in the real world. As such, metaphor is considered as a matter of language alone, specifically poetic language. However, Lakoff and Johnson (1980) convincingly propose that metaphor is conceptual and mundane in nature. That is to say, metaphor is a cognitive mechanism that allows humans to make sense of the world of abstraction by using their experience of more concrete entities to help define the abstraction. Conceptual metaphor is prevalent in everyday life, so prevalent in fact that metaphorical expressions used in every language often go unnoticed, as in the example *Mary has a sweet voice* mentioned above.

2. Previous studies on linguistic synaesthesia

One of the most interesting topics about synaesthesia in language is its directionality of transfer. As Yu (2003: 21) noted, although "there should be twenty theoretically possible kinds of cross-modal transfers, with four targets from each of the five sources," not all of those kinds of transfers have been attested in literary and everyday language. It can, therefore, be hypothesised that there are certain constraints that govern the directional possibilities of synaesthetic transfer. One of the first studies that investigated these constraints was Ullmann (1959). Utilising the literary work of English, French, and Hungarian poets, he discovered three overall tendencies (Ullmann 1959: 276–284). First, synaesthetic transfers are hierarchically distributed, i.e. they tend to go from the lower to the higher sensory modes, that is, TOUCH > TASTE > SMELL > SOUND > SIGHT. The second and third tendencies involve the predominant source and target of synaesthetic transfer, which according to Ullmann's investigation, are TOUCH and SOUND, respectively. These regularities, he concludes, can be observed in different writers of different languages, and thus might be reflective of "the main forces presiding over the general movement of these transfers" (Ullmann 1959: 284). It should be noted that Ullmann's notion of "main forces" is suggestive of cognitive universals underlying the semantic structures of human language in modern-day terms.

Another important work on linguistic synaesthesia is Williams's (1976), which shifted the focus to non-literary language. Particularly, he investigated synaesthetic adjectives in daily English and attempted to reconstruct the routes of diachronic semantic change that were involved. Incorporating Ullmann's distribution tendency of synaesthetic transfer, a summary of Williams's findings is seen in Figure 1 below.

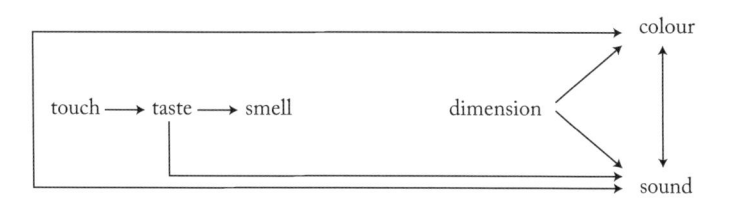

Figure 1. Williams's (1976) routes for synaesthetic transfer.

It should be noted that Williams made a distinction between DIMENSION and COLOUR, previously subsumed under SIGHT by Ullmann. In line with Ullmann's findings, synaesthetic transfers tend to move upward, with TOUCH as the predominant source, transferring to TASTE, SOUND, and COLOUR, and also SOUND as the predominant target transferred from TOUCH, TASTE, DIMENSION, and COLOUR. Besides the major generalisations proposed above, Williams made an interesting point concerning the problem of multiple-order transfers (Williams 1976: 465–467). For example, it is difficult to determine if the SOUND meaning of *sharp* directly relates to that of TOUCH or TASTE, or it might be "in some way a result of their dual influence, and therefore not uniquely attributable to one or the other" (Williams 1976: 465). However, post-first-order transfers, it is postulated, do "obey the same general constraints as first-order transfers" (Williams 1976: 465), unless the evidence suggests otherwise. As in the case of *sharp*, the pathway TOUCH → TASTE → SOUND is then postulated.

Williams's model is confirmed by Yu (2003), who studied synaesthetic expressions in Chinese novels. He found 11 kinds of cross-modal mapping, 8 of which are upward transfers that occur in high frequency and conform to the routes proposed by Williams. The other three kinds, however, are downward transfers representing isolated occurrences. Yu thereby argues that there is a general similarity between literary and everyday language in terms of the constraints that govern synaesthetic transfer. Nevertheless, poetic synaesthesia is special in that it is often more extended, elaborated, and combined than is its non-poetic counterpart. That is to say, many of the synaesthetic expressions in Chinese novels studied by Yu extend to long sentences or paragraphs, cooperate with other figurative devices like oxymoron in creating aesthetic effect, and/or are composed of more than one source domain. Examples of composite synaesthesia are COLOUR + TOUCH → SOUND, DIMENSION + TOUCH → COLOUR, and DIMENSION + TOUCH + COLOUR → SOUND (Yu 2003: 29). Lastly, Yu argues for the major role of conceptual metaphor for motivating synaesthetic transfer, both in upward and downward pathways.

3. Research questions, objectives and methodology

Three important issues can be raised regarding the study of linguistic synaesthesia. The first is the adequacy of data for analysis. The data that have been used as evidence of synaesthetic expressions come from a small number of languages, which are still far from being representative of the world's languages. Indeed, many authors' studying linguistic synaesthesia are aware of this inadequacy and even suggest the necessity of studying more languages to confirm or disprove their findings (Yu 2003: 23). The second issue concerns the motivation that underlies synaesthetic transfer. As noted above, synaesthesia is often attributed to conceptual metaphor, that is, the conceptualisation of a more abstract (less embodied) mental domain in terms of a more concrete (more embodied) mental domain on the basis of "a fixed set of ontological correspondences between [the] entities in the source domain and [the] entities in the target domain" (Lakoff 1993: 309). While most cases of synaesthetic transfer are metaphorically motivated, others, particularly those of downward transfer, cannot be accounted for by relying only on metaphor. The last issue is concerned with how the universals and specifics of linguistic synaesthesia can be explained in terms of embodied cognition and cultural models.

In view of the three problematic issues raised here, this study has the following objectives. First, it aims to investigate the possible transfer pathways for linguistic synaesthesia in Thai, determine the predominant source and target domains, and identify the overall distributional hierarchy of transfer. Secondly, the findings from the Thai data are compared with those from previous studies. Third, potential universals and language specifics that arise from such a comparison are accounted for in reference to cognitive and cultural factors. To fulfil these objectives, the following methodological procedures were conducted for this study. Two groups of five native-speaking Thai students from the University of Cambridge, United Kingdom, participated in a single half-hour brainstorming session. They were given information on the definition and examples of synaesthetic expressions and asked in turn to provide more examples of synaesthetic expressions in Thai in two constructions: N+Adj (attributive construction) and V+Adj (predicative construction). The data collected from these two sessions were tested against the 13-million-word Thai National Corpus and the web-based search engine Google (http://www.google.com/) for actual occurrences and more contexts.

4. Analysis of synaesthetic expressions in Thai

The collected data were two constructions of synaesthetic expressions: attributive and predicative. The attributive construction consisted of a head noun denoting the target domain and a modifying adjective denoting the source domain, as in Example (1).

(1) kŭajtĭaw núaj **rót** **cèp** phétcháʔbùʔrī:
noodle beef taste hurtful Petchaburi
"The beef noodle with an astringent taste (literally hurtful taste) at Petchaburi."
(http://www.bloggang.com/mainblog.php?id=chim&month=01-02-2011&group=43& gblog=10)[4]

In Example (1), the adjective "hurtful" modifies the noun "taste," and hence is a transfer from the tactile modality to the gustatory modality (TOUCH → TASTE), linguistically realised as an attributive construction. The predicative construction, on the other hand, consists of a linking verb denoting the target domain and a complement adjective denoting the source domain, as in Example (2).

(2) lípsàʔtìk dū: wǎ:n nâ: límfot
lipstick look sweet worth taste
"The lipstick looked sweet and was worth tasting." (PRNC083)

In Example (2), the adjective "sweet" complements the verb "look," and hence is a transfer from the gustatory modality to the visual modality (TASTE → SIGHT), linguistically realised as a predicative construction. One problematic issue that can be raised concerns the conventionality of synaesthetic expressions. That is to say, some synaesthetic expressions are relatively more conventionalised than are others. For example, the expression "look-sweet" has 8 tokens in the Thai National Corpus while "look-bitter" has only 1. However, as this study's main focus is on the possibility of synaesthetic transfer and not frequency, the conventionality problem is not immediately relevant, and all the expressions that were provided by the language consultants and were attested by the Thai National Corpus and/or Google are thus treated equally in this study.

In total, 10 pathways of synaesthetic transfer were found in the data. There are 4 possible source modalities: TOUCH transfers to 4 modalities: TASTE, SMELL, SOUND, and SIGHT.[5] TASTE transfers to 3 modalities: SMELL, SOUND, and SIGHT. SMELL transfers to 1 modality: TASTE; and SIGHT transfers to 2 modalities: SMELL and SOUND. SOUND, however, is not a possible source. The 'transferor' hierarchy is thus as follows:

(3) TOUCH > TASTE > SIGHT > SMELL > SOUND

On the other hand, there are 4 possible target modalities: TASTE is transferred from 2 modalities: TOUCH and SMELL; SMELL is transferred from 3 modalities: TOUCH, TASTE, and SIGHT; SOUND is transferred from 3 modalities: TOUCH, TASTE, and SIGHT; and SIGHT is transferred from 2 modalities: TOUCH and TASTE. TOUCH, however, is not a possible target. The 'transferee' hierarchy is thus as follows:

(4) SOUND, SMELL > SIGHT, TASTE > TOUCH

The hierarchies in (3) and (4) are transfer-type-based, that is, based on only the possible types of transfer. They should be distinguished from expression-type-based and token-based hierarchies. In an expression-type-based hierarchy, the numbers of types of synaesthetic expressions that belong to each transfer type are taken into account, while a token-based hierarchy takes into account the numbers of tokens of each synaesthetic expression-type.

Table 1. Ten Possible Pathways for Synaesthetic Transfer in Thai with Examples

No	Pathway of Transfer	Examples
1	TOUCH → TASTE	rót-nûm (taste-smooth) rót-ʔɔ̀:n (taste-soft: mild taste) rót-phèt-rɔ́:n (taste-spicy-hot) rót-cèp (taste-hurt: astringent taste)
2	TOUCH → SMELL	klîn-ʔɔ̀:n (smell-soft) klîn-yēn-yēn (smell-cool-cool: mild, relaxing smell)
3	TOUCH → SOUND	sǐaŋ-nûm (sound-smooth) sǐaŋ-ʔɔ̀:n (sound-soft) sǐaŋ-khǎɛŋ (sound-hard: harsh-sounding)
4	TOUCH → SIGHT	dū:-nûm (look-smooth) dū:-ʔɔ̀:n (look-soft) dū:-khǎɛŋ (look-hard) sǐ:-nûm (colour-smooth) sǐ:-ʔɔ̀:n (colour-soft) sǐ:-rɔ́:n (colour-hot: warm colour) sǐ:-jēn (colour-cool)
5	TASTE → SMELL	klìn/hɔ̌:m-wǎ:n (smell/fragrant-sweet) klìn/měn-prîaw (smell/stink-sour)
6	TASTE → SOUND	sǐaŋ-wǎ:n (sound-sweet) sǐaŋ-khǒm (sound-bitter)

7	TASTE → SIGHT	dū:-wǎ:n (look-sweet) dū:-khǒm (look-bitter) dū:-prîaw (look-sour: vibrant, fashionable-looking) sǐ:-wǎ:n (colour-sweet) sǐ:-prîaw-prîaw (colour-sour-sour: vibrant, fashionable colour)
8	SMELL → TASTE	rót(châat)-hɔ̌ɔm-wǎan (taste-fragrant-sweet)
9	SIGHT → SMELL	měn-khǐaw (stink-green: unpleasant smell of leaves)
10	SIGHT → SOUND	sǐaŋ-jā:w (sound-long) sǐaŋ-sân (sound-short) sǐaŋ-sǔ:ŋ (sound-high) sǐaŋ-tàm (sound-low) sǐaŋ-nǎ: (sound-thick) sǐaŋ-bā:ŋ (sound-thin) sǐaŋ-thùp (sound-opaque) sǐaŋ-khùn (sound-unclear) sǐaŋ-sǎj (sound-clear)

Those two kinds of hierarchies, however, cannot be accurately formulated using this study's methods and data, and thus require further research for their accurate formulation. Table 1 above provides examples of synaesthetic expressions of each of the 10 pathways of transfer found in the data. Table 2 below summarises the possible sources and targets of linguistic synaesthesia in Thai.

Table 2. Possible Sources and Targets of Synaesthetic Transfer in Thai

Source \ Target	TOUCH	TASTE	SMELL	SOUND	SIGHT
TOUCH		√	√	√	√
TASTE	X		√	√	√
SMELL	X	√		X	X
SOUND	X	X	X		X
SIGHT	X	X	√	√	

Note. √ = possible, X = impossible, ■ = non-transfer.

5. Discussion of linguistic synaesthesia across languages

First, consistent with Ullmann (1959), Williams (1976) and Yu (2003), TOUCH is the predominant source of transfer. However, the targets to which TOUCH transfers are different. According to Ullmann and Yu, TOUCH transfers to

SMELL, SOUND, and SIGHT.[6] According to Williams and this study, it also transfers, besides the other three senses, to TASTE. This is in line with another finding of this study, also unanimously confirmed by the other studies mentioned here, namely, that TOUCH is the least likely target of a transfer. The status of TOUCH as the 'best transferor' and also the 'worst transferee' can be accounted for on a cognitive basis. Among the five sense modalities, TOUCH is the most embodied (most concrete), and thus makes the best candidate for being the source mental domain from which most target mental domains are metaphorically mapped. That is to say, TOUCH is the most mentally accessible sense modality, and, in the case of linguistic synaesthesia, it is generally hypothesised to constitute the 'best access' to other senses. This accessibility hypothesis was confirmed by the experimental work of Shen and Gil (2008). Table 3 below provides a comparison of the possible targets of TOUCH transfer found in Ullmann (1959), Williams (1976), Yu (2003) and this study.

Table 3. Possible Targets of TOUCH Transfer according to Ullmann (1959), Williams (1976), Yu (2003) and This Study

TOUCH →	TASTE	SMELL	SOUND	SIGHT
Ullmann	X	√	√	√
Williams	√	√	√	√
Yu	X	√	√	√
This study	√	√	√	√

Note. √ = possible, X = impossible.

Secondly, it was found here that SOUND and SMELL are the predominant targets. This finding is partly in line with Ullmann, Williams, and Yu, which all attribute target predominance singly to SOUND. It is then assumed that the predominance of the auditory modality as the most possible target still holds. Nevertheless, the sources from which SOUND is transferred are different. According to Ullmann, SOUND is transferred from all the other four senses. However, according to Williams, Yu, and this study, it is transferred from TOUCH, TASTE, and SIGHT, but not SMELL. This finding is in line with another from this study, which is also unanimously confirmed by the other studies mentioned here earlier, that SOUND is the least likely source of transfer. The status of SOUND as the 'best transferee' and the 'worst transferor' seems to contradict the traditional distributional hierarchy that places SIGHT, not SOUND, as the highest sense modality. Though admitting that this contradiction is unexpected, Ullmann (1959) reasonably argues that "visual terminology is incomparably richer than its auditional counterpart," and so there is less motivation for SIGHT to be synaesthetically transferred to. On the contrary, SOUND "stands more in need of external support," and "hence the greater frequency of the intrusion of outside elements" into the auditional terminology takes place (Ullmann 1959: 283). Considering the findings of the linguistic synaesthesia studies, including this one, it can be proposed that the hierarchy be revised with SOUND ranking highest and replacing SIGHT. Table 4 below provides a comparison of the possible sources of SOUND transfer found in Ullmann (1959), Williams (1976), Yu (2003) and this study.

Table 4. Possible Sources of SOUND Transfer according to Ullmann (1959), Williams (1976), Yu (2003) and This Study

→ SOUND	TOUCH	TASTE	SMELL	SIGHT
Ullmann	√	√	√	√
Williams	√	√	X	√
Yu	√	√	X	√
This study	√	√	X	√

Note. √ = *possible*, X = *impossible*.

An alternative hypothesis is that both SOUND and SIGHT rank highest universally, but cultural variations do play a major role in formulating culture-specific hierarchies. That is to say, some cultures might value SIGHT as their highest sense modality, while others might prefer SOUND. As noted by Ong (1991: 26–27), cultures vary greatly "in their exploitation of the various senses and in the way in which they relate their conceptual apparatus to the various senses." In terms of our hierarchy of synaesthetic transfers, it is hypothesised that the highest ranking sense modality is closest to what each linguistic community holds as its own conceptual apparatus. A community that does conceptualise "hearing" as its primary source of perception and understanding is, according to Ong, the Hebrews. Moreover, Evans and Wilkins (2000), in their studies on the semantic extension of perception verbs, found that in many of the Australian languages, it is the auditory modality, not vision, that is the primary source of the lexicalisation of certain high-level cognitive concepts like "understand" and "know." Indeed, this argument for cultural variability is in line with what was found in this study, that is, SOUND is the predominant target for transfer. However, it is also suggested that further research, especially cross-linguistic research, is needed before a universal claim can be made regarding the highest sense modality in the hierarchy.

Additionally, some data seemed to provide counter-evidence for the distributional hierarchy. Specifically, there are three transfers that do not move upward as predicted. That is to say, they involve transfers from a higher sense modality to a lower one, i.e. SIGHT > SOUND, SIGHT > SMELL, and SMELL > TASTE. The following example illustrates a case of such a downward transfer.

(5) sǐaŋ　sǔ:ŋ　kɔ̄:n　pāj　lɛ́ʔ　lɛ̌:m　lék　mâj　sû:
voice　high　exceed　go　and　pointed　small　not　fight
nâ:　fāŋ
worth　listen
"Too high and sharp voice is not really worth listening to." (NACHM092)

Ullman's (1959: 281) tables of distribution show the occurrence of SIGHT > SOUND transfer. He considered this occurrence as an unpredicted case, but did not give any explanations for its unexpectedness. Williams's (1976) model, moreover, predicts that SIGHT > SOUND transfer is totally possible in English and some other languages. To that effect, this counter-example might lend evidence against the universal claim of SIGHT as the highest-ranking sense modality, at least in some cultures. According to both this study and Williams, SOUND is the "worst" transferor, as it does not transfer to any sense modality at all, although Yu (2003) did find one example showing that SOUND can transfer to TOUCH. On the other hand, SIGHT does transfer to other senses, i.e. SOUND, according to Williams, and SOUND and SMELL according to this study and Yu.

Moreover, in this study and also in Yu, COLOUR transfers downward to SMELL. One example of the COLOUR > SMELL transfer from this study is as follows:

(6) wē:lā:　tàt　jâ:　tāmmāj　měn　khǐaw
when　cut　grass　why　stink　green
'Why do we smell "green stink" when we cut the grass?' (NWRP_CR006)

Additionally, Yu's example is as follows:

(7) In the chilly air were floating strands of **dark red smell** of blood.

(Yu 2003: 27)

In (6), the COLOUR "green" transfers to the olfactory sense, "smell/stink," giving the meaning of "an unpleasant smell like that of green leaves." In (7), the transfer from "red" to SMELL evokes a particular kind of smell/stink associated with blood. As COLOUR (SIGHT) is in fact a sense modality that is higher than SMELL, this downward transfer seems to contradict Ullmann's hierarchical distribution tendency. Also, this transfer goes against Williams's routes for synaesthetic transfers, as no link is established between SMELL and COLOUR. One possibility is to treat examples like (6) and (7) as exceptions or cases of historical accident. However, this explanation is not satisfactory, considering the fact that, at least intuitively, the transfer COLOUR > SMELL seems motivated, though not in a way similar to many of the other paths of synaesthetic transfer. As noted above, synaesthesia is often attributed to conceptual metaphor. Indeed, metaphorical analysis works well for most synaesthetic expressions, like "sweet voice," in which sweetness of TASTE, which is a lower sense modality, conceptually corresponds to a certain pleasant quality of SOUND, which is a higher sense modality.

However, two major problems do arise regarding the metaphorical nature of synaesthesia. First, it is apparent that some other synaesthetic expressions like those in Examples (6) and (7) cannot be explained in terms of metaphor. There seems to be no ontological correspondence between greenness and a certain unpleasant kind of smell. Besides, the transfer, according to Ullmann's hierarchy, is downward, that is, from a more abstract domain to a more concrete domain. By definition, every case of synaesthetic transfer is metaphorical, as it invariably involves cross-domain (cross-sense) transfer from a more concrete domain (a lower sense modality) to a more abstract domain (a higher sense modality). Nevertheless, the "green stink" (of grass) expression in (6) or the "dark red smell" (of blood) expression in (7) is by no means unmotivated. One can easily see a contextual link between the two entities in question. The recurrent co-occurrence of a particular odour with a particular colour of an entity gives rise to a metonymic transfer between the two sense modalities. The contextual contiguity of the green colour of grass and its unpleasant kind of smell gives rise to the association between COLOUR and SMELL. Likewise, more often than not, when we have a fresh wound and bleed, a particular kind of smell from the chemical composition of our blood becomes our perception.

Further, the principle of metonymy can also account for one example involving the transfer from SMELL to TASTE:

(8) sàʔtāːbák   nǽʔnām   khrûŋ aŋdùːm   **rótchâːt hɔ̌ːm**   **wǎːn**   màj
    Starbucks introduce drink   taste   fragrant   sweet   new
    "Starbucks introduced a new fragrant-sweet tasting drink." (PRNV068)

In (8), a metonymical link between the two sense modalities is quite clear. The act of drinking (and thus tasting) something allows us to smell it at the same time through the opening between the oral and nasal cavities, and thus is a cross-modal transfer. One possible counter-argument against the role of conceptual metonymy in synaesthetic transfer is that, as every synaesthetic transfer is metaphorical (cross-domain) by definition, it would be paradoxical to claim that some cases of linguistic synaesthesia involve metonymy (same-domain transfer). However, this paradox need not be the case. It was argued by Radden and Kövecses (1999) that, in practice, metaphor and metonymy need not be exclusive of each other. The major reason is that they operate in different dimensions. Metaphor, as widely held, involves domain-crossing transfer. However, metonymy involves a transfer based on contextual contiguity, regardless of the presence or absence of domain boundaries. In this way, it can be posited that although every case of linguistic synaesthesia involves metaphor, cases that reflect downward transfer potentially also involve metonymy.[7]

6. Conclusion

In summary, a synaesthetic expression is defined as a linguistic phenomenon in which a linguistic expression encodes the perception of one sense modality through another. The studies of linguistic synaesthesia are mostly concerned with the issues of distribution and motivation, that is, how linguistic synaesthesia is hierarchically distributed and how it is conceptually and culturally motivated. This study looks at the data from Thai and found 10 pathways of synaesthetic transfer. Then, these findings are compared with those of other major works. In terms of distribution, one potentially universal feature is TOUCH as the predominant source of transfer, while the predominant destination of transfer can be culturally variable: SIGHT for some cultures and SOUND for others. In relation to that variability, the highest domain along the distributional hierarchy might be culture specific, depending on which sense modality the linguistic community conceptualises as the primary apparatus for acquiring knowledge. Lastly, there are cases that contradict the distribution tendency, that is, they move down the hierarchy. These cases, however, can be accounted for by referring to the principle of metonymy. Indeed, it might be potentially universal that although every case of synaesthetic transfer is metaphorical, cases of downward transfer are metonymical. More research, nevertheless, is required to confirm or disprove fully these potential language universals and specifics for synaesthesia.

Acknowledgements

I would like to express my sincere gratitude to Dr Luna Filipović, Associate Professor Kingkarn Thepkanjana, Professor Satoshi Uehara, Professor Tadao Miyamoto, and an anonymous reviewer for their valuable comments on earlier versions of this paper.

Notes

1. Human sensory modalities traditionally refer to the five categories, namely, SIGHT, SOUND, SMELL, TASTE, and TOUCH. Some works on linguistic synaesthesia, however, break down SIGHT into DIMENSION and COLOUR (e.g. Williams 1976), or into DIMENSION, COLOUR, and TEXTURE (e.g. Bretones-Callejas 2001).
2. See, for example, Nelson (1968) and O'Malley (1957) for studies on synaesthesia as a literary device.
3. See, for example, Sakamoto and Utsumi (2009) and Werning et al. (2006) for an experimental psycholinguistic view on synaesthesia.
4. The source of data is indicated at the end of the translation line. It is either an Internet address retrieved by Google or a document code tagged by the Thai National Corpus.
5. A distinction can be made between COLOUR and DIMENSION for the sake of a more refined analysis and comparison with other studies. However, both are subsumed under the umbrella term SIGHT in general discussion.
6. Ullmann (1959) made a distinction between TOUCH (in general) and HEAT. This study, however, does not distinguish between these two tactile and thermal domains, and subsumes both under the single umbrella term, TOUCH.
7. Readers interested in the roles of metaphor and metonymy in diachronic change are referred to Allan (2009).

References

Allan, K. 2009. *Metaphor and metonymy: A diachronic approach.* New Jersey: Wiley-Blackwell.
Baron-Cohen, S. & J. Harrison (eds). 1997. *Synaesthesia: Classic and contemporary readings.* Oxford: Blackwell Publishers.
Bretones-Callejas, C. M. 2001. Synaesthetic metaphors in English. *ICSI Technical Report* 8. September 2001. http://www.icsi.berkeley.edu/techreports. (3 Jan, 2011.)
Cytowic, R. E. 1989. *Synesthesia: A union of the senses.* New York: Springer-Verlag.
Evans, N. & D. Wilkins. 2000. In the mind's ear: The semantic extensions of perception verbs in Australian languages. *Language* 76(3). 546–592.
Howes, D. 2005. *Empire of the senses: The sensual culture reader.* Oxford: Berg.
Lakoff, G. 1993. The contemporary theory of metaphor. In A. Ortony (ed.), *Metaphor and thought.* Cambridge: Cambridge University Press.
Lakoff, G. & M. Johnson. 1980. *Metaphors we live by.* Chicago: University of Chicago Press.
Marks, L. E. 1978. *The unity of the senses.* New York: Academic Press.
Nelson, O. C. 1968. *Literary synesthesia and the twentieth-century Anglo-American poetic consciousness.* M.A. thesis, University of Wyoming.
O'Malley, G. 1957. Literary synesthesia. *The Journal of Aesthestics and Art Criticism* 15. 391–411.
Ong, W. J. 1991. The shifting sensorium. In D. Howes (ed.), *The varieties of sensory experience,* 47–60. Toronto: University of Toronto Press.
Radden, G. & Z. Kövecses. 1999. Towards a theory of metonymy. In Panther, K. & G. Radden (eds), *Metonymy in language and thought,* 17–59. Amsterdam & Philadelphia: John Benjamins.
Ramachandran, V. S. & E. M. Hubbard. 2001. Synaesthesia: A window into perception, thought, and language. *Journal of Consciousness Studies* 8. 3–34.
Sakamoto, M. & A. Utsumi. 2009. Cognitive effects of synesthetic metaphors evoked by the semantic interaction. *Proceedings of the 31st Annual Meeting of the Cognitive Science Society (CogSci2009).* 1593–1598.
Shen, Y. & D. Gil. 2008. Sweet Fragrances from Indonesia: A Universal principle governing directionality in synaesthetic metaphors. In Auracher, J. & W. van Peer (eds), *New beginnings in literary studies,* 49–71. Newcastle: Cambridge Scholars.
Ullmann, S. 1959. *The principles of semantics* (2nd ed.). Oxford: Clarendon.
Williams, J. M. 1976. Synesthetic adjectives: A possible law of semantic change. *Language* 52. 461–478.
Yu, N. 2003. Synesthetic metaphor: A cognitive perspective. *Journal of Literary Semantics* 32(1). 19–34.
Werning, M., J. Fleischhauer & H. Beşeoğlu. 2006. The cognitive accessibility of synaesthetic metaphors, 2365–2370. *Proceedings of the 28th Annual Conference of the Cognitive Science Society.*

Chapter 12

A neuro-typological approach to writing systems

Tadao Miyamoto

1. Introduction

In the field of linguistics, writing systems have not been well studied under the assumption that while language is innate, writing systems are mere cultural artifacts, lacking the intrinsic nature associated with human language, which uniquely separates us from other species of animals (cf. Carreiras et al. 2009). In spite of his false assumption of alphabeto-centrism, it is Gelb (1963), who first claimed that the study of writing systems could be a meaningful sub-discipline for understanding the nature of language (cf. Miyamoto 2007).

In this paper, we would like to show that even though writing systems are divided into various types based generally on script types, they could also be classified based on the notion of orthographic depth, which in turn is uniquely manifested in terms of brain activation. In other words, it would be possible to classify writing systems based on the difference in brain activation patterns, employing neuro-imaging for the classification of writing systems. An implication of this suggestion is that it may be possible to establish a new linguistic sub-field, which could be termed 'neuro-typology', where neuroimaging techniques are utilized for linguistic-typological studies.

The following is the outline of this paper. Section Two will explain basic concepts of writing systems, while introducing the simplest classification of written symbols. Section Three will examine the notion of orthographic depth, while introducing our Orthographic-depth Hypothesis. Section Four will look at cerebral functions in general and also a neuroimaging technique of how fMRI (functional Magnetic Resonance Imaging) works. Section Five, the core of this paper, will then review the previous neuro-imaging studies of various writing systems to examine correspondences between the degrees of orthographic depth and neuro-imaging findings. The last Section will suggest the establishment of a linguistic new field, i.e. 'neuro-typology'.

2. Writing systems in general

2.1 Simplest classification of visual symbols

Various ways of classifying writing systems or written symbols have been proposed (Coulmas 1989, 2003; Daniels & Bright 1996; DeFrancis 1989; Sampson 1985); however, as pointed out by Sproat (2000), none of them is satisfactory. Figure 1 below is the simplest classification of visual or written symbols we can think of. In this Figure, these are first classified either as 'semasiographic' or 'glottographic'. Semasiographic symbols, where 'semasio-' refers to 'meaning', are those easily found, for instance, at international airports. Washroom and custom-control signs are a couple of examples; these symbols could be recognized universally regardless of what viewers' native tongues are. Being devoid of language-specific auditory contents, these symbols are 'language-independent'. Hence, these are not part of any writing systems. In contrast, glottographic symbols, where 'glotto-' refers to 'tongue', are those associated with speech sounds of languages; hence, these are symbols of writing systems. These glottographic symbols are then classified either as 'phonographic,' where 'phono' refers to 'sound', or 'logographic', where 'logo' refers to 'word'. Whereas phonographic symbols stand for speech sounds without assuming any semantic contents, logographic symbols stand not only for sounds but also for lexical meanings. As we will see shortly, these phonographic symbols could be regarded as part of so-called 'shallow orthography' or 'deep orthography', depending on how transparent (or opaque) a given orthography is in grapheme-to-sound mapping. Meanwhile, logographic symbols could be divided into 'pictographic' and 'non-pictographic', meaning that every logographic symbol is not a pictogram as generally assumed.

```
                    ┌─────────────────┐
                    │ Visual Symbols  │
                    └─────────────────┘
                    ┌────────┴────────┐
            ┌──────────────┐   ┌──────────────┐
            │ Glottographic│   │Semasiographic│
            └──────────────┘   └──────────────┘
            ┌──────┴──────┐
    ┌─────────────┐  ┌─────────────┐
    │ Phonographic│  │ Logographic │
    └─────────────┘  └─────────────┘
     ┌─────┴─────┐    ┌─────┴──────┐
┌─────────┐ ┌─────────┐ ┌─────────────┐ ┌─────────────────┐
│ Shallow │ │  Deep   │ │ Pictographic│ │ Non-pictographic│
│(e.g.    │ │(e.g.    │ │ (e.g. 山)   │ │  (e.g. 清)      │
│Indonesian)│ │English)│ │             │ │                 │
└─────────┘ └─────────┘ └─────────────┘ └─────────────────┘
```

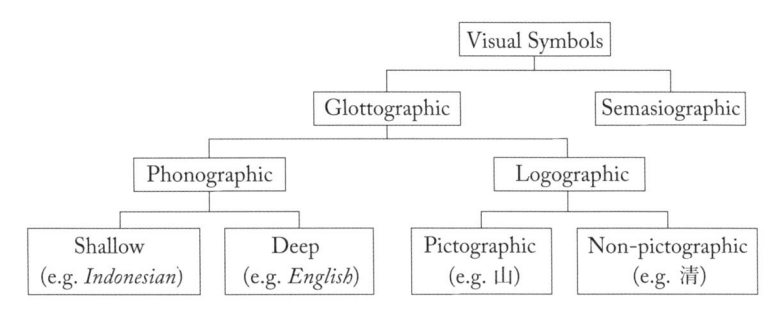

Figure 1. The simplest way of classifying written symbols.

2.2 Writing systems of our concern

Here we will look at very basic characteristics of the writing systems, which we will examine later from neuro-imaging perspectives: i.e. Alphabet, Japanese Kana, Korean Hangul, Chinese Hanʒi and Japanese Kanji. Writing systems differ from each other in terms of the size of linguistic units, which their visual symbols represent. These units are phonetic, phonemic, moraic, syllabic, morpho-syllabic and lexical.

The smallest linguistic unit represented by visual symbols could be 'phonetic'. For instance, it would not be impossible for a writing system to phonetically represent segments, as exemplified by the following description of the three allophones of the English phoneme, /p/.

(1) [pʰ]   (e.g. *pen*)

(2) [p]   (e.g. *spot*)

(3) [p̚]   (e.g. *stop*)

However, there exists in the world no 'phonetic writing system', due possibly to its impracticality. 'Phoneme' is then the smallest linguistic unit utilized by an existing writing system, i.e. alphabetic system. In an alphabetic writing system, based on an orthography-specific set of grapheme-to-phoneme conversion rules, graphemes are mapped onto phonemes. Alphabetic words are then read out *in principle* by way of *assembling* phonemic units.

The linguistic unit one step larger than 'phoneme' must be a tempo-prosodic unit called 'mora'. Japanese Kana is a prototypical example of moraic writing systems. The examples below demonstrate the size difference between 'mora' and 'syllable'.

(4) *hon* 'book'   (two morae (ほ-ん) vs. one syllable)

(5) *kitte* 'stamp'   (three morae (き-っ-て) vs. two syllables)

In the mono-syllabic word *hon* 'book' (4), each of the two morae (i.e. *ho-n*) is individually aligned to a Kana grapheme; and so is in the bi-syllabic word *kitte* 'stamp' (5), where each of the three morae (i.e. *ki-t-te*) is aligned to an individual grapheme. Hence, in Kana writing, graphemes are aligned not to syllables, as generally assumed, but to morae (cf. Kess & Miyamoto 1999).

Chinese Hanʒi graphemes are rather ambiguous concerning the linguistic units they represent. For instance, 山 (/shan/) is a mono-syllabic word, which means 'mountain'; hence, this grapheme is obviously 'syllabic' as well as 'lexical'. However, in its compound case, for instance, of 山脈 (mountain range), the same grapheme 山, *does not stand, obviously, for a word, but for a morpheme*, while retaining its mono-syllabicity. Given the fact that most of Chinese words are compounds, the appropriate designation of Chinese Hanʒi ought not to be 'syllabic', as is generally assumed, but to be 'morpho-syllabic'. Furthermore, concerning the structure of Hanʒi graphemes, roughly 5% of the present-day graphemes are 'simplex', while the remaining 95% of them are 'complex'. Complex graphemes are formed in principle by combining two simplex graphemes, which are then termed phonetic and semantic radicals. For instance, 銅 is a complex grapheme, consisting of a semantic radical 金, which means 'metal' and a phonetic radical 同, which is pronounced as /ton/. However, the function of phonetic radicals is quite opaque in the sense that merely 30% of the pronunciation of phonetic radicals sounds the same as that of their corresponding simplex graphemes.

While Hanʒi is defined as 'morpho-syllabic', Korean Hangul, consisting of 28 basic graphemic components, is defined as 'alpha-syllabic'. Unlike Hanʒi, however, consonantal and vowel strokes are stacked and combined into groups of two to five to create syllabic graphemes. This alpha-syllabicity can be demonstrated by the following example: 김치. This word *kimchi*, 'Korean spicy pickle', consists of two syllabic graphemes, i.e. /kim/ and /chi/. The individual strokes of these syllabic graphemes function alphabetically. For instance, in the grapheme 김 (/kim/), the left upper stroke stands for /k/, the right upper stroke /i/ and the bottom square /m/. Furthermore, given the fact that these alphabetic, more specifically, consonantal strokes depict the shape of the speech organs (i.e. the mouth, tongue and throat), Hangul is regarded as the most logical writing system in the world. In our case of the grapheme 김 (/kim/), the /k/-stroke depicts the tongue-shape required for its pronunciation with a velar constriction at the highest (i.e. right-most) point; and the bottom square depicts the labial configuration of the nasal /m/ with the release of occlusion.

In the case of Chinese complex Hanʒi, even though the function of phonetic radicals is somewhat opaque, its functionality is still retained. Contrastively, in the case of Japanese Kanji, its functionality is highly obscure since each Japanese Kanji assumes multiple readings associated with both Chinese (*on*) and Japanese (*kun*) readings. We can demonstrate the point, for instance, by using the complex grapheme 頭, which generally means 'head'. This character is associated with the following eleven pronunciations: /atama/, /kashira/, /gashira/, /kabu/, /kaburi/, /koube/, /zu/, /tsuburi/, /tsumu/, /tsumuri/ and /tou/. Only one of them, /tou/, is represented by the phonetic radical placed on the left side of the complex grapheme. Hence, in the case of Japanese Kanji, the phonetic radicals are to a large extent unable to function as phonetic indicators, compelling its readers to depend on word-specific memory association between graphemic and lexico-semantic representations. In this sense, Japanese Kanji could possibly be the deepest orthography we have in the present-day world.

3. Orthographic depth

3.1 Shallow vs. deep orthography

From the perspective of lexical processing, writing systems can be classified into two types: so-called 'shallow orthography' and 'deep orthography'. This notion of 'orthographic depth' generally applies to phonographic writing systems, referring to the extent to which a given system deviates from a clear grapheme-to-phoneme mapping relationship. That is whether what is written and how it is pronounced have a one-to-one mapping or one-to-many (or many-to-one) mapping relationship. If a given system has a tendency toward the former mapping relationship, it is called 'shallow orthography'. Well-known examples of shallow orthography are Indonesian, Italian and Finish. For instance in Indonesian, how words are spelled and how these are pronounced are almost the same; hence, the following words are pronounced exactly the same as how they are spelled.

(6) buku-buku   'book-book' (various kinds of books)

(7) kereta-angin   'wheel-wind' (bicycle)

(8) orang-hutan   'man-forest' (orangutan)

Contrastively, if a given system has a tendency toward the latter mapping relationship, then, it is called 'deep orthography'. Well-known examples of deep orthography are French, Arabic and Hebrew; and so is English, as exemplified below.

(9) ryme   (ought to be 'raim')

(10) receipt   (ought to be 'resiit')

(11) philosopher   (ought to be 'filosofar')

3.2 Dual-route hypothesis

In the field of psycholinguistics, the notion of orthographic depth is commonly formulated in terms of the so-called Dural-route Hypothesis (e.g. Besner & Smith 1992; Coltheart et al. 2001; Houghton & Zorzi 2003). According to this hypothesis, lexical processing is conducted by either one of two routes: an 'indirect route,' or 'non-lexical route,' and a 'direct route' or 'lexical route'. The non-lexical route takes part in so-called 'assembled phonology'; it is only thorough the pronunciation of lexical items that their meanings are accessed. This route is employed by non-words and regularly spelled words. However, for the processing of irregularly spelled words, the above route is inappropriate in the sense that rules of regular correspondence between graphemes and their pronunciations would not lead to successful access to corresponding lexical meanings. Hence, these words require the other route, which participates in so-called 'addressed phonology', i.e. the direct association between visual forms and corresponding lexico-semantics. Familiar words also depend on this lexical route, regardless if these are spelled regularly or irregularly. Concerning the notion of orthographic depth, if a given orthography depends mostly on the indirect route for its lexical processing, then such orthography is termed *shallow*. Contrastively, if it depends extensively on the direct route, then it is termed *deep*. Furthermore, if a given orthography depends totally on the direct route, such orthography must be deepest in orthographic representation.

3.3 Orthographic-depth hierarchy

Oddly, there are very few attempts to rigorously quantify the notion of orthographic depth. One such rare attempt is van den Bosch et al. (1994). This study quantizes orthographic depth based firstly on letter-to-phoneme alignment: how difficult it is to convert graphemic strings (i.e. words) to phonemic strings, and secondly on grapheme-to-phoneme correspondence: how to align a phonemic transcription to its spelling counterpart (van den Bosch et al. 1994). Their data-oriented approach is claimed to extract the degree of orthographic depth at both graphemic and phonemic levels. Another attempt is Borgwaldt et al. (2005), in which orthographic depth is quantified by computing the entropic degree of grapheme-to-phoneme conversion exclusively at 'word onsets'. The advantage of using 'word onsets' as a measuring point is that it would make it possible to compare different orthographic and phonological structures, since any words in any writing systems have word onsets. These attempts are, however, formulated to deal exclusively with alphabetic writing systems. Contrastively, encompassing both alphabetic and non-alphabetic writing systems, Sproat (2000: 138) classifies these by presenting the Chart in Figure 2, where the type of phonography is represented as the primary dimension, and the amount of logography as the secondary dimension.

It is our interpretation that the 'logographic dimension' corresponds squarely to 'orthographic depth' in that the greater the amount of logographicity, the deeper the depth of a given orthography. Simply, then, borrowing Sproat's (2000) 'logographic dimension' as a means to express 'orthographic depth,' we will rank the writing systems of our concern as the Orthographic-depth Hierarchy in Figure 3.

Admittedly, the same as with Sproat's Chart, our Orthographic-depth Hierarchy is highly impressionistic, lacking rigorous quantification. However, it is our contention that this Hierarchy would adequately serve our aim: i.e.

218 Tadao Miyamoto

Type of Phonography

Amount of Logography ↓	Consonantal	Polyconsonantal	Alphabetic	Core Syllabic	Syllabic
	W. Semitic		English	LinearB	Modern YI
			Greek		
			Korean		
			Devanagari		
	Perso-Aramaic				
					Chinese
		Egyptian		Sumerian	
				Maya	
				Japanese	

Figure 2. From Sproat's (2000) classification of writing systems.

to show that the notion of orthographic depth is associated with neurological correlates. We will, hence, depend on this Hierarchy for now, and leave any rigorous formulation of orthographic depth for our future study.

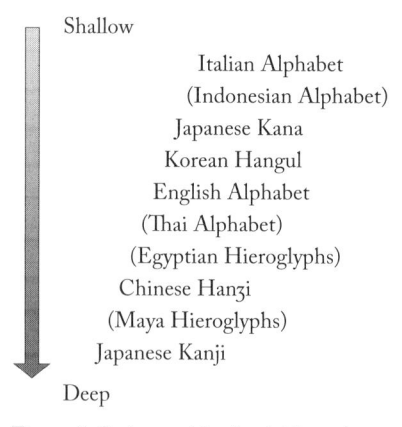

Shallow
↓
Italian Alphabet
(Indonesian Alphabet)
Japanese Kana
Korean Hangul
English Alphabet
(Thai Alphabet)
(Egyptian Hieroglyphs)
Chinese Hanʒi
(Maya Hieroglyphs)
Japanese Kanji
Deep

Figure 3. Orthographic-depth hierarchy.

As for Indonesian, Thai, Egyptian and Maya orthographies, which are shown in parentheses, we do not have fMRI studies, a few of which are for an obvious reason. Hence, these are not in the scope of our inquiry. Our intention in including these as part of its entries is to provide the Chart with the notion of universality. As briefed in Section 3.1, Indonesian orthography is quite shallow. Other than having 18 unique letter combinations (e.g. *ny, ng, ngg, tj*) for representing sounds, which are uniquely Indonesian, it employs the 26-letter Latin alphabet. The correspondence between these letters and the phonemes of 27 consonants and six vowels is quite transparent. Hence, we regard it as being slightly deeper than the Italian alphabet. Thai orthography involves the graphemes of 44 consonants and 15 basic vowels, which are diacritically written above, below, before, or after the consonant they modify. Thai orthography is also uniquely endowed with tone-marking. The correspondence between these graphemes and the phonemes of 21 consonants and nine vowels is quite opaque in both grapheme-to-phoneme and phoneme-to-grapheme conversions (cf. Wutiwiwatchai & Furui 2007). Hence, we regard it being far deeper than the English alphabet, but not as deep as Chinese Hanʒi since, in principle, Thai orthography is not concerned with logographicity. The Egyptian Hieroglyphic system is relatively transparent in grapheme-to-phoneme conversion despite the facts that its graphemic inventory consists of mono-, bi- and tri-consonantal symbols, which function either as phonographic or logographic symbols, and that their graphemic lexical representations can additionally contain so-called 'determinatives' and 'sound complements'. Since it involves both phonographic and logographic components, we regard it being deeper than Thai orthography but not as deep as Chinese Hanʒi. The Maya Hieroglyphic system consists of both syllabic and logographic symbols, both of which are intricately combined into so-called 'compound glyphs'. However, it is not as deep as Japanese Kanji, many of which are associated with multiple readings, as exemplified with the complex Kanji 頭.

4. Our brain

4.1 Basic structure and function

This Section provides the reader with the very basic concepts of brain sciences. The cortex, the largest part of our brain, is divided into four 'lobes', i.e. the frontal, parietal, occipital and temporal lobes. The frontal lobe is associated with such functions as reasoning, planning, speech production and movement; the parietal lobe with the integration of sensory information from various senses; the occipital lobe with visual processing; and the temporal lobe with such functions as auditory and speech comprehension as well as memory. These four lobes can also be grouped merely into two: the posterior cerebral cortex and anterior cerebral cortex. The occipital, parietal and temporal lobes are located in the posterior section of the cortex, to a large extent, organizing sensory information to produce our meaningful experience of the world. Meanwhile, the frontal lobe is located in the anterior section of the cortex, largely performing abstract thinking as well as formulating and executing our intentions into meaningful actions.

Furthermore, various areas of the cortex are often labeled by using so-called 'Brodmann areas'. These are the most frequently cited cytoarchitectural classifications of our cortex; and they correlate to a large extent with functional cerebral areas. For instance, Brodmann areas 1, 2 and 3 correspond to the primary somatosensory cortex; area 4 to the primary motor cortex; area 17 to the primary visual cortex; areas 41 and 42 to the primary auditory cortex; area 22 to so-called Wernicke's area; and areas 44 and 45 to the so-called Broca's area.

With respect to Wernicke's area and Broca's area, these are often regarded as housing our language faculty: the former related with language comprehension and the latter with its production. However, the latest research indicates that language production and comprehension take place in much wider areas of our brain based presumably on various neuroanatomical networks. One instance of such networks is the so-called 'dual-route cortical system' (cf. Saur et al. 2008). Starting from the superior temporal gyrus, which engages in initial stages of lexical processing, this system diverges into two pathways. One is a dorsal pathway, which projects dorso-posteriorly toward premotor cortices in the frontal lobe, and is concerned with *assembled phonology*. The other is a ventral pathway, which projects ventro-laterally to the middle and inferior temporal cortices, and is concerned with *addressed phonology*.

4.2 How fMRI works

Before moving to the following Section, we will very briefly look at how fMRI (functional Magnetic Resonance Imaging) works (cf. Huettel et al. 2003). It is too invasive to directly observe neural activity in our brain, for instance, by inserting shanks directly into our cortex. fMRI is one of the noninvasive techniques developed in recent years, which enables us to indirectly detect the areas of neural activity by way of measuring the often used BOLD (blood-oxygen-level dependence) signal.

For neurons to fire, both glucose and oxygen are required as energy resources. However, since neurons do not store these nutrients, they depend on a constant supply of these through the blood stream. When there is neural activity and neurons are firing, a large amount of energy supplied by glucose is consumed, and glucose is switched to the energetically less effective glycolysis. Responding to this energy utilization, there is a local increase of blood flow and volume to supply oxygen to the regions associated with the increased energy utilization. This hemodynamic response results in changes in the local ratio of oxyhemoglobin (oxygen-rich hemoglobin) and deoxyhemoglobin (oxygen-poor hemoglobin).

Depending then on the level of oxygenation, the magnetic resonance (MR) signal of blood (i.e. the contrast in magnetic strength between these two types of hemoglobin) is manifested. Even though this contrast is slight, based on statistical methods, it would become possible to determine the cerebral areas showing the difference in BOLD signal, which, in turn, makes it possible to determine which cerebral regions are active when we engage in such neural activity as single word reading.

5. Neuro-imaging correlation

5.1 Generalization

What we would like to show in this Section is as follows. The different degrees of 'orthographic depth' associated with individual writing systems is manifested as differences in cerebral activation; and the following contrasting features help us characterize such differences:

1. Dorsal pathway vs. Ventral pathway;
2. Posterior cerebral cortex vs. Anterior cerebral cortex; and
3. Assembled phonology vs. Addressed phonology.

Table 1 below then summarizes our argument in this Section.

Table 1. Activation Patterns Associated with the Writing Systems of Our Concern

	Dorsal (Ass.)	Ventral (Add.)	Posterior	Anterior
Italian Alphabet	x			
Japanese Kana	x	x	x	
Korean Hangul	x	x	x	
English Alphabet	(x)	x	x	x
Chinese Hanzi	(x)	x	x	x
Japanese Kanji		x	(x)	

The Italian alphabet, which is the shallowest orthography in our list, activates the area associated only with a part of the **Dorsal** pathway, which is concerned with **Ass**embled phonology. Japanese Kana activates the areas along the dorsal pathway as well as the **Ventral** pathway, which are concerned with **Add**ressed phonology. Such dependence on the dual-route would result in activating a large portion of the **Posterior** cerebral cortex. Korean Hangul shows a similar activation pattern to that of Japanese Kana. However, it also shows a difference (which cannot be stipulated in the Table): within the posterior cerebral cortex, the activated regions are much wider due to Hangul's graphemic complexity. While depending rather negligibly on a dorsal pathway, the English alphabet employs mostly the ventral stream of the dual-route cortical system for both phonological and semantic processing. Significantly, however, its phonological processing additionally activates a part of the **Anterior** cerebral cortex. Chinese Hanzi employs the same posterior-anterior network as the English alphabet does. The difference (which cannot be stipulated in the Table) is, however, that the actual anterior phonological area differs from the one employed by the English alphabet. Lastly, Japanese Kanji, which is the deepest orthography in our list, activates neither the dorsal pathway in the posterior cortex nor the anterior cerebral cortex. Circumventing phonological areas, it activates a part of the ventral pathway, which extends itself directly to the hippocampus in order to conduct straightforward grapheme-to-semantics conversion.

5.2 Default mode of activation

One thing we would like to make clear is that processing of any orthography could not possibly be carried out without a 'default mode of activation'. Such a default mode consists of functional contributions from, at least, the following cerebral areas: (1) the left superior posterior temporal gyrus (BA22); (2) the left occipitotemporal region (BA19); and (3) the left inferior frontal gyrus (BA6/BA9). These are the very areas that form the dual-route cortical system and its extension to the anterior cerebral cortex (e.g. Binder et al. 2005; Friederici & Alter 2004; Saur et al. 2008, and references cited therein). In other words, processing of any orthography concerns, as a default mode of processing, the dual-route cortical system, part of which is extended to the anterior cerebral cortex. However, there are also specific areas that are selectively and robustly activated by an individual orthography; such a selection may be termed a 'non-default mode of activation'. What we would like to show in the following subsections is such robust activation patters, i.e. 'non-default modes of activation', associated with the individual orthographies of our concern.

5.3 Italian alphabet

We would like to start with the Italian alphabet. Italian is probably one of the shallowest orthographies in the world. Its grapheme-to-phoneme correspondence is extremely transparent, judging from the fact that 33 graphemic symbols are adequate enough to represent 25 phonemes of the language (Lepschy & Lepschy 1981). As for neuroimaging, there is Paulesu et al.'s (2000) study which, using university students as subjects, contrasts single word reading between English and Italian. A noted finding with the Italian alphabet is the presence of robust activation at the junction between the left inferior parietal cortex (BA 40) and the left superior temporal gyrus (BA 41/42), which overlaps with the planum temporale.

Concerning these three regions, first, locating itself at the junction of the auditory, visual, and somatosensory areas, the left inferior parietal cortex is essentially multimodal, processing auditory, visual and sensorimotor stimuli simultaneously. Second, coinciding with part of Wernicke's area, the left superior temporal gyrus is concerned with auditory short-term memory and lexical phonology (Leff et al. 2008.) Third, the crucial function of the planum temporale is also language related, made clear from the fact that lesions at the area bring about various deficits associated with auditory discrimination and speech comprehension (Griffiths & Warren 2002: 352). In essence, forming part of the dorsal pathway, these three regions are crucial for conducting assembled phonology, i.e. the transformation of visual words into corresponding auditory counterparts. Since in the Italian alphabet its grapheme-to-phoneme conversion constitutes the main portion of the lexical processing effort, this effort is manifested as the activation of the areas associated *partially* with a dorsal pathway.

5.4 Japanese Kana

Japanese Kana contains 46 basic symbols and those with diacritics, totaling 110 or so kana configurations, which squarely corresponds to the number of morae. Hence, Japanese Kana is a relatively shallow orthography, though not as shallow as the Italian alphabet. So we expect some similarity in activation between these two types of orthography. However, there must also be some differences since they differ at least in the size of linguistic units their graphemes represent. As for similarity, activating the temporo-parietal system, both orthographies engage in a dorsal pathway of the dual-route cortical system. The presence of a dorsal pathway in contrast with its ventral counterpart in Japanese orthographic processing was originally proposed by Iwata (1984) in his aphasic study, which claimed that Kana relies on the former and Kanji the latter. Finding activation at the temporo-parietal regions, the results of previous neuro-imaging studies on Kana processing agree with Iwata's assessment (e.g. Nakamura et al. 2005; Sakurai et al. 2000). (Neuro-anatomically, modifying Iwata's proposal, Sakurai et al. (2000: 114), for instance, define these pathways as follows: the middle occipital gyrus and deep perisylvian temporo-parietal area constitute a dorsal route for phonological processing; whereas, the inferior occipital, fusiform and posterior inferior temporal gyri constitute a ventral route for lexico-semantic processing.) Since the employment of a dorsal pathway is also suggested for Italian orthographic processing (Paulesu et al. 2000), the activation pattern of the Italian alphabet and that of Japanese Kana are similar.

There is, however, a difference; the activated areas are wider for Japanese Kana than for the Italian alphabet. This spreading of activation into the areas associated with a ventral pathway was observed in our own fMRI study (Jeong et al. 2007), which employed a two-by-two factorial design that manipulated both word types (Kanji vs. Kana) and task types (semantic vs. phonological). Our finding was that differential phonological-semantic activation was greater for Kana than Kanji at the angular gyrus and left inferior occipital gyrus (i.e. the ventral pathway.) A significance of this finding is that as some recent studies on Kana processing indicate, the activation of the dual-route is sensitive to whether task-demands are phonological in nature or semantic in nature (e.g. Coderre et al. 2008; Ino et al. 2009). In other words, Kana orthography employs either one of the dual-routes, depending on the types of tasks it is required to perform. In this sense, Kana processing differs from the processing of the Italian alphabet, which merely activates part of the dorsal pathway, regardless of tasks involved (Paulesu et al. 2000).

5.5 Korean Hangul

In Korean Hangul, individual strokes of syllabic graphemes function alphabetically, and this alphabeticity is highly transparent. Despite the presence of such transparency, Korean Hangul is deeper than Japanese Kana, due to the fact that the number of possible syllabic graphemes created out of 17 consonantal and 11 vowel strokes is quite large, being estimated to be around 2,300. This orthographic characteristic of Korean Hangul is observed with cerebral activation, which spreads to wider areas than those observed with Japanese Kana. As for neuro-imaging, Lee (2004) contrasted i) Hangul and Hanʒi and ii) Hangul and English word readings, and reported robust activation in the following cerebral areas:

1. supramarginal gyrus (BA40);
2. angular gyrus (BA 39);
3. middle temporal gyrus (BA 21); and
4. precuneus and posterior cingulate gyrus (BA 24).

First, (1) the supramarginal gyrus (BA40) is part of the inferior parietal lobe, forming an integral part of the dorsal stream of the dual-route cortical system. This area is essential for visual word recognition; however, it also contributes to phonological processing, automatically computing lexico-phonology even when a task does not explicitly require it (Stoeckel et al. 2009). Second, like the supramarginal gyrus, (2) the angular gyrus (BA39) is essential for visual word recognition (Horwitz et al. 1998). However, functionally and structurally these two gyri are heterogeneous, differentially contributing to word reading. While the supramarginal gyrus, which is a part of the dorsal pathway, contributes to a large extent to phonological processing, the angular gyrus, which is a part of the ventral pathway, contributes to a large extent to semantic processing. Furthermore, the angular gyrus functionally shares the ventral pathway with (3) the middle temporal gyrus, which functions in a diverse manner, for instance, contemplating distance and recognizing known faces. However, the middle temporal gyrus also functions to access lexical meaning in reading.

Third, the activation, which is observed neither with Italian alphabet nor with Japanese Kana is the one at (4) the precuneus and posterior cingulate gyrus (BA 24). The precuneus (i.e. the medial area of the superior parietal cortex) is associated with such functions as attention shift and episodic memory retrieval (Lundstrom et al. 2003). However, the region is also known for its function of processing visuospatial imagery. Meanwhile, the posterior cingulate gyrus, which is part of the limbic system, is noted for the function of attention-shift, cognitive-memory and visuo-spatial activities. Hence, it is quite likely that these two regions, which are associated with visuo-spatial processing, are activated due to graphemic processing demands of Korean Hangul, which is visually highly rich. In sum, Korean Hangul utilizes both dorsal and ventral pathways, as Japanese Kana does; however, unlike Kana, it utilizes the medial and limbic areas of the cortex for processing its visually rich alpha-syllabic graphemes.

5.6 English alphabet

In the English alphabet, there are 1,120 graphemic combinations to represent 40 phonemes (Nyikos et al. 1988). Because of this opacity in grapheme-to-phoneme conversion, in the Orthographic-depth Hierarchy we rank the English alphabet as being deeper than Korean Hangul, whose alphabeticity represented by graphemic strokes is highly transparent. Also, when we compare the English alphabet with its Italian counterpart, the opacity of the former is manifested as a couple of significant differences in activation from the latter despite the fact that both are alphabetic. The following are some details.

It is a well-recognized fact that any alphabetic writing system activates the temporo-parietal system, which constitutes a part of the dorsal pathway of the dual-route cortical system (Bolger et al. 2005; Paulesu et al. 2000). This activation is the cerebral signature of Italian alphabetic processing, which relies totally on assembled phonology for its lexical processing. Contrastively, however, the contribution of this temporo-parietal system is negligible for English lexical processing, which is concerned to a large extent with addressed phonology. This addressed phonology then depends on a ventral pathway, as elaborated by Saur et al. (2008): the ventral stream projects ventro-laterally to the middle and inferior temporal cortices and serves as a sound-to-meaning interface by mapping sound-based representations of speech to widely distributed conceptual representations. In other words, deeper orthographies such as English engage a ventral pathway via the left middle and inferior temporal cortex; along this pathway not only phonological processing but also semantic processing is conducted (Bolger et al. 2005).

As seen in the previous sub-section, Korean lexical processing also depends on a ventral pathway. What differentiates the English alphabet from Korean Hangul in terms of cerebral activation is that in the case of the English alphabet the anterior cerebral region, to be more specific, the posterior portion of the inferior frontal gyrus (BA 44) is also activated. This area is said to be secondary to the initial temporal lobe phonological area, and is associated with working memory's phonological rehearsal mechanism (Costafreda et al. 2006). An indication is then that the ventral stream is extended to the anterior cerebral cortex to form a posterior-anterior network. In other words, given the much deeper nature of the English alphabet, its assembled phonology requires a network of posterior-anterior cerebral cortices, which is not the case with Korean Hangul.

In sum, the lexical processing of the English alphabet, which is far deeper than the Italian alphabet and even deeper than Korean Hangul, can be stated as follows in terms of cerebral activation: i) it primarily relies on the ventral pathway for both phonological and semantic processing; however, ii) its assembled phonology additionally requires a posterior-anterior network, which is an extension of the ventral pathway.

5.7 Chinese Hanʒi

Like the English alphabet, Chinese Hanʒi is deep in orthographic representation. It is far deeper than the English alphabet in the sense that their graphemes are not phonographic but logographic, mapping visual representations directly onto semantic representations. Hence, we expect some similarities and also differences in activation between these two types of orthographies. The similarities are that both orthographies mostly activate a ventral pathway, and extend its activation to the anterior cerebral cortex. A difference is that the actual phonological areas in the anterior cerebral cortex are not the same. The following are some details.

As for neuro-imaging of Chinese Hanʒi, Tan et al.'s (2005) meta-analysis is most resourceful, examining 19 studies: six of these are with Chinese and 13 with alphabetic orthographies. They come up with the following four regions associated with lexical processing of Chinese Hanʒi (Tan et al. 2005: 87):

1. dorsal aspect of left inferior parietal system (BA 40);
2. (bilateral) ventral occipitotemporal system including portions of fusiform gyrus and middle occipital gyrus (BA 19);
3. left ventral prefrontal system covering superior portions of inferior frontal gyrus (BA 44); and
4. left dorsal lateral frontal system (BA9).

The activation at (1) the left inferior parietal system, which constitutes a dorsal pathway, is not uniquely Chinese, and its significance is negligible; and the activation at (2) the ventral occipitotemporal system is not uniquely Chinese, either, since it constitutes part of the ventral pathway of the dual-cortical system. As for (3) the left ventral prefrontal system, its activation is observed with the English alphabet as part of its posterior-anterior network; hence, the activation in this area itself is not uniquely Chinese, either. Deep orthographies, such as English and Chinese, obviously require such a network for conducting their addressed phonology. The reason why Chinese Han3i actives this region must be that despite Hanji being logographic, the phonetic radicals of complex Hanji characters perform their duty, to a certain extent, as phonetic indicators. This grapheme-to-phoneme conversion of Chinese Han3i must be a condition for activating the left ventral prefrontal system.

Uniquely Chinese is the activation at (4) the left dorsolateral frontal region (BA9). Recent studies of Chinese Han3i reading have targeted this region. This cerebral area has then been claimed to underlie the addressed phonology system in Chinese reading by way of serving as a long-term storage center for phonological lexicon and, at the same time, serving for *look-up* process of addressed phonology (e.g. Siok et al. 2004; Tan et al. 2005). If the indication of recent research is correct, then, the activation in the region could be regarded as a neurological support for our assessment that Chinese Han3i, which is logographic, is deeper than the English alphabet, which is phonographic. In sum, Chinese Han3i activates all the cerebral areas associated with a default-mode of lexical processing. However, Chinese Han3i relies on the left dorsolateral frontal region (BA9) for its addressed phonology; and the activation at the area is the cerebral signature of Chinese Han3i processing.

5.8 Japanese Kanji
Lastly, we will examine a cerebral activation pattern associated with Japanese

Kanji reading. To do so, we will depend on our own fMRI study (Jeong et al. 2007), which indicates that even from a neuroimaging perspective, Japanese Kanji is the deepest orthography among all the orthographies of our concern. It neither activates the posterior phonological areas, as the Italian alphabet and Korean Hangul do, nor requires a posterior-anterior phonological network, as the English alphabet and Chinese Hanzi do. It mostly activates the areas along the semantic route, which extends from the left inferior temporal gyrus directly to the left Hippocampus.

As mentioned earlier, in our own study (Jeong et al. 2007) we employed a two-by-two factorial design that manipulated both word types (Kanji vs. Kana) and task types (semantic vs. phonological). Concerning Kanji processing, a significant finding was that differential semantic-phonological activation was far greater for Kanji than Kana at the following regions:

1. anterior fusiform gyrus (BA 37);
2. left inferior temporal gyrus (BA 20);
3. left parahippocampal gyrus; and
4. left hippocampus.

Such a finding suggests that Kanji processing initiates to activate a ventral pathway, which then extends its activation not to the anterior cerebral cortex but directly to the areas associated with lexical memory. The following are some details.

First, as for the activation of (1) the anterior fusiform gyrus and (2) the left inferior temporal gyrus, the recruitment of this occipitotemporal system, particularly, that of the fusiform gyrus is reported also by previous studies on Kanji processing (e.g. Nakamura et al. 2002, 2005; Sakurai et al. 2000; Thuy et al. 2004). The fusiform gyrus is often termed 'VWFA (Visual Word Formation Area)' due to its sensitivity to the perception of visually rich symbols, especially, to that of non-alphabetic symbols. Since the fusiform gyrus constitutes a part of a ventral pathway, which participates in assembled phonology, Japanese Kanji must utilize this pathway as a part of the direct link between the graphemic representations of Kanji and their lexico-semantics.

Second, as for the activation at (3) the left parahippocampal gyrus, this gyrus is noted for its function of memory recollection, or to be more specific, the encoding and decoding of scenes (e.g. images of places). Its most important cerebral function is, however, to send information from the association areas to the hippocampus. In other words, it is a crucial part of the semantic route, which connects the graphemic representation processed at the fusiform gyrus to corresponding (traces of) semantic information stored at the hippocampus.

Third, as is well-known, the hippocampus, which belongs to the limbic system, plays crucial roles in consolidating short- and long-term memory and in spatial navigation. It is also highly lateralized, and its left portion is largely concerned with verbal memory consolidation. In other words, the left hippocampus is the essential part of semantic processing in the sense that it serves lexical storage of Kanji words. In essence, Kanji reading is conducted by a network between the occipitotemporal region, which includes the fusiform gyrus, and the hippocampus via the left parahippocampal gyrus.

In sum, the activation pattern associated with Japanese Kanji reading indicates that graphemic information is converted into corresponding semantic information with no active recruitment of the areas responsible for phonological processing. Hence, this activation pattern itself constitutes a neurological support for the claim that Japanese Kanji is the deepest orthography among the orthographies of our concern.

6. Conclusion

In this paper, based on our Orthographic-depth Hierarchy, we have shown that so-called 'orthographic depth' was not a mere psycholinguistic concept, but was associated with neurological correlates. We characterized such correlation, based on previous neuro-imaging studies of lexical processing. What we have shown is that activation patterns differed systemically according to the degree of orthographic depth, and, to be more specific, that they could be defined in terms of whether they were involved with either or both of the dual-route of cortical system as well as with the posterior-anterior cerebral network. By way of obtaining such characterization, we suggest that neuro-imaging be employed for the classification of writing systems. An implication of this suggestion is then: it may be possible to establish a new linguistic sub-field, which could be termed 'neuro-typology,' where neuroimaging techniques are utilized for linguistic-typological studies. Such a research field should concern not only with writing systems but also with intrinsic properties of languages.

Acknowledgements

This work was originally supported by a Grant-in-Aid (B) for Scientific Research from the Japan Society for the Promotion of Science (No. 18320062).

References

Besner, D. & M. C. Smith. 1992. Basic processes in reading: Is the orthographic depth hypothesis sinking? In R. Frost & L. Katz (eds), *Orthography, phonology, morphology and meaning*, number 94 in Advances in Psychology, 45–66. Amsterdam: North-Holland.

Binder, J. R., C. F. Westbury, K. A. McKiernan, E. T. Possing & D. A. Medler. 2005. Distinct brain systems for processing concrete and abstract concepts. *Journal of Cognitive Neuroscience* 17. 905–917.

Bolger, D. J., C. A. Perfetti & W. Schneider. (2005). Cross-cultural effect on the brain revisited: Universal structures plus writing system variation. *Human Brain Mapping* 25. 92–104.

Borgwaldt, S., F. M. Hellwi & A. M. B. de Groot. 2005. Onset entropy matters: Letter-to-phoneme mappings in seven languages. *Reading and Writing* 18. 211–229.

Carreiras, M., M. L. Seghier, S. Baquero, A. Estevez, A. Lozano, J. T. Devlin & C. J. Price. 2009. An anatomical signature for literacy. *Nature* 461. 983–986.

Coderre, E. L., C. G. Filippi, P. A. Newhouse & J. A. Dumas. 2008. The Stroop effect in kana and kanji scripts in native Japanese speakers: An fMRI study. *Brain and Language* 107. 124–132.

Coltheart, M., C. Rastle, C. Perry, R. Langdon & J. Ziegler. 2001. DRC: A dual route cascaded model of visual word recognition and reading aloud. *Psychological Review* 108. 204–258.

Costafreda, S. G., C. H. Fu, L. Lee, B. Everitt, M. J. Brammer & A. S. David. 2006. A systematic review and quantitative appraisal of fMRI studies of verbal fluency: Role of the left inferior frontal gyrus. *Human Brain Mapping* 27. 799–810.

Coulmas, F. 1989. *The writing systems of the world*. Oxford: Blackwell.

Coulmas, F. 2003. *Writing systems: An introduction to their linguistic analysis*. Cambridge: Cambridge University Press.

Daniels, P. & W. Bright. 1996. *The world's writing systems*. New York: Oxford University Press.

DeFrancis, J. 1989. *Visible speech: The diverse oneness of writing systems*. Honolulu: University of Hawai'i Press.

Friederici, A. D. & K. Alter. 2004. Lateralization of auditory language functions: A dynamic dual pathway model. *Brain and Language* 89. 267–276.

Gelb, I. J. 1963. *A study of writing*. 2nd edition. Chicago: University of Chicago Press.

Griffiths, T. D. & J. D. Warren. 2002. The planum temporale as a computational hub. *Trends in Neurosciences* 25. 348–353.

Horwitz, B, J. Rumsey & B. C. Donohue. 1998. Functional connectivity of the angular gyrus in normal reading and dyslexia. *Proceedings of National Academy of Sciences* 95. 8939–8944.

Houghton, G. & M. Zorzi. 2003. Normal and impaired spelling in a connectionist dual-route architecture. *Cognitive Neuropsychology* 20. 115–162.

Huettel, S., A. W. Song & G. McCarthy. 2003. *Functional magnetic resonance imaging*. Massachusetts: Sinauer Associates Inc.

Ino, T., R. Nakai, T. Azuma, T. Kimura & H. Fukuyama. 2009. Recognition and reading aloud of kana and kanji word: An fMRI study. *Brain Research Bulletin* 78. 232–239.

Iwata, M. 1984. Kanji versus kana: Neuropsychological correlates of the Japanese writing system. *Trends in Neurosciences* 7. 290–293.

Jeong H., M. Sugiura, Y. Sassa, M. Miyamoto, C. Bai, K. Horie, S. Sato & R. Kawashima. 2007. Two distinct neural networks for semantic access during visual word recognition. *Proceedings of the Japan Neuroscience Annual Meeting,* July, Yokoyama.

Kess, J. F. & T. Miyamoto. 1999. *The Japanese mental lexicon: Psycholinguistic studies of kana and kanji processing*. Amsterdam & Philadelphia: John Benjamins.

Lee, K.-M. 2004. Functional MRI comparison between reading ideographic and phonographic scripts of one language. *Brain and Language* 91. 245–251.

Leff A. P., T. M. Schofield, K. E. Stephan, J. T. Crinion, K. J. Friston & C. J. Price. 2008. The cortical dynamics of intelligible speech. *Journal of Neuroscience* 28. 13209–13215.

Lepschy, A. & G. Lepschy. 1981. *La Lingua Italiana*. Milan: Bompiani.

Lundstrom, B. N., K. M. Petersson, J. Andersson, M. Johansson, P. Fransson & M. Ingvar. 2003. Isolating the retrieval of imagined pictures during episodic memory: Activation of the left precuneus and left prefrontal cortex. *Neuroimage* 20. 1934–1943.

Miyamoto, T. 2007. The evolution of writing systems: Against the Gelbian hypothesis. In A. Sakurai, K. Hasida & K. Nitta (edt), *New frontiers in artificial intelligence*, 345–356. Berlin & Heidelberg: Springer.

Nakamura K, M. Honda, S. Hirano, T. Oga, N. Sawamoto, T. Hanakawa, H. Inoue, J. Ito, T. Matsuda, H. Fukuyama & H. Shibasaki. 2002. Modulation of the visual word retrieval system in writing: A functional MRI study on the Japanese orthographies. *Journal of Cognitive Neuroscience* 14. 104–115.

Nakamura, K., S. Dehaene, A. Jobert, D. L. Bihan & S. Koulder. 2005. Subliminal convergence of kanji and kana words: Further evidence for functional parcellation of the posterior temporal cortex in visual word perception. *Journal of Cognitive Neuroscience* 17. 954–968.

Nyikos, J. 1988. *The Fourteenth LACUS Forum 1987*, 146-163. In S. Empleton (ed.), Linguistic Associations of Canada and the United States, Lake Bluff, Illinois.

Paulesu, E., E. McCrory, F. Fazio, L. Menoncello, N. Brunswick, S. F. Cappa, M. Cotelli, G. Cossu, F. Corte, M. Lorusso, S. Pesenti, A. Gallagher, D. Perani, C. Price, C. D. Frith & U. Frith. 2000. A cultural effect on brain function. *Nature Neuroscience* 3. 91–96.

Petersen, S., P. Fox, M. Posner, M. Mintun & M. Raichle. 1989. Positron emission tomographic studies of the processing of single words. *Journal of Cognitive Neuroscience* 1. 153-170.

Sakurai, Y., T. Momose, M. Iwata, Y. Sudo, K. Ohtomo & I. Kanazawa. 2000. Different cortical activity in reading of kanji words, kana words and kana nonwords. *Brain Resarch Cognitive Brain Research.* 111–115.

Saur, D., B. W. Kreher, S. Schnell, D. Kummerer, P. Kellmeyer, M.-S. Vry, R. Umarova, M. Musso, V. Glauche, S. Abel, W. Huber, M. Rijntjes, J. Hennig & C. Weiller. 2008. Ventral and dorsal pathways for language. *Proceedings of National Academy of Sciences* 105. 18035–18040.

Sampson, G. 1985. *Writing systems.* Stanford: Stanford University Press.

Siok, W. T., C. A. Perfetti, Z. Jin & L. H. Tan. 2004. Biological abnormality of impaired reading is constrained by culture. *Nature* 431. 71–76.

Sproat, R. 2000. *The computational theory of writing systems.* Cambridge: Cambridge University Press.

Stoeckel, C., P. M. Gough, K. E. Watkins & J. T. Devlin. 2009. Supramarginal gyrus involvement in visual word recognition. *Cortex* 45. 1091–1096.

Tan, L.-H., A. R. Laird, K. Li, & P. T. Fox. 2005. Neuroanatomical correlates of phonological processing of Chinese characters and alphabetic words: A meta-analysis. *Human Brain Mapping* 25. 83–91.

Thuy, D., K. Matsuo, K. Nakamura, K. Toma, T. Oga, T. Nakai, H. Shibasaki & H. Fukuyama. 2004. Implicit and explicit processing of kanji and kana words and non-words studied with fMRI. *NeuroImage* 23. 878–889.

van den Bosch, A., A. Content, W. Daelemans & B. de Gelder. 1994. Measuring the complexity of writing systems. *Journal of Quantitative Linguistics* 1. 178–188.

Wutiwiwatchai, C. & S. Furui. 2007. Thai speech processing technology: A review. *Speech Communication* 49. 8–27.

Index

A

accessibility hypothesis   203
a change-of-state event   107
actional   82, 87
addressed phonology   216, 228
adjacency pair   159, 171
affectedness   80
Afro-Asiatic   60, 61
agency   80
Agency Hierarchy   80
alphabetic writing system   213
alphabeto-centrism   211
alpha-syllabic   214
ambivalent verbs   91
anaphoric agreement   45
argument omission   145, 153
aspect   80
assembled phonology   216
asynchronous communication   178
attenuation   59
augmentation   59
Austro-Asiatic   66, 72
Austronesian   60, 61, 66

B

best transferee   203
best transferor   203
bi-clausal motion construction   115
blogs   180
blog writer   189
BOLD signal   221
bounded path   109
Broca's area   220
Brodmann areas   220

C

camera angle   122
causative transitive verbs   91
Chinese Hanʒi   227, 228
Chinese language   37
clitics   19, 20
CMC   175, 178, 179, 186, 189
coherent anaphor   139, 140
collectivism   174
communal-focused directive   161, 162, 169, 170
directives   161
communicative functions   160
complete reduplication   59, 72
Computer Mediated Communication   175
conceptual metaphor   206
conflict management   163
constructional approach   124
contextual contiguity   207
cross-modal transfer   207
culture-specific hierarchies   204
cyberspace   180

D

deep orthography   212, 216
default mode of activation   222
default unstressed form   25
degree of transitivity   86
deictic argument   127
deictic predicate   126, 127, 133
deictic zero   127, 129, 131, 133, 134
deixis   120
diminution   59
directional motion   112
directives   159
direct object arguments   77
distributional hierarchy   205
Dong Dam Pwo Karen pronominal system   44
Dong Dam Pwo Karen ʔàʔ-   42, 46
dorsal pathway   224
downward transfer   205
Dravidian   61
dual-cortical system   228

dual-route cortical system 226
Dural-route Hypothesis 216

E

Eastern Kayah Li 42, 46, 47, 50, 51, 52
Egyptian Hieroglyphic system 219
ellipses 142
emoticons 177, 178, 181
emotion predicates 129, 131
encoding strategies 108, 112
English alphabet 226, 227
English subject pronouns 141
epenthesis 21
etymological inquiry 38
etymology of *black* 32, 33
Eurasian languages 70
event-framing patterns 105
event-framing typology 108
experiencing speaker 125, 126, 128, 129, 132, 133
explicit reference 120
expressing sensations 131

F

face 160

face-threatening act 160
final particle 13, 14, 15, 18, 21
first-order transfers 198
first person pronoun 120, 121, 147
first person restriction 129
first-person subject 140
fMRI 220
focus 24
framing typology 109
free function words 20
functional Magnetic Resonance Imaging 220
functional range of ʔàʔ- 53
function words 19
fusiform gyrus 228, 229

G

Genuine ambivalent verbs 97
glottographic 212
goal-of-motion reading 112
grammaticalization 119, 120
grapheme-to-phoneme conversion 228

H

high context communication 178, 192
high context cultures 174

higher sense modality 206
high-low context continuum 173
highly affected DOs 83
Hpa-An Pwo Karen 46, 47

I

iconic description 30
iconic motivation 122
iconic similarity 58
iconization of sound 31
illocutionary force 159
imitation of the sound 30
implicit reference 120, 121, 122, 123
incremental theme 82
independent style 167
individual-focused directive 161, 165
individualism 174
Indo-European 71
Indo-European (IE) root *bhel- 36
inferior parietal system 228
interlocutor 183
internal state predicates 120, 128, 139, 140
internal state predicates 128
interrogative particles 13
intonational clitics 15
intonational phrase 16, 17
intransitive verbs 77

ISPs   128, 129, 131, 132
Italian alphabet   223, 226

J

Jackendovian semantic structure   112
Japanese Kana   224, 225, 226
Japanese Kanji   228, 230
Japanese lexicon   109
Jingpho   43

K

kaomoji   184, 186
Karenic family   41
Karenic languages   43, 46
kinesis   80
kin terms   166
Korean Hangul   225, 229

L

Lahu ɔ̀-   43
Lai Chin ʔa-   43
Lamphun province   41
lexical form   137
lexicalization patterns   128, 132
lexical resources   114
lexical resource view   108, 110
lexical route   216
lexical words   19
light final particles   23
linguistic iconicity   58

Linguistic typology   127
location PP   111
logographic script   179
lower sense modality   206

M

macro-events   104
main function of *ʔa-   48
MANNER   103, 106
manner-of-motion verbs   113
MANNER verb   104
markers of intention   129
Maya Hieroglyphic system   219
metaphor   196
metonymy   207
metrically light   26
Middle English   32
modality particles   13
moderately affected DOs   84
morpho-syllabic   214
MOTION   103
motion construction   104

N

narrator's viewpoint   153
neuro-typology   230
nicknames   144, 153, 166, 171
nominal plurality   60, 64
nominal pluralization   60
nominal plural reduplication   57
nominal plural reduplication   58
non-affected DOs   84
non-alphabetic symbols   229
non-default modes of activation   223
non-genuine ambivalent verbs   92, 94, 97
non-isomorphism   16
non-lexical route   216
non-punctual   82
non-standard spellings   176
non-synaesthetes   195
null form   137

O

objective construal   122, 133
objectivity   123
occupational title   148, 150, 153, 154
Old English   32
online communication   173
online interaction   188
onomatopoeia   30
orthographic depth   217
Orthographic-depth Hierarchy   217, 226
Orthographic-depth Hypothesis   211
overt pronouns   142
overt referential forms   152

P

parallel conflation 107, 108
parallel system of conflation 106
parameters of transitivity 79
participatory styles 167
PATH 103
path compensation 114
path-denoting PPs 111
perceptual representation 29
personal pronouns 138, 139, 155
personal pronouns proper 141
person reference 152, 153
phonesthemes 37
phonetic radical 214
phonetic writing system 213
phonological "bulk-provider" 48
pika-don 29, 30, 31
politeness strategy 184
Politeness Theory 160
posterior-anterior network 228
post-first-order transfers 198
postverbal particles 128
prefix ʔàʔ- 51
primary stress 19
pronominal form 137, 138, 141, 142, 144, 155
prosodic constituents 16, 17
Prosodic Phonology 15, 16
prosodic structure 26
prosody 18
Proto-Agent 81
Proto-Patient 81, 82
proto-roles 81
Proto-Tibeto-Burman 41
Proto Tibeto-Burman *ʔa- 47
prototype approach 79
punctual 87
punctuality 80

R

rapport management 164, 167
Rapport Management Theory 160
reciprocal style 167
recoverability 145
redressive action 160
reduplication 57
referential choices 139
referential expressions 137, 139
referential form 142, 147, 155
referential strategies 138
referential system 144
repair strategies 25
RESULT 106
resultant state 110
resultative construction 104, 116
resultative event 104
resultatives 110
rightmost syllable 23

S

satellite-framed 106
satellite-framing 108, 112
satellite-framing option 115
satellite phrase 104
second-person pronominal forms 140
second-person pronouns 147
second-person reference 142
self-monitoring speaker 124, 129, 133
self-reference 147
semantic map 53
semantic radical 214
semasiographic systems 182, 212
sense modalities 196
sentential stress 24
Serbo-Croatian 20
shallow orthography 212, 215
Sino-Tibetan 61, 66, 71, 72
sound imitation 31
sound-symbolic value 37, 39
sound symbolism 30
speaker's attitude 140, 149, 152, 153, 155
speaker's perspective 140
speaker's perspective-oriented language 140
stand-alone particles 24
STATE CHANGE 106

stative event   127
stative PP   111
stative verbs   89
status particles   13
stress-governed alternation   22
subjectification phenomena   121
subjective construal   121, 122, 125, 127
subjective perspective   150
subjectivity   119, 123, 133, 139, 140
suggestive value   30
symbolic image   38
symbolic representations   38
symbolic value   35, 37
synaesthesia   195
synaesthetic expressions   198, 199
synaesthetic transfer   197, 199, 207
synesthetic   30
syntactic constituents   16
syntactic structure   26

T

Tai-Kadai   66, 72
telic   82, 87
temporo-parietal system   224, 226
Thai National Corpus   200
Thai orthography   219
third-person pronouns   140
third-person reference   142, 147
Tibeto-Burman languages   41
transferee hierarchy   201
transferor hierarchy   200
transitive verbs   77
transitivity   79
transitivity continuum   99
transitivity feature   86
translational motion   109
turn taking   171

U

UMC   176, 177, 178, 180, 181, 184, 190, 192
Unconventional means of communication   176
unconventional spelling   182, 187
universality of human cognition   38
Uto-Aztecan   60

V

ventral occipitotemporal system   228
ventral pathway   224, 229
ventral prefrontal system   228
verb-framed   106
verb-framed language   103, 114
verb-framing   108, 112
visual modality   200
Visual Word Formation Area   229
volitional   82, 87
volitionality   80
vowel lengthening   21

W

weblogs   177
weight requirement   24
Wernicke's area   220
word creation   31
word/root-creation   38
World Atlas of Language Structures   62
worst transferee   203
worst transferor   203
writing systems   211

Z

zero pronominal language   123, 129, 132
zero pronominals   133
zero pronouns   138, 139, 153

Hituzi Linguistics in English No. 19

Typological Studies on Languages in Thailand and Japan

発行	2012 年 7 月 30 日　初版 1 刷
定価	9000 円＋税
編者	ⓒ 宮本正夫・小野尚之・Kingkarn Thepkanjana・上原聡
発行者	松本 功
組版者	内山彰議（4&4,2）
印刷製本所	株式会社 シナノ
発行所	株式会社 ひつじ書房
	〒 112-0011 東京都文京区千石 2-1-2 大和ビル 2F
	Tel.03-5319-4916　Fax.03-5319-4917
	郵便振替 00120-8-142852
	toiawase@hituzi.co.jp　http://www.hituzi.co.jp/

ISBN978-4-89476-607-5　C3087

造本には充分注意しておりますが、落丁・乱丁などがございましたら、小社かお買上げ書店にておとりかえいたします。ご意見、ご感想など、小社までお寄せ下されば幸いです。

刊行案内

Hituzi Linguistics in English No.11
Chunking and Instruction
The Place of Sounds, Lexis, and Grammar in English Language Teaching
中森誉之 著
978-4-89476-404-0　定価 8,800 円＋税

Hituzi Linguistics in English No.12
Detecting and Sharing Perspectives Using Causals in Japanese
宇野良子 著
978-4-89476-405-7　定価 12,000 円＋税

Hituzi Linguistics in English No.13
Discourse Representation of Temporal Relations in the So-Called Head-Internal Relatives
石川邦芳 著
978-4-89476-406-4　定価 9,400 円＋税

Hituzi Linguistics in English No.14
Features and Roles of Filled Pauses in Speech Communication
A corpus-based study of spontaneous speech
渡辺美知子 著
978-4-89476-407-1　定価 11,000 円＋税

Hituzi Linguistics in English No.15
Japanese Loanword Phonology
The Nature of Inputs and the Loanword Sublexicon
六川雅彦 著
978-4-89476-442-2　定価 12,000 円＋税

Hituzi Linguistics in English No.16
Derivational Linearization at the Syntax-Prosody Interface
塩原佳世乃 著
978-4-89476-485-9　定価 12,000 円＋税